Introducing Maya 5:
3D for Beginners

Introducing Maya® 5:
3D for Beginners

DARIUSH DERAKHSHANI

SAN FRANCISCO | LONDON

Associate Publisher: Dan Brodnitz
Alias Books and Training Product Manager: Danielle Lamothe
Acquisitions Editor: Mariann Barsolo
Developmental Editor: Jim Compton
Production Editor: Elizabeth Campbell
Technical Editor: Chris Wells
Alias Technical Editor: Vivien May
Copyeditor: Pat Coleman
Compositor: Happenstance Type-O-Rama
CD Coordinator: Dan Mummert
CD Technician: Kevin Ly
Proofreaders: Emily Hsuan, Laurie O'Connell, Nancy Riddiough
Indexer: Nancy Guenther
Book Designer: Caryl Gorska
Cover Designer: Bob Gundu

Dear Reader,

Thank you for choosing *Introducing Maya 5*. This book is part of a new wave of Sybex graphics books, all written by outstanding authors – artists and professional teachers who really know their stuff, and have a clear vision of the audience they're writing for.

Att Sybex, we're committed to producing a full line of quality books on 3D graphics and animation. With each title, we're working hard to set a new standard for the industry. From the paper we print on, to the animators we work with, to the visual examples our authors provide, our goal is to bring you the best graphics books available.

I hope you see all that reflected in these pages. I'd be very interested in hearing your feedback on how we're doing. To let us know what you think about this, or any other Sybex book, please visit us at www.sybex.com. Once there, go to the product page, click on Submit a Review, and fill out the questionnaire. Your input is greatly appreciated.
Best regards,

Dan Brodnitz
Associate Publisher
Sybex Inc.

Acknowledgments

It's really tough trying to acknowledge everyone who has in some way or another helped in the creation of this book. Over the years, so many people have given me so much to bring me here. I would like to thank the teachers I have and have had in my life for everything they have showed me. Education is the cornerstone of a happy life. ■ I would like to thank my students for teaching me as much as I have tried to teach them. In particular, thanks to Juan Gutierrez, Victor J. Garza, and Robert Jauregui who helped me create the images used in this book. Without their talented assistance, this book would still be a work in progress. Thanks to my bosses, colleagues, and friends at work for showing me everything I've learned and making it fun to be in the effects business. ■ Thanks kindly to my editors at Sybex and Alias for their support and help and for making this process fun. (Jim, Mariann, Elizabeth: I'm looking in your direction.) And thanks to Danielle Lamother, Vivien May, Carla Sharkey, and Michael Stamler at Alias. Thanks to my family, my mom, and brothers for their support and encouragement, and special mad props to my friends Bill, Mark, Frank, Terry, and Brett. ■ And a special thank you to my lovely fiancée and soon-to-be wife Randi for putting up with the long nights at the keyboard, the grumpy, sleep-deprived mornings, and the blinking and buzzing of all my machines in our apartment. A better woman cannot be found.

About the Author

Dariush Derakhshani is an effects animator and educator in Los Angeles, California. Previously using CAD software in his architecture days, Dariush migrated to using 3D programs after Alias PowerAnimator version 6, when he enrolled in USC Film School's Animation program, from which he received an MFA. Dariush also holds a BA in Architecture and Theatre from Lehigh University in Pennsylvania and worked at a New Jersey architecture firm before moving to LA to go to film school.

Foreword

Welcome to the world of 3D animation, and thanks for choosing Maya. With Maya software, you've selected a tool where the possibilities are limited only by your imagination. You've probably already discovered that before you can unleash your creations, you'll need to learn some basic skills. Don't worry, though, this book is a great way to get there.

Introducing Maya 5: 3D for Beginners is an approachable, affordable way for you to start building your skills. You'll explore modeling, animation, rendering, and much more. You'll be inspired by a color gallery displaying a variety of works by Maya artists, many of whom have only recently completed their education. In *Introducing Maya 5: 3D for Beginners*, you'll learn by doing. You'll be presented with step by step exercises, helpful scene files, and theory explained in a straightforward manner. Harness all of the power, technology, and innovation of Maya to express your own creative vision.

With Maya Press, Alias Systems is pleased to work with Sybex in order to bring you a wealth of options in the study of Maya. *Introducing Maya 5: 3D for Beginners* is our first joint publication and a stepping-stone to mastering Maya. Check your local bookstore shelves for additional Maya Press titles as you continue along your learning path.

—Danielle Lamothe
Product Manager
Books and Training
Alias

CONTENTS AT A GLANCE

Contents

Introduction

Welcome to *Introducing Maya 5: 3D for Beginners* and the world of computer-generated imagery (CGI). Whether you are new to 3D graphics or are venturing into Alias' powerhouse animation software Maya from another 3D application, you'll find this book a perfect primer. It introduces you to Maya and shows how you can work with Maya to create your art, whether it is animated or static in design.

This book is the first in the Maya Press series, a new collaboration between Sybex and Alias to create books dedicated to teaching artists all over the world how to use Maya.

This book exposes you to all the facets of Maya by introducing and explaining its tools and functions to help you understand how Maya operates. In addition, you'll find several hands-on examples and tutorials that give you first-hand experience with the toolsets. Working through these will give you skills as well as knowledge. These tutorials expose you to various ways of accomplishing tasks with this intricate and comprehensive artistic tool.

And finally, this book explains workflow—not only how specific tasks are accomplished but why—that is, how they fit into the larger process of producing 3D animation. By doing that, these chapters should give you the confidence to venture deeper into Maya's feature set on your own or using any of Maya's other learning tools and books as a guide.

Above all, however, this book aims to inspire you to use Maya as a creative tool to achieve and explore your own artistic vision.

What You Will Learn from This Book

Introducing Maya 5: 3D for Beginners will show you how Maya works and introduce you to every part of the toolset to give you a glimpse of the possibilities available with Maya.

You'll learn the basic concepts underlying animation and 3D and how to work with the Maya interface. You'll then learn the basic methods of modeling—creating objects and characters that appear to exist in three-dimensional space and that can be animated. You'll also explore shading and texturing, the techniques of applying surfaces to the objects you create, and you'll learn how to create lights and shadows in a scene. Animation is an enormously rich topic, but the practice and theory provided here will give you a solid footing. Then you'll learn how to control the process of rendering, turning your images into files that can be viewed. Perhaps

Maya's most dazzling capability is its dynamics engine, software that allows you to make objects behave as if controlled by the real-world laws of physics.

Once you've finished this book and its exercises, you will have some experience in almost everything Maya offers, giving you a solid foundation on which to base the rest of your Maya and CGI experience.

Quite simply, the goal of this book is to get you familiar enough with all the different parts of Maya to get you working on your own and to start a long, healthy education in a powerful and flexible tool.

You will, however, have the greatest to learn from yourself.

Who Should Read This Book

Anyone who is curious about learning Maya or who is migrating from another 3D software package can learn something from this book. By being exposed to everything Maya has to offer, you will better understand how you can use its toolset to create or improve on your art and work.

If you already have a cursory or even an intermediate experience with Maya, culled from time spent learning at home, you can fill many holes with the information in this book. Self-education is a powerful tool, and the more you expose yourself to different sources, opinions, and methods, the better educated you will be.

How to Use This Book

Introducing Maya 5: 3D for Beginners approaches the subject in a linear fashion in line with how most animation productions are undertaken. But the book has numerous cross-references to make sure the chapters make sense in any order you might want to tackle them. You can easily open this book to any chapter and work through the tutorials and examples laid out for the Maya task being covered. Feel free to browse the chapters and jump into anything that strikes your fancy.

Although you can learn a lot just by reading the explanations and studying the illustrations, it is best to read this book while you are using Maya 5 or Maya 5 Personal Learning Edition so that you can try the exercises for yourself as you read them. This book also includes a CD that contains all the example files and support files you'll need for the tutorials in the text. You can use these example files to check the progress of your own work, or you can use them as a starting point if you want to skip ahead within an exercise. You'll also find it valuable to examine these files in depth to see how scenes are set up and how some of the concepts introduced in the book are implemented. Because Maya is a complex, professional software application, the tutorials are both realistically ambitious and simple enough for new users to complete. Take them one step at a time and find your own pace. Remember, you're not working on deadline—yet.

How This Book Is Organized

Chapter 1, "Introduction to Computer Graphics," introduces you to the common computer graphics terms and concepts to give you a basic overview of how CG is facilitated and how Maya relates to the overall process. This chapter explores the basics of CG creation and its core concepts. In addition, it describes the process of CG production and discusses how to establish a commonly used workflow.

Chapter 2, "The Maya Interface" presents the entire Maya interface and shows you how it is used in production. Beginning with a roadmap of the screen, this chapter also explains how Maya defines and organizes objects in a scene.

Chapter 3, "Your First Maya Animation," creates a simple animation to introduce you to Maya workflow and give you a taste of how things work. By animating the planets in our solar system, you will learn basic concepts of creating and animating in Maya and how to use its object structure.

Chapter 4, "Modeling with NURBS," is an introduction to modeling concepts and workflows in general as well as an explanation of how to model with NURBS by learning to model an axe.

Chapter 5, "Modeling with Polygons," will take your lesson in NURBS modeling a step further by showing you how to model using polygonal geometry to create various objects, from a human hand to a complex catapult.

Chapter 6, "Further Modeling Topics," will round out your modeling lessons by showing you how to use lattices to model your objects. In this chapter, you'll learn how to model a starfish and a teakettle using subdivision surfaces.

Chapter 7, "Maya Shading and Texturing," shows how to assign textures and shaders to your models. Using the axe you created in Chapter 4, you'll learn how to texture it to look like a real axe.

Chapter 8, "Introduction to Animation," covers the basics of how to animate a bouncing ball using keyframes and moves on to creating more complex animation—throwing an axe and firing your catapult model from Chapter 5. You will also learn how to import objects into an existing animation and transfer animation from one object to another. In addition, you'll learn how to use the Graph Editor to edit and finesse your animation.

Chapter 9, "Further Animation Topics," expands on Chapter 8 to show you how to use Maya's skeleton and kinematics system to create a walk cycle. Also covered is how to animate objects by using relationships between objects.

Chapter 10, "Maya Lighting," begins by showing you how to light a 3D scene and shows you how to use the tools to create and edit Maya lights for illumination, shadows, and special lighting effects.

Chapter 11, "Maya Rendering," explains how to create image files from your Maya scene and how to achieve the best look for your animation by using proper cameras and rendering settings.

Chapter 12, "Maya Dynamics," introduces you to Maya's powerful dynamics animation system. You will animate pool balls colliding with each other using rigid body dynamics, and, using particle animation, you will create steam to add to your teakettle scene from Chapter 6. This chapter also introduces you to Maya's amazing Paint Effects module and shows how to use Paint Effects to create animated flowers and grass within minutes.

Hardware and Software Considerations

Because computer hardware is a quickly moving target, and Maya now runs on four distinct operating systems (Windows 2000/XP, Irix, Linux, and Mac OS X), specifying which particular hardware components will work with Maya is something of a challenge. Fortunately, Alias has a "qualified hardware" page on their website that describes the latest hardware to be qualified to work with Maya for each operating system. Go to this URL:

```
http://www.alias.com/eng/support/maya/qualified_hardware/index.jhtml
```

Although you can find specific hardware recommendations on these web pages, some general statements can be made about what constitutes a good platform on which to run Maya. First, be sure to get a fast processor; Maya eats through CPU cycles like crazy, so a fast processor is important. Second, you need lots of RAM (memory) to run Maya; 512MB is a minimum, but 1GB is a good amount to have, especially if you are working with large scene files.

Third, if you expect to interact well with your Maya scenes, a powerful video card is a must; although Maya will putt along with a poor graphics card, screen redraws will be slow with complex scenes, which gets frustrating quickly. You might want to consider a "workstation graphics card" as opposed to a consumer-grade gaming video card for the best compatibility. Several companies make entry-level through top-performing workstation cards to fit any budget. A large hard disk is also important, but most computers these days come with huge drives anyway. Some suggested setups might be as follows (current at the time of writing):

- Windows or Linux
    - AMD Athlon XP 2000+; 1GB RAM; ATI FireGL T2; 80GB hard disk
- Intel Pentium IV 2.4Ghz; 1GB RAM; nVidia Geforce FX; 80GB hard disk
- Mac OS X
    - PowerMac G4 dual 1.25Ghz; 1GB RAM; nVidia Geforce 4 Ti (4600); 80GB hard disk, third-party three-button mouse
- Irix
    - Silicon Graphics Octane 2; dual 600Mhz; 1GB RAM; built-in graphics; 40GB hard disk

Fortunately, computer hardware is so fast these days that even laptop computers can now run Maya well. Additionally, even hardware that is not officially supported by Alias can often run Maya—just remember that you will not be able to get technical support if your system does not meet their qualifications chart.

The CD accompanying this book has been tested on Windows, Mac, and Linux machines and should work with most configurations of these systems.

The Book's CD

The CD in the back of this book provides all the sample images, movies, and files that you need to work through the projects in *Introducing Maya 5: 3D for Beginners*, as well as Maya Personal Learning Edition 5.

The CD is organized into project folders. Each folder contains all the scene and support files for that project. The folders are arranged as Maya projects, so you can copy them to your hard drive and then work directly from them.

Maya Personal Learning Edition 5

If you don't already have a version of Maya, you might want to install the Maya Personal Learning Edition 5 (Maya PLE 5) software, which you can find on the CD at the back of this book. Maya PLE 5 is a special version of Maya that gives you free access to Maya Complete for noncommercial use. Maya PLE 5 works on Windows 2000/XP Professional and Mac OS X. Please see the back of the book for more information.

Contact the Author

You can contact the author through his new Maya-centric community website MayaFAQ.com to post any questions about learning Maya or even help other users with their questions. MayaFAQ.com is dedicated to posting tutorials and frequently asked questions on Maya to foster a creative educational community. You're invited to drop by and join the discussions.

CHAPTER 1

Introduction to Computer Graphics and 3D

Throughout this book you'll learn how to work with the tools and techniques that Maya software offers. This chapter will prepare you for the hands-on study that follows by introducing the most important computer graphics (CG) concepts and the roles they will play in your Maya work. You'll start with the most important concept of all—that learning how to work with Maya is a process of learning how to channel the artist within yourself. Topics include:

- Embrace the Art
- What Is CG?
- The Stages of Production
- The CG Production Workflow
- Core Concepts

Embrace the Art

Transcending the medium becomes art. Learning to look past what you're working *with* and seeing what you're working *for* is key to learning CG or any other art form.

As you begin learning 3D with Maya, you're acquiring a new language, a new way of communicating. Always keep in mind that the techniques you'll begin to master are only a means to the end of artistic creation. The most important thing before you start learning about 3D is to relax and enjoy the show.

Although computer tools begin with logic and explicit numbers, your exploration of Maya is not limited to a logical path. Your exploration should be about learning what *you* can do and not what the *software* can do. Don't make this a lesson in how to make a software program work; make it about how you work with the software.

Most CG studios hiring professional 3D artists look primarily for a strong artistic sense, usually exhibited in a traditional portfolio. As such, it is paramount to embrace the artistic streak in yourself and brush up on life drawings, photography, painting, sculpture, and so on and to understand the core principles introduced in this first chapter. Keep in mind that the computer you'll be using for 3D work is nothing more than a tool.

In the past decade, interest in 3D has surged, primarily as a result of the availability of more powerful machines at lower costs. Since 3D can be intensive on the entire computer system, few machines have been powerful enough all around and accessible enough (that is, inexpensive enough) to most until now. Beginning with the late 1990s, production-level equipment has become available to the home market at reasonable prices, and that has helped to spur on interest in 3D.

With that emergence of powerful, cheap computing, a lot of artists are adding the language of CG to their skill set. So, before you embark on learning how Maya software can help you channel the artist within, let's look at some core 3D concepts that will give you a solid foundation.

What Is CG?

Also known as CGI, CG is simply the abbreviation for Computer Graphics (Imagery). Basically, CG refers to any picture or series of pictures that are generated with the aid of a computer. By convention, however, the terms *CG* and *CGI* generally refer to 3D graphics and not to images created using 2D image or paint programs such as Photoshop or Fractal Painter. That's because most 2D graphics software is bitmap-based and all 3D software is vector-based. Bitmap software creates an image as simply a mosaiclike grid of pixels, to be filled in one at a time. Vector software creates an image as a series of mathematical instructions from one calculated point to another. This is a much more powerful method for creating graphics, and it's behind all the dazzling Maya images you've seen—and the ones you'll create. You'll learn more about vectors and bitmaps in "Computer Graphics Concepts" later in this chapter.

If you're familiar with 2D graphics software such as Adobe Illustrator or Macromedia Flash, you know that those programs also use vectors. What Maya and other 3D graphics tools add is the appearance of depth. Instead of being drawn on a flat plane, objects seem to exist in three-dimensional space. This makes the artist's job, and the process of creation, very different than it is with 2D art.

A Preview of the 3D Process

The process of creating in 3D demands that you create objects in a scene, give them color and light, and render them through a virtual camera to make an image. In essence, you need to create a scene that tells the computer what is where, what colors and textures are on these objects, what kind of lighting there is, and what kind of camera you want to use to shoot the scene.

Instead of a virtual canvas on which to paint or copy and paste images, you are given a 3D space—an open area in which to define your own objects, colors, textures, and lights almost as if you were setting up for a photo shoot. As a matter of fact, CG is remarkably analogous to the art and practice of photography and filmmaking.

Photographers lay out their scene by placing the subjects to form the frame. They light the area for a specific mood and to account for the type of film stock and lens they are using and the colors of the scene. They choose the camera, film, and lenses according to their desired result. They snap a picture, develop the negative, and print it to paper, and a photo is born.

Once you build your scene in 3D using models, lights, and a camera, the computer *renders* the scene, converting it to a 2D image. Through rendering, CGI is born.

Rendering is the process of calculating lights and shadows, the placement of textures and colors on models, the movement of animated objects, and so on to give you a sequence of 2D pictures that effectively "shoot" your virtual scene. Instead of an envelope of 4×6 glossy prints, you get a sequence of 2D computer images (or a movie file like a QuickTime or AVI [Audio Video Interleave] file) that sit on your hard drive waiting to be seen.

And that, in a nutshell, is the CG process. It requires a certain amount of planning and patience, as its convention is so different from painting programs and image editors.

Animation

Although Maya can be used to produce amazingly lifelike 3D still images, most Maya artists also work with the fourth dimension, time. That is, most Maya art is animated. Animation is *change over time*. Underlying all animation, from paper flipbooks to film and on to Maya, is the principle that when we see a series of rapidly changing images, we perceive the motion or change as continuous. In creating CG animation, you create scene files with objects that exhibit some sort of change, whether through movement, color shift, growth, or other behavior. But just as with flipbooks and film animation, the change you are animating occurs between static images, called *frames* by analogy with film. You define the object's animation using a "timeline" measured in these single frames.

You'll learn more in "Basic Animation Concepts" later in this chapter.

The Stages of Production

The CG animation industry has inherited from the film industry a pipeline, or way of doing things, that consists of three broad stages: preproduction, production, and postproduction. In film, *preproduction* is the process in which the script and storyboards are written, costumes and sets are designed and built, actors are cast and rehearsed, a crew is hired, and the equipment rented and set up. In the *production* phase, scenes are shot or filmed, in the most convenient and efficient order. *Postproduction* (often called simply "post") describes everything that happens afterward: the scenes are edited into a story; a musical score, sound effects, and additional dialogue are added; special visual effects may also be added. (In a film that has special effects or animation, the actual CG creation is usually accomplished in post.)

Although the work performed at each stage is radically different, this is a useful framework for understanding the process of creating CG.

Preproduction

Preproduction for a CG animation means gathering all reference materials, motion tests, layout drawings, model sketches, and such together to make the actual CG production as straightforward as possible.

Since the CG artist must define 3D scenes in the program, it is essential the artist have a succinct plan of attack for a well-organized production. The more time that is spent planning and organizing for CG, the better.

In the real world, preproduction is part of every CG animation project. For the tutorial projects in this book, you'll work with sketches and other files supplied on the accompanying CD. Even for these tutorials, however, you're encouraged to gather as much information as you can about the objects you'll create.

The Script

To tell a story, CG or not, you need to put it in words. A story need not contain dialogue for it to benefit from a script. Even abstract animations can benefit from a simple explanation of timings and colors laid out in a script. The script serves as the initial blueprint for the animation.

The Storyboard

A storyboard is a further definition of the script. First, you break the script into scenes, and then you break those scenes into shots. You then sketch out each shot on a panel of a storyboard. The panels are laid out in order according to the script to give a visual and linear explanation of the story. Storyboards are useful for planning camera angles (framing a shot), position of characters, lighting, mood, and so on. Even rudimentary boards with stick figures on notebook paper are useful to a production.

The Conceptual Art

Conceptuals are the design elements that are needed for the CG production. Characters are drawn into character sheets in typically three different neutral poses from the front, from the side, and from an angle called a ¾ view. Some are even sculpted into clay for better reference. Props and sets are identified from the script and boards and sketched out into model sheets. The better the conceptual art is visualized, the easier it will be to model and texture everything in CG.

Production

Production begins when you start creating the models from the boards, model sheets, and concept art. You model the characters, the sets, and the props, and you assign everything textures (colors, patterns). The animators take the models and animate everything according to the boards and script. The sequences are rendered in low quality for dailies and checked for accuracy and content.

CG production itself has an involved number of steps, which are usually defined by the needs of the production. We'll peer into 3D workflow in the next section, but to make a long story short, the 3D scenes are created, lit, and animated in the production phase.

Most of the CG techniques you'll learn in this book are part of the production phase.

Postproduction

Once all the scenes have been set up with props and characters and everything is animated, postproduction can begin. Post production for a CG project is similar to film. This is where all the CG film's elements are brought together and assembled into final form.

Rendering

All the CG scenes need to be rendered to their final image or movie files. Again, this is the process by which the computer calculates how everything in the scene should look and displays it. It is a process that makes great processing demands on your computer, usually requiring the full attention of your PC and can take a good amount of time. As you'll learn throughout this book, decisions you make in creating the objects in a scene can make a big difference in how the rest of the process goes.

You can render one scene while another scene is in production, but working on a system that is rendering is not advisable. But when everything is rendered properly, the final images are sorted, and the assembly of the CG project begins. Rendering is the subject of Chapter 11. Three more postproduction activities are advanced topics, beyond the scope of *Introducing Maya*: compositing, editing, and adding sound.

Compositing

Quite often, CG is rendered in different layers and segments and needs to be put back together. In a particular scene, for example, multiple characters interact. Each character is rendered separately from the others and from the backgrounds. They are then all put together in *compositing*, the process of bringing together scene elements that were created separately, to form the final scene.

Compositing programs such as Shake and After Effects not only allow you to compose CG elements together, but also give you some additional control over color, timing, and a host of other additions and alterations you can make to the scene. Compositing can greatly affect the look of a CG project, and most professionals considered it an integral part of CG creation.

Editing

The rendered CG footage is collected and edited together to conform to the script and boards. Some scenes are cut or moved around to heighten the story. This process is essentially the same as in film editing, with one big difference: the amount of footage.

Live-action filmmakers shoot much more footage than is needed for the film, to make sure they have adequate coverage for all their scenes and leave a little extra room for creativity in the editing. The editor and the director sift through all the scenes and arrange them to assemble the film in the best way with what they have shot. A typical film uses a small fraction of all film or video that is shot.

Because CG creation and rendering can be much more time-consuming and expensive to generate than shooting live action, scenes and shots are typically tightly arranged in preproduction boards so there is not much wasted, if any. The entire production is edited with great care beforehand, and the scenes are built and animated to match the story. Consequently, the physical editing process consists mostly of assembling the scenes into the sequence of the story.

Sound

Sound design is important to CG. Viewers like to associate visuals with audio. A basic sound track can add a significant punch to a simple animation by helping provide realism, mood, narrative, and so on.

Sound effects such as footsteps are added to match the action on the screen, also known in film as *foley sound*. Music is scored and added to match the film. Again, this is much the same procedure as in film, with one exception.

In the event that a CG project requires dialogue, the dialogue must be recorded and edited *before* CG production can begin. Dialogue becomes a part of the preproduction phase as well as post. This is because animators need to hear the dialogue being spoken to be able to match the lips of the characters speaking, known as *lip synch*. Quite often the dialogue or musical score also inspires a character's actions, or body language.

How It All Works Together

The process behind making a *South Park* episode makes for a perfect pipeline example. Although the show appears to be animated using paper cutouts, as was the original Christmas short, the actual production work is now done using Maya. In preproduction on a typical episode, the writers hammer out the script, and the voice talent records all the voices before the art department creates the visuals for the show. The script is storyboarded, and copies are distributed to all the animators and layout artists.

Beginning the production phase, each scene is set up with the proper backgrounds and characters in Maya and then handed off for lip-synch, the first step in the animation of the scene. The voices are digitized into computer files for the lip-synch animators to use to animate the mouths of the characters in the show using Maya. The lip-synched animation is then passed to character animators who use the storyboards and also the sound track to animate the characters in the Maya scene.

The animation is then rendered to start the post, edited together following the boards, and sent back to the sound department for any sound effects and such to round out the scene. The episode is assembled together and then sent off on tape for a broadcast.

The CG Production Workflow

Because of the nature of CG and how scenes must be built, a certain workflow works best. Modeling almost always begins the process (except for perhaps scenes with particles only), which then can lead into texturing and then animation (or animation and then texturing). Lighting should follow, with rendering pulling up the rear, as it must. (Of course, the process isn't completely linear; you'll often go back and forth adjusting models, lights, and textures throughout the process.) Chapters 4 through 12 follow this overall sequence, presenting the major Maya operations in the same order you'll use in real-world CG projects.

Modeling

Modeling, the topic of Chapters 4 through 6, is usually the first step in creating CG. You most often start a CG scene by creating the objects you need to occupy your space. It can end up taking the majority of the time in your process.

There are many different modeling techniques, each of which could be the subject of their own book, and the choice of which to use usually depends on the modeler's taste and preferred workflow. As you'll see, the major choice is between NURBS modeling (Chapter 4) and polygon modeling (Chapter 5). A third method, combining elements of the first two, is subdivision surface modeling (Chapter 6).

Having a good idea of your whole story via a storyboard helps a great deal in figuring out how to proceed with the modeling. Knowing how an object is being used in a scene will give you its criteria for modeling. You never want to spend more time on a model than is needed. Beginning with a highly detailed model for a far-away shot will only waste your modeling time and expand your rendering times. For example, if a park bench is to be seen in a wide shot from far away, it does not need abundant detail or complicated surfacing. You can usually create any required details by adding textures. However, a park bench that is featured prominently in a close-up needs as much detail as possible. The viewer will see more of the bench, so more detail needs to be added. You'll learn more about this aspect of modeling in Chapter 4. The more you use models in scenes, the better eye you will develop for knowing exactly how much detail to give them. As you begin your CG experience, however, it's a good idea to lavish your attention on detail. The detailing process will teach you perhaps 70 percent of what you can learn of modeling, which in turn will benefit your overall speed and technique.

Character Modeling

Character modeling usually involves a lot of organic forms such as animals, human, aliens, and such. Practically anything that will be animated to be a character in a scene can be referred to as a character model. You need to create these with animation techniques in mind, as well as accuracy of form.

Most organic characters (as opposed to robots with mechanical parts and hard edges, for example) are built with patches of surfaces stitched together or as a single object that is stretched and pulled into shape. Character models need to look seamless since most character animation requires the model to deform in some way—to bend and warp at certain areas such as the joints.

A character modeler needs to keep the future of the character in mind, to allow for particular character animation methods that will be used. Always try to build your characters with the proper amount of detail appropriate to the scene.

Quite frequently, you will create several models for a character to account for different uses of the character and to keep the scene efficient and workable. You might create one character with fine facial detail for the close-up speaking scenes and another with hardly any details for walk cycles in distant shots.

Architectural and Environment Modeling

This includes architectural previsualization for the design of buildings, but also the generation of backgrounds for sets and environments. Typically it involves modeling buildings or interiors as well as mountains or anything that is required for the scenery such as benches, chairs, lampposts, and so on.

Again, you should not create incredibly detailed environments if they are not featured in a shot, especially in environments that use a lot of geometry. The greater the amount of geometry, the slower your computer will run, and the longer your rendering will take.

You can create a good deal of the environment using clever textures on simple geometry. Games frequently use detailed maps on bare surfaces for environments. The rule of thumb for all kinds of CG is "whatever works."

> Since your computer stores everything in the scene as vector math, the term *geometry* refers to all the surfaces and models in a scene.

Props Modeling

This covers almost everything else needed in the scene. In theater and film terms, a *prop* is an object used by a character in the action; anything relegated to the scenery or background is a *scenic*.

For example, a prop can be a purse a character is carrying, a leash on an animated dog, or a car a character is driving. If the car or purse were just sitting in the background, they would be considered scenics.

Texturing

Once the models are complete, it's a good idea to begin *texturing* and *shading*, the process of applying colors and textures to an object to make it renderable. When you create an object in Maya, for example, a simple gray shader is automatically assigned to it that will let you see it when you light and render the scene.

Because the textures may look different after animating and lighting the scene, it's wise to leave the final adjusting for later.

Just as a painter will rough in an image before adding details, you don't need to make all the shading adjustments right away, since you can return to any part of your scene in Maya and adjust it to fine-tune the picture.

You'll learn more about texturing in Chapter 7.

Animation

Although modeling takes the biggest part of an animator's time, you can really make or break your scene with its animation.

We all have an innate sense of how things move. Culled from years of perception and observation, we understand how physics applies to things and how people and animals move around. Because of this, viewers tend to be much more critical of CG's motion than of anything else.

To animate something properly though, there may be quite a lot of setup beyond the modeling. Depending on the kind of animating you'll be doing, you may need to set up the models for however you'll be animating them. For example, for character animation you will need to create and attach an armature, or skeleton, to manipulate to make the character move, like a puppet.

Taking the models you've spent hours detailing and reworking and giving them life is thrilling and can make any detailed modeling and setup routine well worth it.

Chapters 8 and 9 cover animation techniques in Maya.

Lighting

Lighting is another important part of CG. During this step, you set up virtual lights in your scene to illuminate your objects and action. Lighting can drastically alter the look of your scene. It can greatly increase the believability of your models and textures and can create and heighten mood for your scene.

Although you may set up some initial lights during the texturing of the scene, the serious lighting should be the last thing you do for you scene, aside from changes and tweaks.

The type and number of lights you use in a scene greatly affect not just the look of your scene, but also the amount of time the scene takes to render. Lighting becomes a careful dance between pragmatics and results. It is perhaps the subtlest part of CG to master.

Once you gain more experience with lighting, you'll notice it will affect every other part of your CG creation. You'll find that you'll start modeling differently—modeling with thoughts of the final lighting of the scene in mind. Texturing will change when you keep lighting techniques you've learned in mind. Even your animation and staging will change a bit to take better advantage of efficient, but powerful lighting.

And this is because CG is fundamentally all about light. Manipulating how light is created and reflected is what you're doing with CG. Without light we would not see anything, so it makes sense that simulating it is the most influential step in CG.

As you'll learn in Chapter 10, virtual lights in Maya are similar to lights used in the real world, from single points of light such as a bulb to directed beams such as spot lights.

Rendering

At this stage, your computer takes your scene and does all the computations to create raster images for your movie. Rendering time depends on how much geometry is used in the scene, as well as on the number of lights and the quality and size of your output. The more efficient your scene is, the better the render times.

A lot of people ask how long they should expect their renders to take or how long is too long for a frame to render. It's a subjective question with no answer. Your frames will take as long as they have to take for them to look they way you want. Of course, if you are in a tight time or budgetary constraint, you want simple scenes to keep the render resources and times to a minimum.

As you learn, use as many lights and as much geometry as you can handle for your scenes. The more experience you pick up, the better your eye will become for efficiency. It's important to understand how a scene is put together before you learn how to *efficiently* put a scene together.

Core Concepts

3D animation draws from many disciplines. In learning Maya, you'll work with concepts derived not only from computer graphics but also from design, film and cinematography, and traditional animation. Here's a summary of the most important of those concepts as they apply to Maya.

Computer Graphics Concepts

Knowing a bit about the general terminology and methodology of computer graphics will help you understand how Maya works. Let's begin with the crucial distinction between raster (bitmapped) and vector graphics and how this distinction affects you as a Maya user.

Raster Images

Raster images (synonymous with bitmapped images) make up the world of computer images today. These images are displayed through the arrangements of colored pixels on screen or dots on a print to display an image to the viewer. Everything you create in Maya will eventually be seen as a raster image, even though you create it using vectors.

Raster image programs such as Painter or Photoshop let you adjust existing settings such as color, size, and position for all or a part of an image. They let you paint onto a scanned picture or a virtual canvas to adjust or create the pixels yourself. These programs essentially affect pixels directly, giving you the tools to change pixels to form images. For instance, you can use Photoshop to paint the side of your house red using a scanned photo to see what it might look like before you run down to the local paint store.

Recall from the beginning of this chapter that a raster or bitmap image is a mosaiclike grid of pixels, each pixel corresponding to a mosaic tile. The *resolution*—fineness of detail—of an image is defined by the number of pixels per inch (or other unit of measure) in the horizontal and vertical directions. Because they are based on a grid of a fixed size, raster images do not scale up very well. The closer you get to a raster image, or the larger a raster image is

Figure 1.1

A raster image at its original size (left) and blown up two to three times (right)

scaled, the bigger the pixels become, making the image look blocky, or *pixelated*. To make large raster images, you need to increase the resolution, that is, the number of pixels in the image. The higher the resolution, the larger the file size. Figure 1.1 shows what happens when you blow up a raster image.

In light of this limitation, you might wonder why raster images are used. The answer lies in *how* these images are generated. Most common raster displays are television or computer screens. In fact, the term *raster* originally referred to the display area of a television or computer monitor. The electronics in these devices essentially paint an image as a grid of red, green, and blue pixels on a glowing screen to form an image. Every image generated by a computer, therefore, must either begin as a raster image or be rasterized as part of rendering for display.

Vector Images

Vector images are created in a wholly different way. Vector images are created using mathematical algorithms and geometric functions. Instead of defining the color of each and every pixel in a grid of a raster image, a vector image uses coordinates and geometric formulas to define *areas, volumes,* and *shapes.*

Popular vector-based image applications include Illustrator and Flash, as well as practically all computer-aided design (CAD) programs such as AutoCAD or SolidWorks. These programs let you define shapes and volumes and add color and texture to them through their toolsets.

They store the results in files containing coordinates and equations of points in space and the color values that have been assigned. This vector information is then converted into raster images (called *rasterization*) through rendering so you can view the final image or animation.

Scaling vector graphics does not suffer from the same limitations of raster images. As you can see in Figure 1.2, vectors can be scaled with no loss of quality; they will never pixelate.

Motion in vector programs is stored not by a long sequence of image files, but through changes in positions of the geometry and in the math that defines the shapes and volumes. When a Flash cartoon is played on a website, for example, the information downloaded and fed into your computer is in vector form. It contains the position, size, and shapes of all the characters and backgrounds of the animation. Your computer then renders this information on the fly, in real time, into a raster display that you can enjoy on your screen.

In Maya, however, you work with vectors that are displayed as wireframes. When you finish your scene, Maya renders the image, converting the vector information into a sequence of raster images.

When a vector file is edited, its geometric information is altered through the tools of the vector program. This allows for easy manipulation and handling of changes and is perfect for design industries in which collaboration and efficiency in changes are a necessity. Only when the editing is finished will the vector file be rendered into a new sequence of raster images by the computer.

Figure 1.2:

A vector image at its original size (left) and blown up to 200 percent (right)

Image Output

When you're done with your animation, you'll want as many people as possible to see it. To do that you have to render it out into a file sequence or a movie file. The file can be saved in any number of ways, depending on how you intend it to be viewed.

COLOR DEPTH

An image file stores the color of each pixel as three values, representing red, green, and blue. Image type depends on how much storage is allotted to each pixel (the *color depth*). These are the color depths you're most likely to use with Maya:

Grayscale   The image is black and white with varying degrees of gray in between, typically 256. Grayscale images are good for rendering out black-and-white subjects; no extraneous color information is stored in the image file.

16-bit color or High Color   Each color channel (red, green, blue) gets 5 bits of space to store its value, resulting in an image that can display a maximum of 32,768 colors. Each color channel has a limited range of shades, but still gives a nice color image. You may notice the gradation in the different shades of each color that may result in *color banding* in the image.

24-bit color or True Color   Each color channel is given 8 bits for a range of 256 shades of each red, green, and blue channel for a total of 16 million colors in the image. This color depth gives the best color quality for an image and is widely used in most animation applications. It is said that the human eye cannot see quite as many shades of color as there are in a True Color image. Most of your renders from Maya will probably be as 24-bit color files.

FILE FORMATS

In addition to image type, a number of different image file formats are available today. The most common perhaps is JPEG (Joint Photographic Experts Groups), which is widely used on the Internet.

The main difference between file formats is how the image is stored. Some formats compress the file to reduce file size. However, the greater the compression, the poorer the image's color.

The popular formats to render into from Maya are TIFF (Tagged Image File Format), SGI (Silicon Graphics, Inc.), Maya IFF (Maya Image File Format), and Targa. These file formats maintain a good 24-bit color depth, are either uncompressed or hardly compressed, and are frequently used for broadcast or film work.

To see the animation rendered in a sequence of TIFFs, for example, you must play them back using a frame player such as Fcheck or compile them into a movie file.

Ultimately, your final image format depends on the next step in your project. For example, if you plan to composite your CG, you'll need to output a format that can be imported by your compositing or editing program. TIFF files are perhaps the best format to use as they are widely compatible and store uncompressed color.

MOVIE FILES

Animations can also be output to movie files such as those in AVI or QuickTime. These usually large files are self-contained and contain all the images necessary for the animation that they playback as frames. Like image files, movie files can be compressed to keep their sizes to a minimum, but they can suffer from quality loss as well.

Maya can render directly to an uncompressed AVI movie format, saving you the seeming hassle of having to render out a large sequence of files as TIFFs or such. Although this might seem like a good idea, you probably shouldn't render directly to a movie file. It is best to render a sequence of files, which can easily be compiled into a movie file later using a program such as After Effects or even QuickTime Pro.

The reason for this is simple: nothing is perfect, and neither is rendering on your computer. At times, your render will crash or your machine will freeze. In such an event, you need to start your AVI render from the beginning, whereas with TIFFs you can pick up right after the last rendered frame. With a sequence, you also have the option of reordering the frames, or easily adjusting a few individual frames' properties such as hue or saturation, without affecting the entire movie file. It's just a better idea to render to sequences.

Color

Color is what we perceive as the differences in the frequency of light. The wide range of colors that we see (the visible spectrum) result when any of three *primary colors* of light—red, green, and blue—are mixed together. Color can be mixed in two ways, subtractive and additive. These color definitions are most often displayed in *color wheels*, which place primary colors equally spaced around a ring and place the resultant colors when primaries are mixed in between the appropriate primaries.

Knowing more about color will help you understand how your CG's color scheme will work and help you to design your shots with greater authority. (See the reading list at the end of this chapter for some books that expound on color theory and color's impact on composition.)

SUBTRACTIVE AND ADDITIVE COLOR

Subtractive color mixing is used when the image will be seen with an external light source. It's based on the way reflected light creates color. Light rays bounce off colored surfaces and are tinted by the different pigments on the surface. These pigments absorb and reflect only certain frequencies of the light hitting them, in essence *subtracting* certain colors from the light before it gets to your eyes. Pile up enough different colors of paint and you get black; all the color is absorbed by the pigment, and only black is reflected.

With subtractive color mixing for painting, the traditional color wheel's primary colors are *red*, *blue*, and *green*. These three pigments can be mixed together to form any other color pigment. This is the basis for the color wheel most people are exposed to in art education. However, in the world of print production, a CMYK (Cyan, Magenta, Yellow, and blacK) color wheel is used, which places cyan, yellow, and magenta ink colors as the primary colors used to mix all the other ink colors for print work.

Projected light, however, is mixed as *additive color*. Each light's frequency adds upon another's to form color. The additive primary colors are *red*, *green*, and *blue*. These three colors, when mixed in certain ratios, form the entire range of color. When all are equally mixed together, they form a white light.

A computer monitor uses only additive color mixing, mixing each color with amounts of red, green, and blue (RGB). Output for print is converted to a CMYK color model.

Warm colors are those in the magenta to red to yellow range, and *cool colors* are those in the green to cyan to blue range of the additive color wheel. Warm colors seem to advance from the frame and cool colors seem to recede into the frame.

HOW A COMPUTER DEFINES COLOR

Computers represent all information, including color, as sets of numeric values made up of binary 0s and 1s (bits). In a 24-bit RGB color image, each pixel is represented by three 8-bit values corresponding to the red, green, and blue "channels" of the image. An 8-bit binary number can range from 0 to 255, so for each primary color you have 256 possible levels. With three channels you have $256 \times 256 \times 256$ (16.7 million) possible combinations of each primary color mixed to form the final color.

But color value can also be set on the hue, saturation, and value (HSV) channels of a color. Again, each channel holds a value from 0 to 255 (in a 24-bit image) that defines the final color. The hue value defines the actual tint (from red to green to violet) of the color.

The saturation defines *how much* of that tint is present in the color. The higher the saturation value, the deeper the color. Finally, value defines the brightness of the color, from black to white. The higher the value, the brighter the color.

HSV and RGB give you different methods to control color, allowing you to use the method you prefer. All the colors available in Maya, from textures to lights, are defined as either RGB or HSV values for the best flexibility. You can switch from HSV to RGB definition in Maya at any time.

CMYK COLOR SPACE

For print work, a CMYK color wheel is used, referred to as the four-color process, with cyan, magenta, yellow, and black as the ink colors used. Your color inkjet printer produces color printouts by mixing the appropriate levels of these inks on the paper.

All output from a computer, which is RGB based, to a printer goes through a CMYK conversion as it's printed. For professional print work, specially calibrated monitors are used to better preview the CMYK color of an RGB image before it is printed. Fortunately, only the print professionals need to worry about this conversion process because most of it is handled by our graphics software to a fairly accurate degree.

Resolution, Aspect Ratio, Frame Rate

Resolution denotes the size of an image in the number of horizontal and vertical pixels, usually given as # × # such as 640 × 480. The higher the resolution, the finer the image detail.

You will adjust your final render size to suit the final medium for which you are creating the animation. The following are some standard resolutions:

VGA (Video Graphics Array)	640 × 480	Formerly the standard computing resolution and still a popular television resolution for tape output.
NTSC D1 (National Television System Committee)	720 × 486	The standard resolution for broadcast television in North America.
NTSC DV	720 × 480	Close to the NTSC D1 resolution, this is the typical resolution of digital video cameras.
PAL (Phase Alternation Line)	720 x 586	The standard broadcast resolution for most European countries.
1K Academy (1K refers to 1,000 pixels across)	1024 × 768	Typically the lowest allowable resolution for film production at Academy ratio. Since film is an optical format (whereas TV is a raster format), there is no real set defined resolution for film. Suffice it to say, the higher the better.
2K Academy (2K refers to 2,000 pixels across)	2048 × 1556	Most studios output CG for film at this resolution, which gives the best size to performance ratio.
4K Academy (4K is 4,000 pixels across)	4094 × 3072	A high resolution for film, used for highly detailed shots.

Any discussion of resolution must include the matter of *aspect ratio*. Aspect ratio is the ratio of the screen's *width* to its *height*, and, of course, there are standards:

Academy Standard	1.33:1 or 4:3	The most common aspect ratio. The width is 1.33 times the length of the height. This is the NTSC (National Television Standards Committee) television aspect ratio as well as the aspect ratio of 16mm films and some 35mm films, especially classics such as *Gone with the Wind*.
Widescreen (a.k.a. Academy Flat)	1.85:1 or 16:9	The most often used 35mm film aspect today. When it's displayed on a television, horizontal black bars appear above and below the picture so that the edges are not cropped off (letterbox).
Anamorphic Ratio	2.35:1	Using a lens (called an anamorphic lens), the image captured to 35mm film is squeezed. When played back with a projector with an anamorphic lens, the image is projected with a width at 2.35 times its height. On a standard TV, the letterboxing would be more severe to avoid cropping the sides.

How many frames are played back per second determines the *frame rate* of the animation. This is denoted as *fps*, or frames per second. The following shows the three standard frame rates for media:

- NTSC: 30fps
- PAL: 25fps
- Film: 24fps

Knowing your output medium is important when beginning an animation project. Though not crucial, it can give you what you need to know for designing your framing, creating your movements, determining what you'll need to render it all out, and so on. You can change the frame rate and render resolution at any time in Maya, but it's always better to know as best you can what the final resolution and fps will be before you begin.

Playing back a 24fps animation at 30fps will yield a slower moving animation and will either necessitate the repetition of some frames to fill in the gaps or will end the animation early. Conversely, playing a 30fps animation at 24fps will create a faster moving animation that will either skip some frames or will end later than it should.

3D Coordinate Space

It is essential with a 3D program to know where you are at all times. You can do so if you understand the toolset you're working with and the 3D space in which you're working.

3D space is merely the virtual area in which you create your models and execute your animation. It is based on the Cartesian coordinate system, a geometric map of sorts developed by René Descartes.

Space is defined in three axes, X, Y, and Z, representing width, height, and depth. The three axes form a numeric grid in which a particular point is defined by its *coordinates* set forth as (#,#,#) corresponding to (X,Y,Z).

At the zero point of these axes is the *origin*. This is at (0,0,0) and is the intersection of all three axes. The 3D space defined by these three axes is called the *World Axis,* in which the XYZ axes are a *fixed reference.* The axis in *World Space* is always fixed and is represented in Maya by the XYZ axis icon in the lower-left corner of the perspective windows.

But since objects can be oriented in all sorts of directions within the World Axis, it's necessary for each object to have its own width, height, and depth axis independent of the World Axis. This is called the *Local Axis*. Local Axis is the XYZ coordinate space that is attached to every object in Maya. When that object rotates or moves, its local axis rotates and moves with it. This is necessary to make animating an object easier as it moves and orients about in the World Axis.

You'll get a hands-on introduction to Maya's Cartesian coordinate space in the tutorial in Chapter 3 (see Figure 1.3), where you'll re-create the solar system with the sun placed at the origin, the planets orbiting the world axis and rotating on their own local axes, and moons orbiting the planets and also rotating.

Basic Design Concepts

How you lay out your scene and design your colors is what composition is all about. Creating a dynamic frame that not only catches the viewer's eye but informs and intrigues is an art form all its own.

Some background in basic design is definitely helpful, and you'll want to look at some design books as you further your education in 3D. Understanding the fundamentals of layout and design makes for better-looking scenes and easier setup. The concepts presented here will get you started.

Figure 1.3

The sun at the origin, the earth and other planets orbiting the world axis and also rotating on their own axes, and the moon orbiting the earth

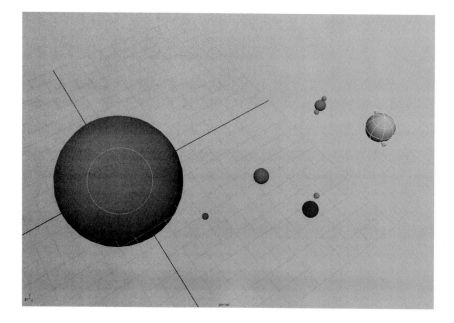

Form, Space, and Composition

Space is defined as your canvas or frame. Since ultimately your canvas will be a rendered image, your design space becomes your image frame. Whether that frames falls into a tiny web window or a huge IMAX screen, the basics of design always apply: How you arrange your forms and divide your space says a lot.

A *form* in design is anything that can be seen; it has some sort of shape, color, or texture that distinguishes it from its frame. Basically any objects you model or animate become a form in your frame when you render the scene. How these objects lie in the frame defines your composition. The space behind and between what is rendered out is the ground or background plane. Objects become *positive space*, and the background becomes *negative space*.

To viewers, positive space tends to proceed forward from the frame, while negative space recedes. Playing with the position of positive and negative space greatly affects the dynamics of your frame. Add to that the element of motion, and you have a terrific chance to play with your canvas.

Design a static frame in which the objects are all centered and evenly spaced, and your viewer will wonder why they're looking at your composition. Arrange the composition so that your subjects occupy more interesting areas of the frame, in which they play with negative space and the viewer's eye can travel the frame, and you create a dynamic composition, with or without animation.

In the tutorial in Chapter 10, you'll use light and shadow to make a still life of fruit a dynamic and interestingly composed frame.

Balance and Symmetry

Balance in a frame suggests an even amount of positive space from one side of the frame to the other. A frame that is heavier on one side can create a more dynamic composition.

Symmetrical objects in a frame are mirrored from one side to another and create a certain static balance to the frame. An asymmetrical composition, therefore, denotes movement in the composition.

A popular technique used by painters, photographers, and cinematographers is called *framing in thirds*, in which the frame is divided into a grid of thirds vertically and horizontally. Interesting parts of the frame or focal points of the subjects are placed at strategic locations in the grid. Placing your subject in the lower third would make it seem small or insignificant. Placing it in the upper third would make the viewer look up to it, magnifying its perceived scale or importance. Figure 1.4 illustrates the difference between a static, symmetric frame and a frame based on thirds.

Figure 1.4

A purely symmetric frame looks static, but framing in thirds helps create a sense of motion.

Contrast

Contrast in design describes how much your foreground subject "pops" from the background. As you can see in Figure 1.5, when you create an area in your frame where there is little variation in color and light, the image will seem flat and uneventful. Using dark shadows and light highlights increases the perceived depth in the image and helps pop out the subject from the background. Animating contrast can help increase or decrease the depth of your frame.

As you'll see in Chapter 10, light plays an important role in creating dynamic contrasts within your frame.

Color

Your use of color also plays a big part in creating impact in your frame. Warm colors tend to come out toward you while cooler colors recede into the frame. Placing a warm color on a subject on a cool background creates a nice color contrast to help the dynamics of your frame.

Colors opposing each other on the color wheel are *complementary* colors and usually clash when put together. Using complementary colors can create a wide variation of contrast in your scene.

Design theory may not seem specifically pertinent to CG right now, but recognizing that there is indeed a way to quantify design elements of a pretty picture greatly helps the design student progress.

Basic Film Concepts

In addition to the design concepts used in framing a shot, you'll want to understand some other filmmaking concepts.

Planning a Production

Understanding the paradigm filmmakers use for their productions will make it easier to plan, create, and manage your own shorts. Most narrative films are broken into acts, which comprise sequences made up of scenes that are made up of shots.

A *narrative film* is a film that tells a story of a hero called a *protagonist* and his or her struggle against an *antagonist*.

Narrative films are typically divided into three *acts*. The first act establishes the main characters and the conflict or struggle that will define the story. Act II covers most of the action of the story as the hero attempts to overcome this conflict. Act III concludes the film by resolving the action in the story and tying up all the loose ends.

Acts can be separated into *sequences*, which are groups of sequential scenes that unite around a particular dramatic or narrative point.

A *scene* is a part of a film that takes place in a specific place or time with specific characters to present that part of the story. Films are broken into scenes for organization purposes by their locations (that is, by where or when they take place). Don't confuse the scene in a film with the word *scene* in CG terms, which refers to the elements in the 3D file that make up the CG.

Scenes are then broken into *shots*, which correspond to a particular camera angle, or *framing*. Shots break up the monotony of a scene by giving different views of the scene and its characters. Shots are broken by *cuts* between the shots.

Shots are defined by angle of view, or the POV (Point of View) of the camera. Shots change as soon as the camera's view is changed.

CG productions of even the simplest topics can follow this simple organization. By following a similar layout in the scripting and storyboarding of your own short, you will find the entire production process will become easier, and the effect of your film stronger.

Figure 1.5

With low contrast, the subject seems to disappear into the background. Add shadows and highlights, and the subject will "pop out."

Lighting

Without lights, you can't capture anything on film. How you light your scene affects the contrast of the frame as well as the color balance and your overall design impact. For most scenes, a typical lighting solution called the *three-point system* is used.

This method places a *key* light in front of the scene as the primary illumination and to cast the shadows in the scene. The key light is typically placed behind the camera and off to one side to create a highlight on one side of the object for contrast's sake.

The rest of the scene is given a *fill* light. The fill acts to illuminate the rest of the scene, but is typically not as bright as the key light. The fill also helps soften harsh shadows from the key light.

To pop the subject out from the background, a *back* light is used to illuminate the silhouette of the subject. This is also known as a *rim* light because it creates a slight halo or rim around the subject in the scene. It's a faint light compared with the key or fill lights.

Create lights in your scene that are too flat or even, and you can greatly weaken your composition and abate your scene's impact. The more you understand how real lights affect your subjects in photography, the better equipped you will be in CG lighting. Although CG lighting techniques can vary wildly from real life, the desired results are typically the same. You'll learn more about Maya lighting techniques in Chapter 10.

Basic Animation Concepts

As mentioned at the beginning of this chapter, animation is the representation of change over time. That's a simple view of an amazing art that has been practiced in one way or another for some time. Although this section cannot cover all of them, here are a few key terms you will come across numerous times on your journey into CG animation.

Frames, Keyframes, In-betweens

Each drawing of an animation, or in the case of CG, a single rendered image, is called a *frame*. A frame also refers to a unit of time in animation, whose exact chronological length depends on how fast the animation will eventually playback (frame rate). For example, at film rate (24fps) a single frame will last 1/24 of a second. At NTSC video rate (30fps) that same frame will last 1/30 of a second.

Keyframes are key frames at which the animator creates a pose for a character (or whatever is being animated). In CG terms, a keyframe is a frame in which a pose, a position, or some other such value has been saved in time. Animation is created when an object travels or changes from one keyframe to another. You will see how creating poses for animation works first hand in Chapter 9, when you create the poses for a simple walking human figure.

In CG, a keyframe can be set on almost *any* aspect of an object—its color, position, size, and so on. Maya will interpolate the *in-between* frames between the keyframes set by the animator. In reality, you can set several keyframes on any one frame in CG animation. Figure 1.6 illustrates a keyframe sequence in Maya.

Keyframe at frame 1

Figure 1.6

Keyframing. In the first frame of this sequence, a keyframe is set on the position, rotation, and scale of the cone. On frame 30, the same properties are again keyframed. Maya calculates all the movement in between.

Frame 5

Frame 10

Frame 15

Frame 20

Frame 25

Keyframe at frame 30

Weight

Weight is an implied facet of design and animation. The weight of your subject in the frame rests on how it is colored and its contrast, shape, and location in the frame and the negative space around it. In animation, the idea of weight takes on a more important role. How you show an object's weight in motion greatly affects its believability. As you'll see in the axe tutorial in Chapter 8, creating proper motion to reflect the object's weight goes a long way toward creating believable animation.

Weight in animation is a perception of mass by the audience. An object's movement and how it reacts in motion and to other objects need to convey the feeling of weight. Otherwise the animation will look bogus, or as they say, "cartoonish."

Weight is created with any number of techniques developed by traditional animators over the years that in some ways distort the shape of the character to make it look as if it is moving. Although it may seem strange to distort an object's dimensions as with *Squash and stretch*, it lends the motion of the character more realism of motion. Chapter 8 will touch more on creating weight in animation; here's a quick preview.

SQUASH AND STRETCH

The character responds to gravity, movement, and inertia by literally squashing down and stretching up when it moves. For example, a cartoon character will squeeze down when it is about to jump up, stretch out a bit while it is flying in the air, and squash back down when it lands to make it look as if the character is reacting to gravity.

EASE-IN AND EASE-OUT

Objects never really suddenly stop. Everything comes to some sort of rest in its own time, slowing before the complete stop in most cases, and is called ease-out.

As objects don't suddenly stop, they also don't immediately start motion either. Most everything needs to speed up a bit before reaching its full speed. This is ease-in. The bouncing ball tutorial in Chapter 8 illustrates ease-in and ease-out.

FOLLOW-THROUGH AND ANTICIPATION

Sometimes exaggerating the weight of an object is necessary in animation. Objects ending an action typically have a follow-through in some way. For example, a cape on a jumping character will continue to move a bit even after the character lands and stops moving. This is similar to the movement of gymnasts. When they land, they need to bend a bit at the knees and waist to stabilize the landing.

Likewise, you can create a little bit of movement in your character or object *before* it moves. Anticipation is a technique in which a character or object winds up before it moves, like a spring that coils in a bit before it bounces. The axe tutorial in Chapter 8 will introduce you to these two concepts.

SUGGESTED READING

The more you know about all the arts that inform CG, the more confident you'll feel among your peers. To get started, check out the following excellent resources.

Art and Design

These books provide valuable insights into the mechanics and art of design. The more you understand design theory, the stronger your art.

Bowers, John. *Introduction to Two-Dimensional Design: Understanding Form and Function*. New York: John Wiley & Sons, 1999.

Itten, Johannes. *Design and Form: The Basic Course at the Bauhaus and Later*. New York: John Wiley & Sons, 1975.

Ocvirk, Otto G, and others. *Art Fundamentals: Theory and Practice*. New York: McGraw-Hill, 1997.

Wong, Wucius. *Principles of Form and Design*. New York: John Wiley & Sons, 1993.

CG

CG has an interesting history and is evolving at breakneck speeds. Acquiring a solid knowledge of this history and evolution is as important as keeping up with current trends.

Kerlow, Isaac Victor. *The Art of 3-D: Computer Animation and Imaging*. New York: John Wiley & Sons, 2000.

Kundert-Gibbs, John; Lee, Peter; et al. *Maya 4.5 Savvy*. San Francisco: Sybex, 2003.

Kuperberg, Marcia. *Guide to Computer Animation*. Burlington: Focal Press, 2002.

Masson, Terrence. *CG 101: A Computer Graphics Industry Reference*. Indianapolis: New Riders Publishing, 1999.

Periodicals

Computer Graphics World (free subscription for those who qualify)

cgw.pennnet.com

cinefex

www.cinefex.com

3D World

www.3dworldmag.com

Websites

www.animationartist.com

www.awn.com

www.highend3d.com

www.3dcafe.com

Film

Block, Bruce. *The Visual Story: Seeing the Structure of Film, TV, and New Media*. Burlington: Focal Press, 2001.

Must Read

Myers, Dale K. *Computer Animation: Expert Advice on Breaking into the Business*. Milford: Oak Cliff Press, 1999.

Physics

As you'll see in Chapter 12, one of Maya's most powerful features is its ability to simulate the dynamics of moving objects. To use that capability effectively, you need a general awareness of the properties of physics—how objects behave in the physical world.

NEWTON'S LAWS OF MOTION

There are three basic laws of motion, the first two of which everyone in animation should and will definitely come to understand to a good degree. Sir Isaac Newton set forth these three laws of motion, summarized here:

- An object in motion will remain in motion and an object at rest will remain at rest unless an external force acts upon the object. This is called inertia, and its understanding is critical to good animation. You'll find more on this in Chapters 8 and 9.

- The more massive an object is, the more force is needed to accelerate or decelerate its motion. This law deals with an object's momentum.

- Every action has an equal and opposite reaction. When you press on a brick wall, for example, the wall exerts an equal amount of force back to your hand. That way your hand doesn't smash through the wall.

MOMENTUM

In particular, it's important to understand what momentum is all about. When an object is in motion, it has momentum. The amount of momentum is calculated by multiplying the mass of the object by its velocity. The heavier something is moving, or the faster it is moving, the more momentum it has.

That's why a tiny bullet can cause such a great impact on a piece of wood, for example. Its sheer speed greatly increases its momentum. Likewise, a slow-moving garbage truck can bash your car, relying on its sheer mass to magnify its momentum.

Basically, when one moving object meets another object that is moving or not, momentum is transferred between them. That means when something hits an object, that target is somehow moved, if there is sufficient momentum transferred to it. For more on this notion, see the axe-throwing exercise in Chapter 8.

Summary

Now that you have a foundation in CG and 3D, you are ready to tackle the software itself. Maya is a capable, intricate program. The more you understand how *you* work artistically, the better use you will make of this exceptional tool.

It seems as if there is a lot to think about before putting objects into a scene and rendering them out. With practice and some design tinkering though, all this becomes intuitive to the artist. As you move forward in your animation education, stay diligent, be patient, and never pass up a chance to learn something new. And above all else, have fun with it.

CHAPTER 2

The Maya Interface

This chapter takes you on a guided tour of all the elements visible on the Maya screen. You will visit the menus, the icons, and the shelves, just to get an idea of what everything is. You'll learn how to work with these tools later in this book, but it's a good idea to go into this at least knowing what everything is called and its purpose.

This chapter can also serve as a good reference for later, when you're wondering what a particular icon does.

If you are already familiar with the Maya interface, you might want to skip this chapter or use it for reference. Topics include:

- ■ **Navigating in Maya**

- ■ **A Screen Roadmap**

- ■ **Panels and Frequently Used Windows**

- ■ **Maya Object Structure**

Navigating in Maya

The key to being a good animator, with the Maya software or with any other tool, is not necessarily knowing where to find all the tools and buttons. It's more about knowing *how* to find the features you need. Don't let the interface intimidate you; it's much friendlier than you might initially think.

Maya is intricate and multifaceted, with layers upon layers of function sets and interface options, separated into categories. The purpose of this chapter is to help you get to know Maya, and how it operates, rather than how to use it.

The best way to start is to explore the interface. Using your mouse, check out the menus, the menu sets, and the tools. Just be careful not to change any settings; the rest of this book and its projects assume your Maya settings are all at the default.

Once you're done clicking around, choose **Window → Settings/Preferences → Preferences**. In the Preferences window, choose **Edit → Restore Default Settings**. That will restore all the settings and interface elements to the default state, just in case settings were changed.

A Screen Roadmap

Let's get to the basics of how Maya is laid out (see Figure 2.1). Running across the top of the screen, right under the application's title bar, are the *main menu bar*, the *Status line*, and the *shelf*.

To the left of the screen, running vertically, is the *Tool Box*, offering quick-view selections, and across from it is the *Channel box/Layer Editor* and sometimes the *Attribute Editor* (not displayed in Figure 2.1). Running horizontally at the bottom of the screen (from the top down) are the *Time Slider*, the *Range Slider*, the *Character Set menu*, the *Auto Keyframe button*, and *Animation Preferences button*.

In the middle of all these elements is the *workspace*, which is host to your *panels* (or scene windows) and their menu options, also known as views or viewports in some other 3D packages. This is where most of your focus will be; this is where you create and manipulate your 3D objects.

MOUSE CONTROLS

You'll want to use a mouse that has three buttons as opposed to a mouse that has a scrolling wheel as a middle button. The wheel may become cumbersome to deal with as a button, and an actual third button is far easier to use.

In Maya, the left mouse button (LM) acts as the primary selection button as it does in many other programs; the right button (RM) activates numerous shortcut menus, and the middle mouse button (MM) lets you move within the Maya interface and move objects themselves.

The Main Menu Bar

Starting with the menu bar, shown here, you'll find a few of the familiar menu choices you've come to expect in many applications, such as File, Edit, and Help.

The one difference in Maya, however, is that menu choices depend on what you are doing. By switching *menu sets*, you change your menu choices and hence your available toolset. You'll find more in-depth information about these later in this chapter, but the menu sets in Maya Complete are Animation, Modeling, Dynamics, and Rendering; Maya Unlimited adds the Cloth and Maya Live menu sets to those four.

Figure 2.1

The initial Maya screen

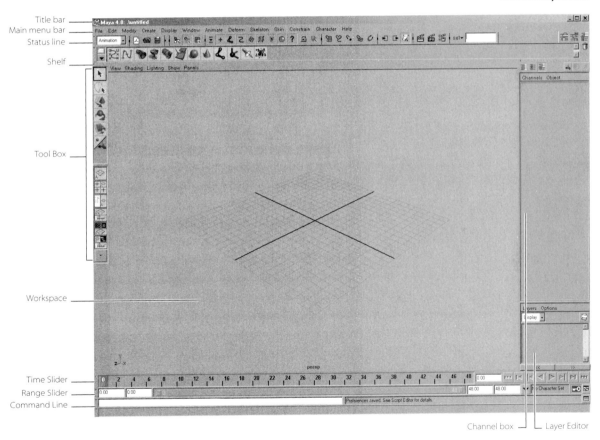

No matter which menu set you are working in, the first six items are constant: File, Edit, Modify, Create, Display, and Window. The last menu, Help, is also constantly displayed, no matter which menu set you choose.

When searching for a particular tool, keep in mind that each menu set controls particular functions. The following menus are always visible:

File Deals with file operations, from saving and opening to optimizing scene size and export/import.

Edit Contains the commands you use to edit characteristics of the scene, for example, deleting and duplicating objects or undoing and redoing actions.

Modify Lets you edit the characteristics of objects in the scene, such as moving or scaling them or changing their pivot points.

Create Lets you make new objects, such as primitive geometries, curves, cameras, and so on.

Display Contains commands for adjusting elements of the GUI (graphical user interface) in Maya as well as objects in the scene, allowing you to toggle, or switch on or off, the display of certain elements as well as components of objects, such as vertices, hulls, pivots, and so on.

Window Gives you access to the many windows you will come to rely on, such as the Attribute Editor, Outliner, Graph Editor, Multilister, and Hypergraph.

Help Gives you access to the help files.

You'll notice two different demarcations to the right of some menu items: arrows and boxes (called *option boxes*). Clicking an arrow opens a submenu that contains more specific commands. Clicking an option box (❑) opens a dialog box in which you can set the options for that particular tool.

ADVANCED TIP: FLOATING MENUS

In Maya you can "tear off" menus to create separate floating boxes, which you can place anywhere in the workspace, as shown here. This makes accessing menu commands easier, especially when you need to use the same command repeatedly. Let's say, for example, that you need to create multiple polygonal spheres. You can tear off the **Create → Polygonal Primitives** menu and place it at the edge of your screen. You can then click the **Sphere** command as many times as you need without opening the dual-layered menu every time. To tear off a menu, click the double line at the top of the menu, and drag the menu where you want it.

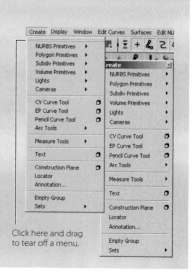

Click here and drag to tear off a menu.

The Status Line

The Status line (see Figure 2.2) contains a number of important and often-used icons.

The Status line begins with a drop-down menu that gives you access to the menu sets in Maya. Selecting a menu set changes the menu set in the main menu bar. You will notice immediately after the Menu Set drop-down menu, and intermittently throughout the Status line, black vertical line breaks with either a box or an arrow in the middle. Clicking a break opens or closes sections of the Status line.

Figure 2.2

The Status line

Scene File Icons

The tools in the first section of the Status line deal with file operations:

Icon	Name	Description
	New Scene	Creates a new, blank scene file.
	Open Scene	Displays a window where you can find any scene file you've saved and open it.
	Save Scene	Displays a window where you can specify a filename and location to save a new scene; or, if the current scene has already been saved and named, saves it to that location.

Selection Modes

The second section between the black horizontal lines is the *Selection Mode field*. This drop-down menu lets you use presets for *selection masks*.

> Using a selection mask, you can select some object types in a scene and not others. For example, in a heavily layered scene, you might want to select only the faces of a polygon and not any other object or object component. You can use a selection mask to isolate polygonal faces as the only selectable object on the screen.

This Selection Mode field gives you some presets that optimize the selection modes for your convenience. But you might prefer to use the individual selection mask icons farther down the Status line; they give you more control.

The next group of icons let you click into three distinct selection modes:

Icon	Name	Description
	Hierarchy Mode	Lets you select groups of objects or parts of a group
	Object Mode	Lets you select objects such as geometry, cameras, lights, and so on
	Component Mode	Lets you select an object's components, such as vertices, faces or the Control Vertices of NURBS surfaces (CVs)

To switch between Object and Component modes, press the F8 key, the default hot key.

Click Hierarchy Mode to select templated objects and the topmost node of a hierarchy. If you have grouped several objects together, being in this mode and clicking any of the member objects selects the entire group.

Individual Selection Masks

The next set of icons between the section breaks deal with individual selection masks, which give you control over which objects or components you want to select. Which icons are displayed depends on the selection mode. If you have many objects in your scene and you are having difficulty selecting a certain type of object with your cursor, you can use these filters to single it out.

Icon	Name	Description
	Set Object Selection Mask	Turns on or off all selection icons
	Select by Handles	Allows selection of object handles
	Select by Joints	Allows selection of joints
	Select by Curve	Allows selection of curves
	Select by Surfaces	Allows selection of surfaces
	Select by Deformations	Allows selection of lattices and other deformers
	Select by Dynamics	Allows selection of particles and dynamic objects
	Select by Rendering	Allows selection of rendering nodes and objects such as lights and cameras
	Select by Miscellaneous	Allows selection of miscellaneous objects such as locators and dimensions
	Lock Selection	Keeps selected objects locked in as selected
	Highlight Selection Mode	Turns off the automatic display of components when selecting in Selection mode

You'll work with these filters throughout the book. For a quick preview, roll your mouse over each of the icons to see a tooltip that gives the icon name and describes its function.

Snapping Functions or Snaps

The icons with the magnets are snaps, which allow you to snap your cursor or object to specific points in the scene. You can snap to other objects, to CVs or vertices, and to grid points and more by toggling these icons. Thus, you can precisely place your objects or points.

Icon	Name	Description
	Snap to Grids	Lets you snap objects to intersections of the view's grid.
	Snap to Curves	Lets you snap objects along a curve.
	Snap to Points	Lets you snap objects to object points such as CVs or vertices.
	Snap to View Planes	Lets you snap objects to view planes.
	Make the Selected Object Live	This has nothing to do with snapping. It lets you create objects such as curves directly on a surface.

Input and Output Connections

The first two icons following the filters list the *input* and *output connections* of an object; the third icon toggles on/off *construction history*, subjects covered later in this book.

Icon	Name	Description
	Input Connections	Lets you select and edit all the input connections for the selected object. That is, you can select and edit any object that directly influences the selected object.
	Output Connections	Lets you select and edit the output connections or any objects the selection affects.
	Construction History	Toggles on/off the construction history.

Input connections are attributes of the object that are being controlled or somehow affected by another object. Output connections are attributes of the object that affect other objects in the scene. Construction history is a feature that keeps track of the nodes and attributes that help make up an object.

Render Controls

The next three icons give you access to render controls:

Icon	Name	Description
	Render Current View	Renders the active viewport at the current frame.
	IPR Render Current View	Renders the active view at the current frame into Interactive Photorealistic Rendering (IPR). You can change certain shading and texturing settings and view real-time updates in the IPR window.
	Render Globals	Opens a window that gives you access to all the rendering switches such as resolution, file type, frame range, and so on.

The Name Selection Field

You use this input window on the Status line to enter object names to make selections. You can enter exact names as well as wildcards such as "sphere*" just in case you forget part of the name of the object.

The Channel Box/Layer Editor

The last part of the Status line deals with the area defined earlier in the chapter as the Channel box/Layer Editor. These buttons toggle through three views in that area of the screen. Clicking the first button displays the Attribute Editor. Clicking the second turns on Tool Options in that column. Clicking the last icon restores the Channel box/Layer Editor.

Icon	Name	Description
	Show/Hide Attribute Editor	Displays the Attribute Editor in this area
	Show/Hide Tool Settings	Displays the current tool's settings
	Show/Hide Channel box/Layer Editor	Displays the Channel box and Layer Editor

The Shelf

The shelf, shown in Figure 2.3, is an area where you keep icons for tools. By default, the shelf contains the icons listed here.

You can point to the icons in the shelf to display a tooltip that gives you the name and a description.

Icon	Name	Description
	CV Curve Tool	Creates a curve using control vertices
	EP Curve Tool	Creates a curve using edit points
	Extrude	Creates an extruded surface
	Revolve	Creates a revolved surface
	Loft	Creates a lofted surface
	Stitch Tool	Allows you to stitch patches together
	Sphere	Creates a NURBS sphere
	Cone	Creates a NURBS cone
	IK Joint Tool	Creates skeletal joints
	IK Handle Tool	Creates IK handles for skeletons
	Spotlight	Creates a spotlight
	Particle Tool	Allows you to create particles
	NURBS Cylinder	Creates a NURBS Cylinder

> **ADVANCED TIP: CUSTOMIZING THE SHELF**
>
> Once you have established a set of favorite Maya tools for routine tasks, you may want to customize the shelf to make those tools immediately accessible. Clicking the Menu icon (▼) opens a menu that you can use to edit the shelf to your liking. To add a menu item to the shelf, press Ctrl+Alt+Shift and select the command from the menu. It will appear on the current shelf. To get rid of an item, MM drag it to the Trash icon. You can create multiple shelves, stack them on top of each other, and access them by clicking the Shelf Tab icon (☐) above the Menu icon to the left of the shelf.

Don't worry too much about the shelf right now; it may be better to use the commands from the menus first before turning to icons and shelves. You'll find that after using Maya for a while, you will create a group of your favorite tools in your own shelves and find the shelf area an invaluable asset to your workflow.

The Tool Box

The Tool Box, shown in Figure 2.4, displays the most commonly used tools: Select, Lasso Select, Translate (or Move), Rotate, Scale, and Show Manipulator. In addition to the common commands, it displays several choices for screen layouts that let you change the interface with a single click. This is quite convenient because different animations call for different view modes. Experiment with the layouts by clicking any of the six presets in the Tool Box.

Icon	Name	Description
	Select	Lets you select objects
	Lasso Select	Allows for a free-form selection using a lasso marquee
	Translate (Move)	Moves selection
	Rotate	Rotates selection
	Scale	Scales selection
	Show Manipulator	Displays an object's specific manipulators
	Current Tool Display	Shows the currently selected tool (shown as blank)

The Channel Box/Layer Editor

The area running vertically to the right of the screen is most usually used for the *Channel box*. This key element lists an object's channels—that is, the attributes of an object that are most commonly animated and used for keyframing—as well as an object's input and output connections. When an object is selected in one of the main views, its name appears at the top

Figure 2.3

The shelf

of the Channel box, and its channels are listed vertically, their names to the left and their values to the right in text boxes. In the Channel box, you can edit all the channel values and rename the object itself. Below these values are the names of the nodes or objects to which the selection has input and output connections.

Immediately under the Channel box is the Layer Editor. This arrangement is quite convenient for scenes that require multiple objects and have layered animations. You can place certain objects on display layers that might be turned on or off to help organize a scene. Get familiar with this feature early on, as it will be a valuable asset when you find yourself animating more complicated scenes.

To create a new layer, click the Create New Layer icon ( ). To add items to a layer, choose **Layers → Add Selected Objects to Current Layer**. You can also use the

layers to select groups of objects by choosing **Layers → Select Objects in Selected Layer(s)**. To change the name and color of a layer, simply double-click the layer to open the Edit Layer dialog box.

You can easily resize this area by clicking either of the double arrow buttons at the bottom of the panel. You can also switch between the Channel box and the Layer Editor by toggling one of the icons in the upper-left corner. (See Figure 2.5.)

Icon	Name
	Show the Channel Box
	Show the Layer Editor
	Show the Channel Box and the Layer Editor

The reason this area of the screen is "most usually" used for the Channel box and the Layer Editor is that you can replace this panel with one of two other windows—the Attribute Editor or the Tool Settings—by clicking one of the three icons (see Figure 2.6) in the upper-right corner of the screen. This gives you quick access to the three windows you find most useful to have on screen all the time. You might want to display the Channel box all the time.

Time Slider/Range Slider

Running horizontally across the bottom of the screen are the Time Slider and the Range Slider, shown in Figure 2.6. The Time Slider displays the range of frames available in your animation and gives you a gray bar, known as the current time indicator, which you can click and then drag back and forth in a scrubbing motion to move through time in your sequence. (When instructed in this book to "scrub" to a certain point in your animation, use this indicator to do so.)

Figure 2.4

The Tool Box

The text box to the right of the Time Slider will give you your current frame, but you can also use the text box to enter the frame you want to access. Immediately next to the current time readout is a set of VCR playback controls that you can use to playback your animation.

Below the Time Slider is the Range Slider, which you use to adjust the range of animation playback for your Time Slider. The text boxes on either side of this slider will give you read-outs for the start and end frames of the scene and of the range selected.

You can adjust any of these settings by either typing in these text boxes or lengthening or shortening the slider with the handles on either end of the bar. When you change the range, you change only the viewable frame range of the scene; you don't adjust any of the anima-tion. Thus, adjusting keyframes and timing is much easier, especially in long animations. By zooming in to a particular section of your time frame, the Time Slider displays only the frames and keyframes for that portion, making it easier to read.

To the right of the Range Slider are the Character Set Selection menu (which deals with the automation of character-animated objects), the Auto Keyframe button (which sets a keyframe automatically when an animated value is changed), and the Animation Preferences button. You'll find information on these features later in this book.

Figure 2.5

The Channel box/Layer Editor

Command Line/Help Line

Maya Embedded Language (MEL) is the user-accessible programming language of Maya. Every action you take invokes a MEL command or script that runs that particular function. You can write your own commands or scripts, using either the Command line or the Script Editor. Use the Command line (see Figure 2.7) to enter single MEL commands directly from

OPENING THE ATTRIBUTE EDITOR IN ITS OWN WINDOW

By default, the Attribute Editor opens in this area of the screen whenever you start Maya. The preferred configuration in this book is to open the Attribute Editor as a separate win-dow instead. To follow along in this book, you'll also want this configuration.

To configure the Attribute Editor to open in its own window, choose **Window → Settings/Preferences → Preferences** to open the Preferences dialog box.

Under the Interface section, set Open Attribute Editor to In Separate Window, and set Open Tool Settings to In Separate Window. If any of your screen elements are missing, you can toggle them on and off through this dialog box.

the keyboard in the white text box portion of the bar. The Command line also displays command feedback and messages from the program, in the gray portion of the bar. The icon at the end of the Command line opens the Script Editor in which you can enter more complicated MEL commands and scripts.

Below the Command line is the Help line. This bar provides a quick reference for most everything on the screen. For the most part, it's a readout of functions when you point to icons. It also prompts you for the next step in a particular function or the next required input for a task's completion.

The Help line is most useful when you're not really quite sure about the next step in a command, such as which object to select next or which key to press to execute the command.

Panels and Frequently Used Windows

The main focus of Maya is, of course, its work windows—the perspective and orthographic views. You use these windows to create, manipulate, and view 3D objects, particles, and animations. By using the mouse, you can navigate in these views rather easily. Navigation in almost all work windows involves a combination of mouse control and keyboard input.

Perspective/Orthographic Windows

The default Maya layout begins with a full-screen perspective view, as shown in Figure 2.8. This view is essentially the view from a camera and expresses real-world depth through the simulation of perspective. In this window, you can see your creation in three dimensions and move around it in real time to get a sense of proportion and depth.

Figure 2.6

The Time Slider and the Range Slider

Figure 2.7

The Command line and the Help line

You can switch your view from the full-screen perspective to the four-panel layout shown in Figure 2.9 by pressing the spacebar. Pressing the spacebar again returns your active view panel to full-screen mode.

Orthographic views (top, front, and side) are most commonly used for modeling, because they are best at conveying exact dimensions and size relationships. Even though the cubes in the perspective window are all the same size, the perspective view, by definition, displays the cubes farther away as being smaller than those closer to you. Orthographic views, however, display exact proportions so that you can see the four cubes as being identical in size and shape.

The four-panel layout gives you accurate feedback on the sizing and proportionality of your models. In general, you'll probably prefer to start your modeling in orthographic view and use the perspective view(s) for fine-tuning and finishing work and for setting up camera angles for rendering.

You can easily adjust the panel layouts of your screen by using any of the six presets in the Tool Box on the left side of the screen or by choosing **Window → Saved Layouts**. Furthermore, you can replace each view panel by choosing another panel name from the list in the Panels menu in the bar at the top of each view. From this menu, you can choose any modeling view, orthographic or perspective, or another window to best suit your workflow. You can also change the size of these windows by clicking and dragging the separating borders between the panels.

By default, each panel displays a grid that you can adjust by choosing **Display → Grid ❏**. The grid is made of actual units of measure that you can adjust. Choose **Window → Settings/ Preferences → Preferences** to open the Preferences dialog box, and in the Settings section make your adjustments.

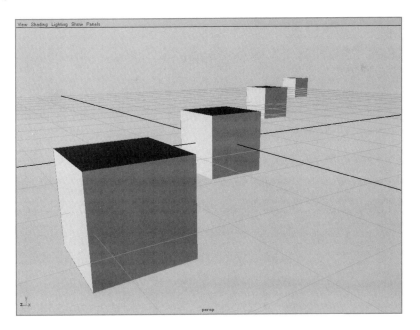

Figure 2.8

The full perspective view

SHORTCUTS TO VIEWING

Here's a quick summary of the most important keyboard shortcuts:

Alt+MM

Tracks around a window. Tracking moves left, right, up, or down in two dimensions; just hold down the Alt key, press and hold the MM, and drag the mouse. This is also called a pan.

Alt+LM+MM

Dollies into or out of a view. A dolly physically moves the camera in and out of the view, practically zooming in and out. However, this is different from an actual zoom in that a zoom function changes the *focal length* of the view's camera lens as opposed to moving the camera closer or farther away. Changing the focal distance can distort the image and change the viewing angle. To dolly, hold down the Alt key, press and hold both the LM and the MM, and drag the mouse.

Alt+LM

Rotates or orbits the camera around in a perspective window. Orbiting lets you get around your object to observe it from different vantage points. To orbit, hold down the Alt key and hold down the LM. This move is called a tumble.

Alt+Ctrl+LM Drag

Dollies your view into the screen area specified in your mouse drag. Hold down the Alt and Ctrl keys while using the LM to outline a window in the panel to execute this "bounding box dolly." This action is commonly referred to as a window zoom in other applications.

Try This: In the four-panel layout (click the second layout icon in the Tool Box), create a NURBS sphere by choosing **Create → NURBS Primitives → Sphere**. A sphere should appear and be selected, as shown in Figure 2.10. You will notice its primary attributes in the Channel box.

Now, press 2, and you will see the wireframe mesh get denser. Press 3, and the mesh gets even denser. You can view all NURBS objects in three levels of display, such as this sphere. Pressing 1, 2, or 3 toggles between detail levels for any selected NURBS object.

> NURBS is a type of surface in Maya that can adjust its detail level at any time to become more or less defined as needed. The display detail keys (1, 2, 3) adjust the level of NURBS detail seen in the panels only.

When you're working in the windows, you can view your 3D objects as either wireframe models (as in Figure 2.10) or as solid, hardware-rendered models, called shaded mode (see Figure 2.11). Wireframe mode is the fastest since the computer doesn't have as much computational overhead. But, depending on your graphics card and your system processor, you'll be surprised at how fast shaded mode can actually be.

Within the shaded mode, you can select from varying degrees of shading detail. You can cycle through the levels of detail by pressing 4, 5, 6, and 7. Wireframe mode is 4, shaded mode is 5, texture shaded mode is 6, and lighted mode is 7.

Pressing 4 or 5 toggles between wireframe and shaded mode in any of the modeling windows. Texture shaded mode (6) displays the actual image textures that have been applied to the object (with quality depending on your video card's capability). Lighted mode (7) is a hardware preview of the object or objects as they are lit in the scene. The detail level hot keys for NURBS objects (1,2,3) apply in shaded mode as well. Here's a quick summary:

Key	Function
4	Toggles into wireframe mode
5	Toggles into shaded mode
6	Toggles into textured mode
7	Toggles into lighted mode

It's always good to toggle between the wireframe and shaded modes to get a feel for the weight and proportion of your model as you are building it. The texture mode is good for the rudimentary lining up of textures, but you may more typically rely on fully rendered frames for that. The IPR renderer in Maya is also great for previewing work because it updates areas of the frame in good-quality renders at interactive speeds. Chapter 11 covers IPR.

Figure 2.9

The four-panel screen layout

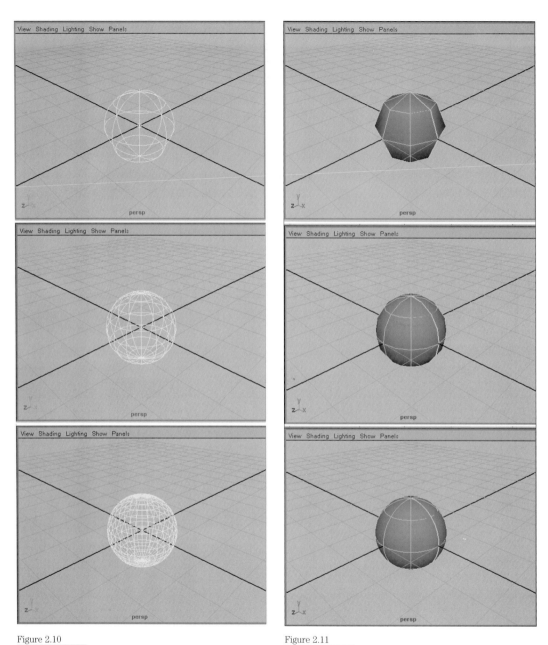

Figure 2.10

NURBS display smoothness

Figure 2.11

Shaded NURBS display detail

The lighted mode however, is useful for spotting proper lighting direction and object highlights when you first begin lighting a scene. It helps to see the direction of lights within your scene without having to render frames all the time. How many lights you see in the modeling window depends on your computer's graphics and overall capabilities. Chapter 10 covers lighting and makes frequent use of this mode.

Other display commands you will find useful while working in the modeling windows are found under the view panel's View menu. **Look at Selection** centers on the selected object or objects, **Frame All** (press A as a keyboard shortcut) moves the view in or out to display all the objects in the scene, and **Frame Selection** (press F as a keyboard shortcut) centers on and moves the view in or out to fully frame the selected object or objects in the panel.

> When using the keyboard shortcuts in the preceding paragraph, *don't* press Shift to generate the capital A or F. Keyboard shortcuts in Maya are described as "case sensitive" because in many cases pressing a single letter key has a different effect than pressing Shift plus the letter (the "uppercase" letter). This book shows all single letters as capitals (the same way they appear on your keyboard), and the Shift key is included when it's part of the shortcut.

The Manipulators

The next thing you should know about the interface deals directly with objects. *Manipulators* are on-screen handles that you use to *manipulate* the selected object, hence the name. Figure 2.12 shows the three distinct and most common manipulators for all objects in Maya: Move, Rotate, and Scale. You use these manipulators to adjust attributes of the objects visually and in real time. Additionally, you can use some manipulators, called special manipulators, or special *manips*, to adjust specific functions while using certain tools or with some objects, such as a spotlight.

You can access the manipulators using either the icons from the Tool Box or the following hot keys:

Key	Function
W	Activates the Move tool
E	Activates the Rotate tool
R	Activates the Scale tool
Q	Deselects any translation tool to hide its manipulator

It may seem strange for the default hot keys to be W, E, and R for Move, Rotate, and Scale, but since the keys are right next to each other on the keyboard, selecting them is easy. These are without a doubt the hotkeys you will use the most, since these are the tools you will be using the most.

Try This: Select the Move tool ( ) from the Tool Box, and the first manipulator shown in Figure 2.12 appears in the middle of the object. The three arrows represent the three axes of movement possible for the object.

Red is for the X axis, green is for the Y axis, and blue is for the Z axis. Cyan is for free movement in both axes of the view of the active panel.

Clicking any of the three arrows lets you move the object *only* on that particular axis. The square in the middle of the manipulator lets you move the object freely about the plane of the view panel, regardless of the axis. When you select a manipulator handle for movement, it turns yellow. The free movement box in the center then turns back to its regular color, cyan.

Next select the Rotate tool ( ) from the Tool Box, and you will see the second manipulator in Figure 2.12. The three colored circles represent the three axes of rotation for the object—red for X, green for Y, and blue for Z. Select a circle to rotate the object on that axis. The yellow circle surrounding the three axis circles lets you freely rotate the object on all three axes. The free rotation handle also turns cyan when an axis handle is active.

Now try selecting the Scale tool ( ) to see the third manipulator in Figure 2.12. By selecting one of the axis handles and dragging the mouse, you can non-uniformly scale the object in that axis, while the middle cyan box will scale the object uniformly on all three axes.

You can scale the manipulator handles to make them more noticeable or less obtrusive. Press the plus key (+) to increase a manipulator's size, and press the minus key (–) to decrease it.

It is much easier, however, to use the default hot keys defined for these transformation tools rather than selecting them from the Tool Box. If the keys ever seem not to work, check to make sure Caps Lock is off. Be sure you are using the lowercase keys.

The Attribute Editor Window

Window → Attribute Editor (Ctrl+A)

The Attribute Editor is one of the most important windows in Maya. Every object is defined by a series of attributes, and you edit attributes using the Attribute Editor. This window displays every attribute of an object and gives you the ability to change them, set keyframes, connect to other attributes, attach expressions, or simply view the attributes.

Figure 2.12

Using manipulators

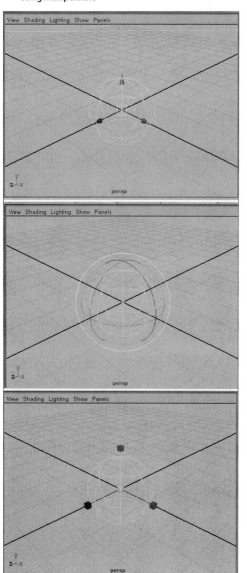

The window has tabs that correspond to the object's node structure. You'll learn more about Maya's object structure later in this chapter, so don't worry about what the tabs mean just yet. As you can see though, each tab displays different attributes of the object.

Try This: Press Ctrl+A to open the Attribute Editor for the sphere (shown in Figure 2.13), and click the makeNurbSphere1 tab.

Now, you'll notice that the Channel box has the primary attributes (**Translate X**, **Translate Y**, **Translate Z**, **Rotate X**, and so on) of the sphere already listed. Below that, you'll find listed the Shapes node named *nurbsSphereShape1* and the Inputs node *makeNurbSphere1*. If you click the *makeNurbSphere1* entry in the Channel box, it will expand to show you some select attributes from that tab in the Attribute Editor. These attributes, despite being shown in two places, are the same. If you edit one in the Channel box, it will be reflected in the Attribute Editor, and vice versa. The Channel box becomes a quick reference, giving you access to the most likely animated attributes of an object, while the Attribute Editor goes into detail, giving you access to everything that makes up that object.

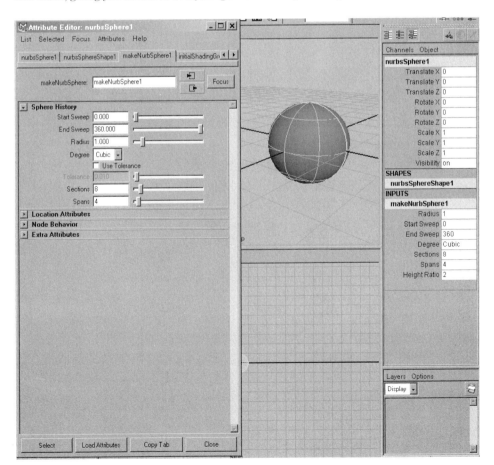

Figure 2.13

The Attribute Editor

Try changing some of the settings in this window and see how that affects the sphere in the view panels. For example, changing the **Radius** attribute changes the size of the sphere. Click the nurbsSphere1 tab, and you will see listed the primary attributes. Try entering some different values for the **Translate** or **Scale** attributes and see what happens to the sphere in the view panels.

On the other hand, press W to activate the Move tool, and move the sphere around one of the view planes. Notice that the respective **Translate** attributes update in almost real time in both the Attribute Editor and the Channel box.

Because you'll use the Attribute Editor constantly, you might want to keep the window open all the time and just move it around, or you can memorize the Ctrl+A hot key to open the window easily.

Outliner/Hypergraph

These two very different windows serve similar functions. They are best used for organizing and grouping scene objects. Basically, these windows let you see every object in your scene in either outline form or flowchart/graph form.

When you are steeped in an animation or model, you will invariably have several elements to your scene. Without a roadmap, it becomes difficult to find the correct object to select or manipulate. Both windows provide this service.

Your needs will typically determine whether you use the Outliner or the Hypergraph. The Outliner is perfect for organizing, for grouping objects together, for renaming nodes, and so forth. The Hypergraph displays all the connections between nodes and is perfect for editing the relationships between nodes.

Figure 2.14

The Outliner

The Outliner

Window → Outliner

The Outliner (see Figure 2.14) displays all the objects in your scene as an outline. You can select any object in a scene by simply clicking its name.

The objects are listed by order of creation within the scene, but you can easily reorganize them by MMB dragging an object to a new location in the window, allowing you to group certain objects together in the list. This is a fantastic way to keep your scene organized.

Additionally, you can easily rename objects by simply double-clicking their Outliner entry and typing their new name. It's crucial to an efficient animation process to keep things well named and properly organized. By doing so, you can quickly identify parts of your scene for later editing and troubleshooting.

A separator bar in the Outliner lets you split the display into two separate outline views. By clicking and dragging this bar up or down, you can see either end of a long list, with both ends having independent scrolling control.

The Hypergraph

Window → Hypergraph

By contrast, the Hypergraph (see Figure 2.15) displays all the objects in your scene in a graphical layout similar to a flowchart. You can see more directly the relationships between the objects in your scene. This window will perhaps be a little more difficult to decipher for the novice, but it affords the user much greater control over object interconnectivity, hierarchy, and input and output connections.

Navigating around the Hypergraph is the same as navigating around any modeling window using the familiar Alt key and mouse combinations for tracking and zooming. The following chapters focus much more on these two windows.

Multilister/Hypershade

As the Outliner and Hypergraph list the objects in the scene, the Multilister and Hypershade windows list the textures and shaders of your scene. Shaders are assigned to objects to give them their visual appearance, their look and feel in other words. Through either of these windows, you can create and edit custom shaders and assign them to any object in the scene. Advantages are associated with each of these two windows, and which you use will depend on personal preference and the particular task.

Maya uses render nodes to create shaders and shader networks for assignment to objects. Render nodes define the characteristics of shaders, which in turn are applied to objects to define how they will look when they're rendered. Shader networks are complex shaders that rely on a network of render nodes to achieve special rendering or texturing effects.

Figure 2.15

The Hypergraph

The Multilister

Window → Rendering Editors → Multilister

The Multilister (see Figure 2.16), true to its name, lays out not just the shaders of your scene, but also lights, cameras, and shaders and their textures in a table format. All the shaders in the scene are displayed under their respective tabs in this window and are represented by named thumbnail icons.

Double-clicking any of the names under the thumbnails lets you change the name of the shader or render node. Remember, keeping objects—including shaders—properly named is critical to good animation workflow and will keep your co-workers happy when you're working in a group.

Clicking any of the thumbnails themselves selects the shader for use, and double-clicking it opens its Attribute Editor. Commands for assigning and such are all located in the Multilister's menu bar, but you can access them by RMB clicking to activate the shortcut menus as well.

The Multilister is in two panels. Both panels let you select what type of shading/render node is displayed. By default, the top panel displays all the shaders in the scene on its General tab—with materials, lights, and camera nodes under their respective tabs. The bottom panel is typically reserved for the display of texture nodes that are available for use or are already connected to shaders.

You can customize both panels using the Display and Filter menus.

Figure 2.16

The Multilister

The Multilister is perfect for quick reference of shaders and lights, but lacks the muscle to easily edit shaders as the Hypershade can. You might want to work more with the Hypershade window and use the Multilister as a quick reference now and then.

The Hypershade

Window → Rendering Editors → Hypershade

The Hypershade (see Figure 2.17) displays the shaders and textures in your scene in a graphical flowchart layout similar to the Hypergraph window. You can easily connect and disconnect render nodes to create anything from simple to complex shading networks. The Hypershade window is in three main areas: the *create panel*, the *render node display*, and the *work area*. The three icons in the upper right let you easily switch views.

THE CREATE PANEL

The Create panel lets you create any shader and its supporting textures by simply clicking the icon for the desired shader or texture. The button at the top selects the type of shader to create: materials, textures, lights, and utility nodes.

THE RENDER NODE DISPLAY

After you create a render node, it appears in the display area as a thumbnail icon and is available for editing. Clicking a render node's icon selects that node for use. Double-clicking the icon opens the Attribute Editor. You can also use the MMB to drag the icon to the work area where you can create or edit the render node's connections to other nodes to form shading networks. Navigating in this area of the Hypershade, as well as the work area, is similar to navigating the Hypergraph and work windows in that you use the Alt key and mouse controls.

THE WORK AREA

The work area is a free-form workspace where you can connect render nodes to form shading networks that you can assign to your object(s) for rendering. This is by far the easiest place to create and edit complex shaders, because it gives you a clear flowchart of the network. You can add nodes to the workspace by MMB dragging them from either the display area of the Hypershade or even the Multilister window.

Figure 2.17

The Hypershade

The Graph Editor

Window → Animation Editors → Graph Editor

Maya's Graph Editor (see Figure 2.18) is an unbelievably powerful tool for the animator, and you use it to edit keyframes in animation.

Since 3D data is stored digitally as vector information—in mathematical form—every movement that is set in Maya generates a graph of value vs. time. The Graph Editor gives you direct access to the curves generated by your animation, which means that you have unparalleled access to editing and fine-tuning your animation.

The Graph Editor is divided into two sections. The left portion, which is much like the Outliner, displays the selected objects and their hierarchy with a listing of their animated channels or attributes. By default, all of an object's keyframed channels are displayed as colored curves in the display to the right of the list. However, by selecting an object or an object's channel in the list, you can isolate only those curves you want to see.

The Graph Editor displays these animation curves, also known as function curves, as value vs. time. Keyframes are represented on the curves as points that can be freely moved about to adjust timing or value. You'll want to tune and refine animation through the Graph Editor, because it gives you the utmost in control over value, timing, and finesse.

The concept of the Graph Editor and the process of editing animation using graph curves may seem daunting at first, especially if you are not mathematically inclined, but this window is truly an animator's best friend. Intimate knowledge of this process will come as you use the Graph Editor, and you will find it much easier to deal with animation. Most, if not all, animation programs make extensive use of a graph or function curve editor.

Figure 2.18

The Graph Editor

The Script Editor

Window → General Editors → Script Editor

You can access the Script Editor (see Figure 2.19) by clicking the icon in the bottom-right corner of the screen at the end of the Command line or by choosing it from the menu. Now, since almost everything in Maya is built on MEL, every command you initiate generates some sort of MEL script or MEL argument. A history of these comments is available in the Script Editor.

This window is handy when you need to reference a command that was issued or an argument or a comment that was displayed. It is also useful in *scripting*, or creating macros of MEL commands to execute compound actions. When you want to create a custom procedure, you can copy and paste MEL from this window to form macros.

The Script Editor is essential in learning how to script. But scripting is a fairly advanced function that you may never need for your work. In any case, tackle scripting only after you establish a comfortable working repertoire in Maya.

The window is in two halves. The top half is the Script Editor's feedback history, and the bottom half is its Command line where new MEL commands can be issued. By highlighting text in the upper window, you can copy and paste the command back into the Command line. You can easily add newly issued commands or macros of commands to the shelf by choosing **File → Save Selected to Shelf**.

Using the Script Editor is also a good way to check on error messages that are too long to fully view in the Command line's feedback box. If you see an error message pop up and something goes wrong, open the Script Editor to see what sort of error(s) have scrolled by.

The Connection Editor

Window → General Editors → Connection Editor

You can use the Connection Editor (see Figure 2.20) to easily connect attributes between almost any two objects. Thus, you can set up almost any sort of relationship between any number of objects. For example, the height of a cube in the Y axis may control the Z axis

Figure 2.19

The Script Editor

A WORD TO THE WISE ABOUT THE HOTBOX

Only when you are comfortable with the interface and you've begun to establish a workflow for yourself should you use the hotbox/marking menus. Once you do, however, you'll find them pleasantly efficient. Many animators prefer to turn off the menu bar entirely to increase screen space for modeling and animating, using the hotbox exclusively. Others use both.

But again, you should use the main menu bar at the top of the screen instead of the hotbox when you're first starting out. It is better to find out where the commands are first. It also helps cut down the clutter of commands and the possibility of confusion about where and how to find them.

rotation of a sphere through a simple click of the mouse. You can set up more complicated connections to automatically rotate the tires of a car as the car moves forward.

The Connection Editor window is separated into two vertical columns, each representing one of two objects. By selecting an object and clicking the Reload Left button, you can load into the Connection Editor's left column all the attributes of the selected objects. By selecting a second object and clicking Reload Right, you can load the attributes of the second object. Clicking attributes in both columns creates a direct relationship between the two objects' attributes.

Connections are the cornerstone of animation and a significant reason for animation being so open-ended in Maya. You can create any kind of relationship between almost any attributes of almost any object to create highly complex, interconnected animations as well as automate animations to simplify a job. And who would argue with simplifying a job?

Figure 2.20

The Connection Editor

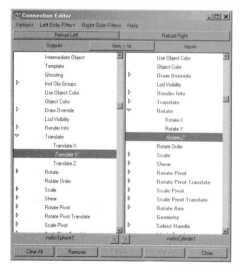

The Hotbox

The hotbox (see Figure 2.21) gives you convenient access to all menu commands in Maya.

To display the hotbox, press and hold down the spacebar in any modeling panel. All the menu commands that are available from the main menu bar are also available through the hotbox. To access a command, simply click it. You can display any or all of the menu headings to give you quick access to whatever commands and features you use most.

As you can see in Figure 2.22, the hotbox is separated into five distinct zones, delineated by the black diagonal lines: North, East, West, South, and Center. Activating the hotbox and clicking a zone displays a set of shortcut menu commands called marking menus, discussed in the next section.

Marking Menus

In addition to menu selections, the hotbox has marking menus in each of the five zones. Using marking menus is yet another way to quickly access the commands you use the most. By default, the marking menu sets deal with changing your selection masks (which objects you can and cannot select), Control Panel visibility, and the type of panel that is being displayed. You can also access predefined (but customizable) key/mouse strokes through the hotbox.

Menu Sets

Recall that menu sets are organized according to function. These menu sets are Animation, Modeling, Dynamics, and Rendering in Maya Complete, with Maya Unlimited adding the Cloth and Maya Live menu sets to those four. Each menu set gives you access to the commands associated with its broader function set. The Animation menu set, for example, displays in the main menu bar all the menu headers that correspond to animation functions, such as the Deform and Skeleton menus.

The menu set drop-down is the first thing on the Status line. Changing between menu sets is easier if you use the default hot keys.

Key	Function
F2	Animation menu set
F3	Modeling menu set
F4	Dynamics menu set
F5	Rendering menu set

Switching back and forth between menu sets may feel a little strange at first, but it makes for a much more organized workspace than having all the menu headers staring at you across the top of the window as you animate. Besides, you can access all the functions through the hotbox anywhere on the screen.

When you find yourself wondering where a particular tool set is, all you need to do is ask yourself, What phase of CG would that function fall under? Since the menu sets are organized in phases of computer animation workflow—modeling, animating, dynamics, and lighting/rendering—the task dictates which menu set includes its toolset.

Figure 2.21

The hotbox and marking menus

Maya Object Structure

Now, on top of everything that you see in Maya—its interface—there is a layer that you don't see: the code.

The layer of code keeps the objects in Maya organized through a network of nodes. And how you relate these nodes defines how you've built your scene. In short, using Maya is essentially programming your computer directly to create 3D objects and animation.

Figure 2.22

Hotbox zones

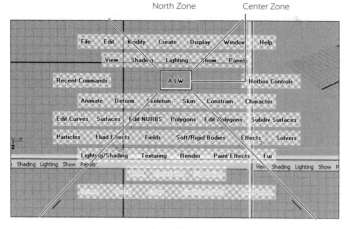

So, having a solid understanding of how Maya defines objects and how they interact is essential to an efficient and successful animation process. And this involves getting an intrinsic understanding of how nodes relate to each other, whether it's a straightforward parent-child hierarchy in which one affects the other directly or a more complicated script-driven expression connecting 15 attributes of several objects together to simplify a task.

When you're beginning to work with a robust program, the learning curve occasionally spikes. With Maya, these spikes typically involve nodes and their interconnections.

Although the interface automates much of the node creation and relationship process, the sooner you are exposed to the implications on the node level of objects, the easier it will be for you to overcome the typical learning curve.

Even though you may not actively see that you're making root level connections between nodes and attributes, you indeed are with every click of a command.

Understanding Nodes

At its core, Maya relies on packets of information called *nodes*, and each node carries with it a group of attributes that in combination define an object. These attributes can be spatial coordinates, geometric descriptors, color values, and so on.

Taken together, an object's attributes define it and how it animates. You can define, animate, and interconnect any or all of these attributes individually or in concert, which gives you amazing control over a scene.

Nodes that define the shape of a surface or a primitive are called *creation nodes* or *shape nodes*. These nodes carry the information that defines how that object is created. For example, a sphere's creation node has an attribute for its radius. Changing that attribute changes the radius of the sphere at its base level. Shape nodes are low on the hierarchy chain and are always child nodes of *transform nodes*. The sphere listens to its creation node attributes first and then moves on down the chain to its other nodes' attributes (such as position, rotation, or scale).

> Not all primitives are created with shape nodes, so changes at the creation level may not be possible on certain objects; some objects are created without a creation node. When you create a new primitive or an object, make sure the History button ⊞ is turned on. If it is crossed out, the primitive will be created without a shape node.

The most visible and used nodes are the transform nodes, also known as DAG nodes. These nodes contain all the transformation attributes for an object or a group of objects below it. Transformations are the values for translation (position), rotation, and scale. These nodes also hold hierarchy information on any other children or parent nodes to which they are attached. When you move or scale an object, you adjust attributes in this node.

Try This: As an example of working with transform nodes, let's create a sphere and see what happens in the Attribute Editor as we adjust its position and size. Follow these steps:

1. Press Ctrl+A to open the Attribute Editor.

   The tabs along the top of the window let you switch between the nodes that are attached to this object. The current tab should be on the sphere's shape node called nurbsSphereShape1. This node contains specific information about the object, but is not typically a node that you edit.

2. Click the nurbsSphere1 tab to access the sphere's transforms node. Press W to select the Translate tool, and move the sphere a little bit in the X direction. Notice in the Attribute Editor that the **Translate** attribute for X has changed. You should also see the change in the channel editor.

3. Press R to select the Scale tool. Scale the sphere uniformly, meaning equally, in all directions by clicking and dragging the center manipulator handle, the cyan box. Notice that the **Scale X**, **Scale Y**, and **Scale Z** attributes of the sphere change in the Attribute Editor. In the Attribute Editor, enter **1.0** for the X, Y, and Z scale values to reset the sphere to its original size.

4. In the creation node of makeNurbsSphere1, change the radius from 1.0 to 2.0. The sphere doubles in size since its radius is doubled. Switch back to the transform node (nurbsSphere1) and take note that the **Scale X**, **Scale Y**, and **Scale Z** attributes are unchanged. This is because you affected the size of the sphere through its **Radius** attribute in the creation node, at its root level and not through the **Scale** attributes in a higher node. Any changes you make to the **Scale** take effect after changes in the lower node.

Parents and Children

A parent node is simply a node that passes its transformations down the hierarchy chain to its children. A child node inherits the transforms of all the parents above it. For example, in the next chapter, you will create a simulation of the solar system. By using hierarchies, you will create a nested hierarchy of parents and children to animate the orbital rotation of the nine planets and some of their moons.

By creating parent-child relationships, you can easily animate the orbit of a moon around a planet while the planet orbits the sun. With the proper hierarchy, the animation of the planet orbiting the sun automatically translates into the moon. In effect, the planet takes the moon with it as it goes around the sun.

Child nodes have their own transformations that can be coupled with any inherited transforms from their parent, and these transformations affect them and any of their children down the line.

Figure 2.23

A simple hierarchy in both the Outliner and Hypergraph windows

The rotation of one of the planets around the sun takes with it its moon, but that moon can have its own animation to spin itself around its planet. It may seem premature to explain this before you see it in practice, but understanding parent-child relationships and hierarchies in general is essential. The more you hear about these concepts in different contexts, the easier they will be.

Figure 2.23 features the Outliner and Hypergraph views with a simple hierarchy of objects for your reference. A top parent node called group1 holds its children nurbsCone1, nurbsSphere3, and the nested group node group2. The node group2 is the parent node of nurbsSphere2 and nurbsSphere1. Chapter 3 will have more information on hierarchies.

Figure 2.24

The best menu...ever!

Summary

Don't worry if you haven't absorbed all of the information in this chapter. Now that you've had some exposure to the Maya user interface, you'll have some familiarity with the various windows once you really get to work. You can always come back to this chaper to refresh your memory. Remember, you should learn the Maya program using its default settings as in Figure 2.24. To start, concentrate on using the menus to access most commands. Once you are really comfortable working in Maya, you can start using hot keys and shortcuts. At this stage, though, you should be focusing on getting a clear understanding of the tools and what they do. You will be introduced to some hot keys and shortcuts as you work thruough the exercises in this book.

CHAPTER 3

Your First Maya Animation

In this chapter you're going to start using Maya software and make some things move. You've spent some time learning how the Maya interface works and how some of the windows operate, and that's really all you need to know to get started. This chapter will take you through the creation of our solar system and the mechanics of animating their orbits. With the solar system exercise, you'll dive into creating simple objects, setting simple keyframes, and stacking your animation to get planets and moons to orbit each other and the sun. This will expose you to object creation, simple modeling, object components, grouping and hierarchies, basic keyframing, and basic timing. Topics include:

- **Project Overview: the Solar System**
- **The Preproduction Process: Planning**
- **Creating a Project**
- **The Production Process: Creating and Animating the Objects**
- **Using the Outliner**

Project Overview: The Solar System

This project focuses on familiarizing you with the fundamentals of object creation, hierarchy, and pivots. You will create and animate a simple simulation of our working solar system.

This tutorial is good practice in getting used to object hierarchies and selections. It will show you how to set up hierarchies and give you experience in working with the proper nodes within a group to create hierarchically layered animation.

The focus in this example is getting used to working with objects.

The Preproduction Process: Planning

As with any good animation you need to begin with a good plan. The more research and information you gather, the better equipped you will be for your given task. For this simple animation, you'll just need to find out where each of the nine planets are in relation to the sun and each other, how they orbit, and how many moons they have.

Starting with the sun in the center, the planets in order are Mercury, Venus, Earth, Mars, Jupiter, Saturn, Uranus, Neptune, and Pluto. They all orbit the sun in ellipses, but for our purposes, you'll be fine with circular orbits. Most planets have a number of moons that orbit them, and one has a large ring that circles around it.

Earth	1 moon
Mars	2 small moons
Jupiter	16+ moons
Saturn	3 large rings and 18+ moons
Uranus	18 moons
Neptune	8 moons
Pluto	1 moon

It may seem overwhelming to create and animate all those objects, but it's a fantastic exercise in getting comfortable with Maya animation. Since the essence of the project is attainable without making every moon, you'll cut most of them out of your scene.

Creating a Project

You'll start by creating a new project for this assignment. Choose **File → Project → New** to open the New Project window. (Figure 3.1 shows the Windows version; the Mac OS X version has the same fields.) In the Maya program files are organized in a particular way. The top level of this organization is the project folder. Within the project folder are numerous file folders that hold your files. The two that stand out are the Scenes and Images folders. The Scenes folder stores your scene files, which contain all the information for your scene, and the Images folder stores images you've rendered out from your scene.

> The scene files mentioned in this chapter are all included on the CD in a project layout explained here. You can copy the scene files into your own project folders once you create the project.

To create a new project, follow these steps:

1. In the Name field in the New Project window, enter **Solar_System** as the name for your project. In the Location box, type the location where you want to store your projects.

   The default location for Windows is `My Documents\maya\projects`; for Macs, the default location is `Home (/Users/<yourname>)` in the `Documents/maya/projects/default` folder. If you prefer, you can put projects in a folder on your second hard drive to keep them separate from your operating system; this allows for easier backup and is generally a safer environment.

2. On a Windows system, create a folder called Projects on drive D through Windows Explorer. On a Mac, select the second drive from the Choose a Folder dialog box (drag the bottom slider all the way to the left to display all your attached and networked hard drives) and create a folder in it called Projects. In the New Project window, click the Browse button and select `D:\Projects` (Windows) or `<Hard Drive Name>/Projects` (Mac) for the location. All the other fields will be filled in for you with defaults; just click the Use Defaults button. Click Accept to create the necessary folders in your specified location. Figure 3.2 shows the complete New Project window in Windows; except for the drive name, the values are the same on a Macintosh.

Figure 3.1

The New Project window on a Windows system. Maya automatically creates a new file system structure for your project.

Figure 3.2

The completed New Project window

How much disk space you require depends on the project. Depending on the complexity and extent of your models and animation, your scene files will typically be on the smaller side. Real disk space starts being consumed when you begin rendering out hundreds of frames at a time. You will need about 10–15MB free for each of these two projects.

> After you create projects, you can switch between them by choosing **File → Project → Set** and selecting the new project. Maya then uses that project's folders until you switch to or create another project.

The Production Process: Creating and Animating the Objects

As discussed in Chapter 1, production is typically divided into phases to make workflow easier to manage. In this project, we'll first create the sun, the planets, and their moons; then we'll animate their respective orbits and rotations.

Creating the Sun and the Planets

The first thing we're going to do is create the sun and the planets. Follow these steps:

1. Choose **File → New Scene**. Maya will ask if you want to save your current scene. Save the file if you need to, or click No to discard the scene.

2. In the four-panel view, press the spacebar with the cursor inside the top view panel to select and maximize it.

3. To create the sun, choose **Create → NURBS Primitives → Sphere**. This will place a NURBS sphere at the origin—that is at a position of 0,0,0 for x,y,z. The origin of the workspace will be the center of the solar system.

4. Select nurbsSphere1 in the Channel Box, and type **Sun**.

Keep in mind that Maya is case-sensitive. An object named *sun* is different from an object named *Sun*.

> Naming your objects right after creation is a good habit to establish. It makes for a cleaner scene file and a more organized workspace. These are particularly important if anyone needs to alter your scene file.

5. Press R to activate the scale manipulator and uniformly scale it up to about twice its current size. For more precision, you can instead highlight the entry fields (the white window next to the attribute) for the **Scale X**, **Scale Y**, and **Scale Z** channels in the Channel box and enter the 4 in any of the three fields. A scale of 4 will be entered in all three fields, as shown in Figure 3.3, and your sun will expand in size by a factor of 4. Entering exact values in the Channel box is a way to scale the sphere precisely. Using the manipulator does the same job but may not be as precise.

Creating the Planets

Next create the planets. Follow these steps:

1. Create a NURBS sphere for Mercury and name it as such.

2. Press W to activate the move manip, and move Mercury a few grid units away from the sun in the positive X direction. (Click the red arrow and drag it to the right.) Leave about two grid units between Mercury and the sun.

3. Since Mercury is the second smallest planet and is tiny compared with the sun, scale it down to 1/20 the size of the sun, or 0.2 in all three axes of scale.

4. Repeat steps 1 through 3 to create the rest of the planets and line them up, each progressively farther out in the X axis. Be sure to keep about 2 grid units of space between each of them. Scale each one to be proportional as follows:

Venus	0.5
Earth	0.5
Mars	0.4
Jupiter	1.0
Saturn	0.9
Uranus	0.7
Neptune	0.7
Pluto	0.15

Now of course this is not a precise proportion to our solar system, but it will do nicely here. Figure 3.4 shows your solar system as it should look now.

Figure 3.3

The sun's Scale values in the Channel box

Figure 3.4

Top view—all the NURBS spheres lined up in place

Using Snaps

This would be the perfect time to start using *snaps,* the icons you looked at in the previous chapter.

Icon	Name	Description
	Snap to Grids	Snaps objects to intersections of the view's grid
	Snap to Curves	Snaps objects along a curve
	Snap to Points	Snaps objects to object points such as CVs or vertices
	Snap to View Planes	Snaps objects to view planes

You use snaps to snap objects into place with precision, by placing them by their pivots points directly onto grid points, onto other object pivots, onto curve points, and so on. Here you will slightly reposition all the planets to center them on the nearest grid line intersection. Follow these steps:

1. Select the first planet, Mercury, and toggle on the *grid snaps* by clicking the grid snap icon: ⊞ .

2. The center of the move manipulator has turned from a square to a circle, signaling that some form of snapping is active. Grab the manipulator in the middle by this circle, and move it slightly to the left or right to snap it onto the closest grid intersection on the X axis.

3. Select the remaining planets, and snap them all to the closest grid intersection on the X axis, making sure to keep about two grid spaces between each of them. Since the sun was created at the origin, and you haven't moved it, you don't need to snap it onto an intersection.

Making Saturn's Ring

You will now create the ring for your Saturn. Follow these steps:

1. Choose **Create → NURBS Primitives → Torus** to get a donut shape. Snap the ring to the same grid intersection as Saturn. This will ensure that both the planet and its ring are on the same pivot point; they share the same center.

2. Select the torus shape you've created, and name it Ring (if you haven't already done so).

3. While the torus shape is still selected, press the spacebar to display the four-panel layout, and maximize the perspective window.

4. Press F to *focus* the perspective display on the ring—and on Jupiter as well.

5. Press 5 to get into shaded mode, and with the torus selected, press 3 to increase the resolution display for the ring.

6. Press R to display the scale manipulator, and scale it down in the Y axis to flatten it.

SAVING MULTIPLE VERSIONS OF YOUR WORK AND *INCREMENTAL SAVE*

As you're working on a project, you may want to save multiple versions of your files at various stages of completion. When working in the professional world, you'll find that clients and art directors are constantly reconsidering animations you've created, so it's always good to keep as many versions of an animation as you can. Scene files are reasonably small, and hard disk space is inexpensive. Just keep your scene folder organized well—for example, by keeping older versions of scenes in separate subfolders—and you should have no problems.

Maya 5's new incremental save feature is an invaluable tool for saving multiple stages of your work, and you should use it as you work through the tutorial projects in this book. Once you've turned on this feature, you can use it to save and create a backup at any stage in your work. If you need to take a break at a point before the instructions tell you to save, you'll be able to start again with the most recent version of your scene file.

Incremental save makes a backup version of your scene file every time you save it. To enable it, choose **File →** **Save** ☐ and click the Incremental Save option box. Once you've done this, Maya will create a new folder within your scenes folder with the name of your current scene file. It will create a backup of your scene in that file and append a number to the filename; for example, planets_001.mb. Every time you save your file, Maya will create a new backup. Once you enable incremental save, Maya will continue to keep the option turned on until you disable it through **File → Save** ☐.

The scene files for the projects in this book on the accompanying CD are provided to give you a reference point for the major stages of each project; compare your own version to those files to make sure you're following the instructions correctly. (In later chapters, some projects also begin with a scene file from the CD.) These files use a slightly different naming system than the names generated by incremental save (for example, planets_v1.mb instead of planets_001.mb), and there is no risk of files overwriting each other.

For important real-world projects, you may decide to supplement the incremental save backups by using Save As to create manually named files, perhaps following a similar naming system, at the stages where you've made significant changes. This may make it easier to identify specific versions of a scene for comparison. Whether you do this or simply use incremental save, it's also a good idea to keep written notes about the differences in each version of a scene file so that whenever you make a large addition or change to a file, you have a record of your work. (If you do name files manually, be sure to use an underscore (_) between the filename and version number instead of a space. Using spaces in your filenames can create problems with the software and with the operating system, especially when you're rendering out a scene.)

You'll notice that the ring is too fat and is cutting into the planet. You need to edit the attributes of the ring to increase the inside radius of the donut shape and create a gap between the planet and the ring.

7. Press Ctrl+A to open the Attribute Editor, and then click the makeNurbTorus1 tab to select its creation node. (See Figure 3.5.)

8. Increasing the **Radius** attribute to about 1.5 and decreasing the **Height Ratio** attribute to about 0.25 will give you the desired effect.

Now, all your planets are complete, and you can move onto the moons.

Changing the original attributes or parameters of an object as you've just done with Saturn's ring is often referred to as "parametric modeling."

Saving Your Work

Now save your work. Saving frequently is another good habit to establish. Power failures and other unforeseen circumstances may not happen often, but they do happen. (As mentioned in the sidebar on the previous page, Maya 5's incremental save feature makes it easy to maintain backups of each stage of your work.) Because you created this as a new project, the Save File window will direct you to the Scenes folder of that project. Save your scene as `planets` in .mb (Maya Binary) format. (If you're working in Maya PLE, you can only save your files as .mp files.)

The file `Planets_v1.mb` in the Scenes folder of the Solar_System project on the CD shows what the scene should look like at this point.

Creating the Moons

For the planets that have moons, you'll create a new NURBS sphere for each moon. For simplicity's sake, you'll only create a maximum of two moons for any planet. However, to get

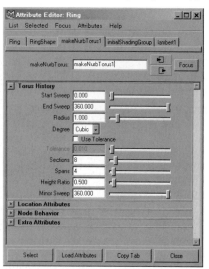

Figure 3.5

Changing the creation attributes of the NURBS torus in the Attribute Editor

more comfortable with this exercise, feel free to make all the moons for all the planets.

The first moon will be the earth's. Follow these steps:

1. Create a NURBS sphere and scale it to about half the size of the earth using the scale manip. There's really no need to type any values for any of the moons' sizes; you can just visually estimate their sizes.

2. Move the sphere to within half a unit of the earth using the move manipulator by the X axis. There's no need to snap it to a grid point, so toggle off the Snap to Grid icon (⌗).

3. Repeat steps 1 and 2 for the remaining moons, placing them each within half a grid unit from their respective planets. When you create two moons for a planet, place one on either side of the planet.

4. Once you're done with all the moons and their placements and sizes, select all the elements in the scene and press 3 to increase the display resolution on all the spheres. When you're done, you should have a scene similar to Figure 3.6.

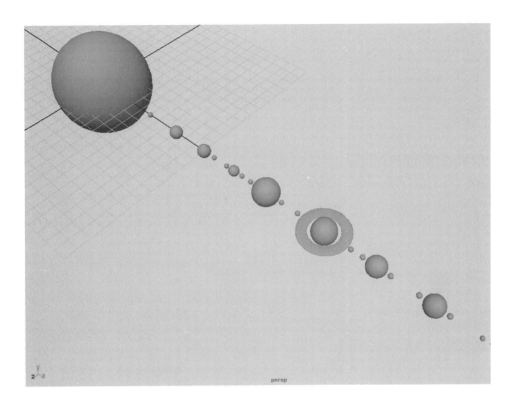

Figure 3.6

The planets and moons in position in perspective view

Applying a Simple Shader

To help distinguish one gray planet from another, you'll need to attach simple shaders to each of the planets. You can easily take care of this task using the Hypershade window. Follow these steps:

1. Choose **Window → Rendering Editors → Hypershade** to open the Hypershade window. You will notice three default, or initial, shader icons already loaded. (See Figure 3.7.)

2. In the Create Panel on the left of the Hypershade window, click the heading bar (labeled Create Textures in Figure 3.7) and change it to Create Materials. In the new selection set, click Lambert to create a new Lambert shader node. It will appear in the top and bottom of the Hypershade window. Click it another eight times to create a total of nine Lambert shading groups in the Hypershade, and then close the window.

Figure 3.7

The Hypershade window

3. Click the first of the new Lambert nodes in the Hypershade window, and then double-click its icon to open the Attribute Editor At the top, replace lambert2 with Mercury_Color. This will identify this material as the one you will use for Mercury.

4. Name each of the remaining eight planets in your animation (Venus, Earth, Mars, Jupiter, Saturn, Uranus, Neptune, and Pluto).

> To rename a node in the Hypershade window, you can also right-click the node's icon and choose **Rename** from the shortcut menu that appears.

Again, keeping a well-named and organized scene is paramount in a smooth animation experience. It's always much more of a chore to go back and root through dozens of unnamed nodes to find the thing you want. When you're done with naming all the material nodes, save your work. You may want to take a break.

Once you've created the shaders, you can assign the appropriate colors to each of them according to the planet they represent.

1. Double-click Mercury to open its Attribute Editor if it's not currently open (see Figure 3.8).

2. To change the color of the shader, click the gray box next to the **Color** attribute. This will open the Color Chooser window from which you can choose a new color from the color wheel or by adjusting values with the HSV sliders. Since Mercury has a brownish red appearance, go with an orange such as in Figure 3.9.

SETTING KEYFRAMES

As with many other functions in Maya, you can set a keyframe in several ways. The best way when you're first starting to learn Maya is to choose **Animate → Set Key □** to display the Set Key Options dialog box:

If you simply choose **Animate → Set Key** instead, Maya sets a keyframe for every single keyable attribute for the selected object. Although this may seem convenient, it makes for a sloppy scene, especially if the scene must be heavily animated.

Having keyframes for attributes that may not actually be animated creates unnecessary clutter. In the Set Key Options dialog box, set the Set Keys On to All Keyable Attributes instead of the default All Manipulator Handles and Keyable Attributes. Set Channels to From Channel Box instead of the default All Keyable. Now, when you choose **Animate → Set Key**, you will set only a keyframe for the channels that you specify explicitly through the Channel box, giving you greater control and efficiency. All you have to do is highlight the channel you want to keyframe and then choose **Animate → Set Key**. Save your settings by choosing **Edit → Save Settings**, and then click Close to close the dialog box.

3. Change the remainder of shaders as follows:

Mercury	Orange Brown
Venus	Beige Yellow
Earth	Blue
Mars	Red Orange
Jupiter	Yellow Green
Saturn	Pale Yellow
Uranus	Cyan
Neptune	Aqua Blue
Pluto	Bright Gray

Figure 3.10 shows the shading groups. Next you will apply shaders to each of the planets.

4. Select a planet in the perspective window, and RM click its corresponding material in the Hypershade window to open a shortcut menu. Select **Assign Material to Selection**. You can also MM drag the material from the Hypershade window to its planet, although assigning material in this way is not preferred in larger scenes. Leave the moons the default gray color. When you're finished, you should have a scene similar to Figure 3.11.

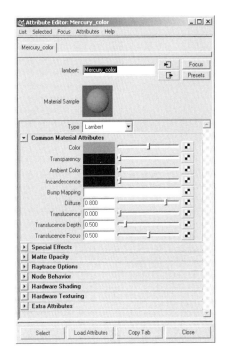

Figure 3.8

Mercury's shading group in the Attribute Editor

Now that you're done with that, you're ready to animate! Just save this file and, if you've enabled incremental save as recommended earlier, it won't be replaced with subsequent saves. If you get lost in your animation and need to start fresh, you won't have to create everything from scratch again. You can just return to the previous version of the file and start your animation again.

Figure 3.9

The Color Chooser window

Figure 3.10

The Hypershade window with all the colored planet shading groups

Figure 3.11

**The shaded planets in
perspective view**

Creating the Animation

To begin this phase of the project, load the file `Planets_v2.mb` in the Scenes folder of the
Solar_System project on the CD, or continue with your own scene file. The animation you'll
be doing for the orbits is really straightforward. Basically you will rotate the planets around
their own axes, you'll then animate the moons around the planets, and finally you'll send the
planets with their moons orbiting the sun.

The basic premise of this exercise deals with hierarchy and pivot points. A *pivot point* is
an object's center of balance of sorts. Every object or node that is created in Maya has a pivot
point at its origin. Since most objects, such as the spheres you created for the planets, will
appear at the origin upon creation, their pivot points are automatically centered.

Once you move an object, as you have done to position the planets and moons, the pivot
point moves with it. Thus, all your planets' and moons' pivot points are already correctly
positioned at the center of each planet and moon.

Now we'll set up our scene file's animation settings:

1. Press F2 to open the Animation menu set.

2. With the Range Slider, set your animation to go from 1 to 240.

3. Click the Animation Preferences icon (🖼), click Settings, and set Time to 30 frames per second, or *NTSC video speed*.

4. Verify that Up-Axis is set to Y and not Z. This ensures that you have designated the Y-axis to be pointing "up" in the perspective window or pointing out at you from the monitor in the Top view. "Y up," as it's called, is Maya's default, but it never hurts to make sure.

> Choose **Window → Settings/Preferences → Preferences** to open the Preferences window. Under Settings: Undo, check the circle for Undo to On (if it isn't already), and set the Queue to Infinite. Setting the Queue to Infinite takes a little more system memory, but it's worth it. With this configuration, you can undo (press CTRL+Z or just Z) as many times as it takes to undo your blunders. To close the Preferences window, click Save.

Mercury's Rotation

Now you're ready to animate Mercury's rotation. Follow these steps:

1. Select Mercury first, and press E to activate the rotation manipulator. Press F to focus on it in the perspective view, or zoom in on it manually.

2. Make sure you are on frame 1 of your animation range. You'll place an initial keyframe here for the first planet.

3. For Mercury, you'll be setting your initial keyframe for the Y-axis rotation. In the Channel box, click the attribute **Rotate Y** and choose **Animate → Set Key**. The **Rotate Y**'s attribute box should turn orange, indicating a keyframe or other input.

4. With the Range Slider, go to frame 240. Grab the rotation manipulator handle by the Y-axis and turn it clockwise a few times to rotate the sphere.

5. Choose **Animate → Set Key** with the **Rotate Y** attribute still selected in the Channel box.

6. To playback your animation, you can *scrub* your timeline. Scrubbing refers to using the mouse to move the time marker back and forth to watch the animation playback in a window. Click in the Timeline, hold down the left mouse button, and move your cursor side to side to scrub in real time. You'll see Mercury rotating around itself in your active view panel.

Clicking so many things just to set two keyframes may seem like a lot or work, but you're doing this the long way right now; you're not using any shortcuts or hot keys. You'll start using those for the next planet.

You have the self-rotation for Mercury worked out, and since there's no moon for Mercury, let's get it orbiting the sun.

Grouping Mercury for a New Pivot Point

You've already learned that every object created in Maya is created with a pivot point around which it rotates, from or to which it scales, and is the placement point for its XYZ coordinates. If the pivot point for Mercury is already at the center of itself, how do you rotate it around the sun?

One idea is to move its current pivot point from the center of itself to the center of the sun. That would, however, negate its own rotation, and it will no longer spin around its own center; so you can't do that. What you need to do is to create a new pivot point for this object by creating a new parent node above it in the hierarchy. For more on object nodes and hierarchy, refer to the end of Chapter 2.

To create a new pivot point, follow these steps:

1. With Mercury still selected, choose **Edit → Group**. The Channel box now displays the attributes for the node called group1. In addition, the rotation manipulator handle has jumped from where it originally was, centered on Mercury, to the origin where the zero points of the X-, Y-, and Z-axes collide. Figure 3.12 shows the new Mercury group and its new pivot location.

You have essentially created a new Maya object by grouping Mercury to itself, and hence have also created a new pivot point placed by Maya at the origin by default. Since an object's manipulator always centers on its pivot point, yours jumped to the origin. That's fortunate for you, because that just happens to be the center of the sun, exactly where you need it to be for Mercury to orbit it properly.

2. Without unselecting Mercury and its moon, click the word *group1* in the Channel box and change the name of this new group to Mercury_Orbit.

Figure 3.12

Grouping Mercury to itself creates a new pivot point at the origin.

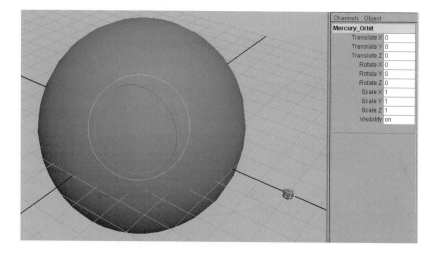

3. Now click anywhere in an empty space in your view window to unselect Mercury_Orbit. Try selecting it again. Notice that when you click Mercury or its moon, you can select only one or the other. If you select one and then Shift+click the other, you select both objects, but you will not select Mercury_Orbit, the group that contains both these objects and has its pivot point at the center of the sun. This is because you are in object selection mode.

> To select the group Mercury_Orbit, you need to switch into Hierarchy Selection by toggling its icon (⬚) on the Status line. Just remember to switch back to Object Mode (⬚).

4. Go back to frame 1 of your animation and set a keyframe for Mercury_Orbit's **Rotate Y** attribute by choosing **Animate → Set Key**.

5. Go to frame 240, grab Mercury_Orbit's rotate manipulator handle by the Y-axis, and spin it around the sun twice.

6. Choose **Animate → Set Key** to set a keyframe at frame 240 for Mercury_Orbit. Scrub your animation to play it back.

    One down, nine to go.

Creating Venus

For your next planet, Venus, follow the same procedure as for Mercury, and animate it so that it orbits itself. Then create a new pivot point by grouping it to itself (and calling the new node Venus_Orbit). Last, animate Venus_Orbit to rotate around the sun.

The Earth and the Moon

You will animate the third planet in much the same way except that this time there is the added complication of a moon. In addition, instead of choosing **Animate → Set Key** to set your keyframes, you'll use the keyboard hot key S.

> Whenever you press S and an attribute is highlighted in the Channel box, you are essentially choosing **Animate → Set Key**.

To animate the earth and the moon, follow these steps:

1. Select the earth and give it its self-rotation animation first by pressing S (instead of choosing **Animate → Set Key**).

2. Select the moon and give it its own self-rotation animation by spinning it around itself as you've just done with the earth.

3. To spin the moon around the earth, follow the steps given earlier in this chapter for spinning a planet around the sun.

4. Group the moon to itself by choosing **Edit → Group** and name it Moon_Orbit.

This time, however, you need the pivot point to be at the center of the earth and not at the center of the sun where it is currently. Follow these steps:

1. Turn on the grid snap, and then press the Insert key to activate the pivot point. The moon's manipulator changes from a rotation handle to the pivot point manipulator. This manipulator acts just like the move manipulator, but instead of moving the object, it moves the object's pivot point.

2. Grab the yellow circle in the middle of the manipulator and move the pivot point to snap it to the grid point located at the center of the earth (see Figure 3.13).

3. Press the Insert key again to return to the rotation manipulator for Moon_Orbit. At frame 1, set a keyframe for the moon's Y-axis rotation. Then, at frame 240, rotate the moon about the Y-axis and set a keyframe. Return to frame 1.

GROUPING THE MOON WITH THE EARTH

To create the animation of the earth's orbit of the sun, you need to make sure that the moon will also follow the earth around the sun. So, instead of just selecting the earth and grouping it to itself as you've done for the other two planets, you need to include Moon_Orbit. Follow these steps:

1. Select the earth and the group Moon_Orbit, and then choose **Edit → Group**. Name this Earth_Orbit.

Make sure you use Hierarchy Mode ( ) when you click the moon object to select Moon_Orbit and not just the moon sphere. Otherwise, you will lose the animation of the moon orbiting the earth.

Figure 3.13

Moving the moon's pivot point to the center of the earth

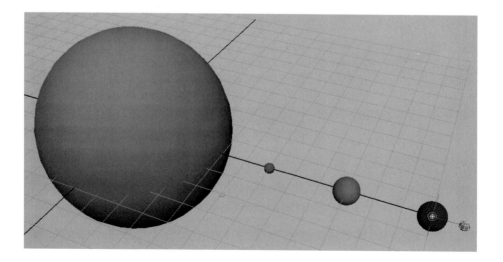

2. Set a keyframe for Earth_Orbit's **Rotate Y** attribute at frame 1 by highlighting **Rotate Y** in the Channel box and pressing S for the Set Key command.

3. Go to frame 240, spin the earth and the moon around the sun a few times, and set a keyframe there as well.

Now the first three planets are going around themselves and around the sun, with a moon in there too. If you haven't been saving your work, save it now. Just don't save over the un-animated version from before.

CREATING THE OTHER PLANETS' MOONS

Repeat this animation procedure for the remaining planets and moons, but leave out Pluto for now.

> If you find that one of your moons is left behind by its planet or that it's no longer rotating around the planet, you most likely made an error when grouping the moon and planet. Undo until you're at the point right before you grouped them, and try again. If that still doesn't work, start over from the earlier version of the file you saved just before you started animating it.

AUTO KEYFRAME

You can also use the Auto Keyframe feature when animating the other planets and moons. Auto Keyframe automatically sets a keyframe for any attribute that has changed from a previously set keyframe. For example, an initial keyframe for an attribute such as **Y-Axis Rotation** needs to be set at some point in the animation. The next time the **Y-Axis Rotation** is changed, Maya will set a keyframe at the current frame.

To turn on Auto Keyframe, click the Auto Keyframe icon ( ), which is to the right of the Range Slider. When the icon is red, Auto Keyframe is active.

To use Auto Keyframe to animate Mars' moon orbiting Mars, follow these steps:

1. Turn on Auto Keyframe

2. Start at Frame 1. Select Mars' moon and set a keyframe for its Y rotation by highlighting **Rotate Y** in the Channel box and pressing S.

3. Got to frame 240. Rotate the moon around Mars several times. Maya will automatically set a frame for Y rotation at frame 240. Save your file.

Using the Outliner

Now, let's look at how to use the Outliner to illustrate the hierarchies for the planets and moons. When all is good and proper, the Outliner should look like Figure 3.14. Choose **Window → Outliner** and take a peek at what you have. If you haven't yet named everything properly, such as the moons, take this opportunity to do so.

Figure 3.14

The Outliner view of the planet hierarchies

Let's take a look at the planet Mars and its layout in the Outliner to better understand the hierarchy for all the planets. All the other planets should be laid out exactly like Mars (except for the planets that have one or no moons).

At the bottom of the hierarchy are Mars' two moons, mars_moon and mars_moon2. Each of those moons is spinning on its own pivot point. You then grouped each moon to itself, creating the mars_moon_orbit and mars_moon2_orbit nodes, and you placed their pivot points at the center of Mars to animate their orbits of Mars.

Mars is spinning on its own pivot point, but it needed another pivot point to be able to orbit the sun. Since you needed to make the moons go with it around the sun, you selected Mars, mars_moon_orbit, and mars_moon2_orbit (the top nodes of the moons that circle the planet Mars) and grouped them all together, placing that pivot point at the center of the sun. This node you called Mars_Orbit. This is the parent node since it is the topmost node for this group. Where this parent node goes, so follow the children nodes that are grouped under it.

Hierarchy such as this is a cornerstone of Maya animation. It is imperative to be comfortable with how it works and how to work with it.

Correcting Hierarchy Problems using the Outliner

One of the most common problems you will run into with this project is a planet rotating around the sun without its moon. The following steps will force you to make this error with the planet Pluto, to illustrate how to fix it using the Outliner—as opposed to undoing and redoing it as suggested earlier.

Go to Pluto, start the same animation procedure as outlined earlier, and then follow these steps:

1. Create Pluto's own rotation by spinning it around itself.

2. Do the same for its moon's rotation.

3. Group the moon to itself and grid-snap the pivot point at the center of Pluto to create the moon's orbit of Pluto.

Once Pluto's moon (pluto_moon) is orbiting Pluto, you're ready to group the moon's orbit and Pluto together to create an orbit of the sun for them both.

4. In object mode, select the sphere for Pluto's moon, and select the sphere for Pluto.

5. Choose **Edit → Group** to group them together, and call that new node Pluto_Orbit like the others.

6. Animate Pluto_Orbit rotating around the sun.

7. Playback the animation.

Figure 3.15

Pluto's incorrect hierarchy

You'll notice that the moon is no longer orbiting the planet. This is because you neglected to include Pluto_moon_orbit in your group Pluto_Orbit. The animation of the moon going around Pluto is stored in that node, and since it is no longer attached to your Pluto_Orbit, there's no moon orbit of Pluto.

Figure 3.15 shows the hierarchy of Pluto and how it's different from the other planets (with the earth showing as an example). The moon's orbit node has been left out of the group.

Using the Outliner, you can easily fix this problem. You will place the pluto_moon_orbit node under the Pluto_Orbit node. Go to frame 1 of the animation, and grab the pluto_moon_orbit node in the Outliner and MM drag it to the Pluto_Orbit node so that it has a black horizontal line above and below it to show a connection, as in Figure 3.16.

You have just grouped pluto_moon_orbit under Pluto_Orbit, a practice known as parenting. Now you need to parent pluto_moon under pluto_moon_orbit as well. MM drag pluto_moon onto pluto_moon_orbit. When you playback the animation, you will see that the moon is rotating around the planet as Pluto and the moon both orbit the sun. Now the layout in the Outliner for Pluto is similar to the other properly working planets.

The file `Planets_v3.mb` in the Scenes folder of the Solar_System project on the CD will give you an idea how this project should now look. The first five planet systems are grouped and animated as reference, leaving the final four for you to finish.

Figure 3.16

Regrouping objects in the Outliner

You can add objects to a group by MM dragging their listing onto the desired parent node in the Outliner. You can also remove objects from a group by MM dragging them out of the parent node to a different place in the Outliner.

GROUPING TERMINOLOGY

Grouping terminology can be confusing. Grouping Node A under Node B makes Node A a *child* of Node B. Node B is now the *parent* of Node A. Furthermore, any transformation, or movement, applied to the parent Node B will be *inherited* by the child Node A.

When you *group* Node A and Node B, both nodes become *siblings* under a newly created parent node, Node C. This new node is created just to be the parent of Nodes A and B and is otherwise known as a *null node*. To group objects, select them and choose **Edit → Group**.

Parenting nodes together places the first selected node under the second selected node. For example, if you select Node A, Shift+select Node B, and then choose **Edit → Parent**, Node A will group under Node B and become its child. This is the same procedure as MM dragging Node B to Node A in the Outliner as you did with Pluto's moon and Pluto itself.

Summary

The planet animation you created is based on a system of layering simple actions on top of each other to achieve a more elaborate result. If you work slowly and in segments, animation becomes more straightforward to produce and generally is of a higher quality. Much of your time in actual animation—as opposed to setup or modeling—will be spent adjusting the small things. These small things give the scene life and character. You will find that finishing 85 percent of a scene will take about 15 percent of the time. The remaining 85 percent of the time goes into perfecting the final 15 percent of the scene.

CHAPTER 4

Modeling with NURBS

Modeling is the process of creating 3D objects so that they are ready to animate. Simple objects call for simple models, and complicated objects call for a complex of simple models. One of the toughest things about modeling is deciding how to represent an object in 3D. Just like a sculptor working with a chisel, you must analyze the object and deconstruct its design to learn how it exists.

Maya software uses three types of modeling: NURBS, polygons, and subdivision surfaces. All three types require planning, a process that begins with deciding which modeling method to use. To help you make that choice, this chapter begins with an overview of modeling, briefly describing the three methods and how they differ. You'll also learn about Maya's prim- itives, which are available with all three modeling methods. In the second part of the chapter, you'll take a detailed look at modeling with NURBS and get plenty of hands-on practice. (The next two chapters cover the process of modeling with polygons and subdivision surfaces.) Topics include:

- **Planning Your Model**
- **Modeling with NURBS**
- **Creating an Axe Using NURBS**
- **Editing NURBS Surfaces**
- **Using Artisan to Sculpt NURBS**

Planning Your Model

The first step to making anything is to understand how it's constructed. The best training for a CG modeler is to visualize the elements that make up an object. By dissecting the components of that object, you can translate its re-creation into 3D terms. You first create the elements in Maya and then join them together to form the desired object.

Gather as much information as you can about the object you want to model. Take pictures from as many angles as possible, get sizes and dimensions, and even write a detailed description of the object. For a further understanding of how your subject is put together, try to re-create it in a sketch or simple clay or balsa wood model. By exploring different ways to create the object, you'll be better able to model it in the Maya interface. Maya has a truly rich toolset for creating models, and it's important to choose the methodology that best matches the modeling task at hand. Be prepared with sketches, pictures, and whatever information you can gather before you sit down to realize your CG model.

How detailed should your model be? This is a crucial question, because a model that's too complex or a scene that has too much detail wastes precious computing time and power, greatly increasing render times.

Begin by deciding the purpose for your model. Then find out to what level of detail it will be *seen* in your CG scene. For example, consider the two scenes in Figure 4.1. If you need to create a park bench that is shown in a far shot (left), it will be a waste of time and effort to model all the details like the grooves in the arm rest. If, however, your park bench is shown in a close-up (right), you'll need those details after all. It is important to plan your model to the level of detail it requires.

Figure 4.1

The level of detail you need to include in a model depends on how it will be seen in the animation.

If you aren't certain how much detail you will eventually need, it is best to create a higher level of detail that you can easily pare down if it becomes unnecessary in the scene. Also keep in mind that you can add detail to your model in the texturing phase of production. You would be amazed at the richness of detail a model can achieve with simple geometry and well-painted texture maps. (Chapter 7 covers texturing.)

As your models become increasingly complex, you will also need to gauge how well your computer can handle them. As the detail increases in a model, the performance demands on your PC can skyrocket. If a slower machine or a weaker graphics card limits you, your models will have to be even better thought out as to their level of detail. Equipped with this decision and hopefully a number of photos, web pictures, and sketches, you will find your modeling experience more productive.

An Overview of NURBS, Polygons, and Subdivision Surfaces

A fundamental decision you'll make in planning is choosing the modeling method. Maya can define a model in three ways: NURBS (the subject of this chapter), polygons (the subject of Chapter 5), or subdivision surfaces (an advanced technique introduced in Chapter 6). Although NURBS modeling is traditionally what Maya modeling is renowned for, polygons are the simplest to describe.

Polygon Modeling

Polygons are made up of *faces*. A single polygon face is a flat surface made when three or more points called *vertices* are connected. The position of each vertex defines the shape and size of the face, usually a triangle. The line that connects one vertex to another is called an *edge*. Some polygonal faces have four vertices instead of three, creating a square face instead of a triangular one.

Polygonal faces are attached along their polygonal edges to make up a more complex surface that constitutes your model (see Figure 4.2). A camping tent is a perfect example. The intersections of the poles are the faces' vertices. The poles are the edges of the faces, and the cloth draped over the tent's frame is the resultant surface.

Polygon models are the simplest for a computer to render, and for that reason they are typically used for gaming applications,

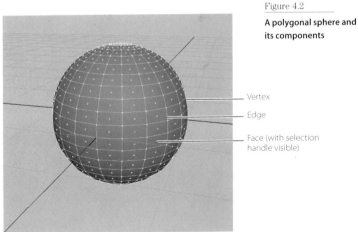

Figure 4.2

A polygonal sphere and its components

Vertex

Edge

Face (with selection handle visible)

which need to render the models as the game is running. The gaming artists create models with a small number of polygons—called *low-count poly models*—that a PC or game console can render in real time. High-resolution polygon models are frequently used in television and film work. In fact, a number of science fiction TV shows use polygonal models almost exclusively for their special effects. And because even complex polygon models can be made of a single surface, they are useful for character animation work as well. Since models in character animation bend and warp a good deal, having a single surface that will not separate at the seams can be advantageous. You'll get hands-on practice with polygon modeling in Chapter 5.

NURBS Modeling

NURBS modeling is based on mathematics that is more complicated than the mathematics for polygons. Because NURBS modeling requires more processing, this method is typically used for applications in which the rendering is done in advance, such as animation for film or television. NURBS modeling excels at creating curved shapes and lines, so it is most often used for organic forms such as animals and people, as well as highly detailed cars and the like.

NURBS is an acronym for *Non-Uniform Rational Bèzier Splines*. NURBS geometry is based on Bèzier curves, a math concept originally developed by the French engineer Pierre Bèzier. Bèzier curves are drawn between *control vertices* (*CVs*) based on equations using cubic polynomials.

In essence, Bèzier curves are created with a starting and an ending CV and at least 2 CVs in between that provide the curvature. As each CV is laid down, the curve or spline tries to go from the previous CV to the next one in the smoothest possible manner.

As shown in Figure 4.3, CVs control the curvature. The *hulls* connect the CVs and are useful for selecting multiple rows of CVs at a time. The starting CV appears in Maya as a closed box, and the second CV, which defines the curve's direction, is an open box, so you can easily see the direction in which a curve has been created. The curve ends, of course, on the end point CV. The start and end CVs are the only CVs that are always actually on the curve.

Figure 4.3

A Bèzier curve and its components

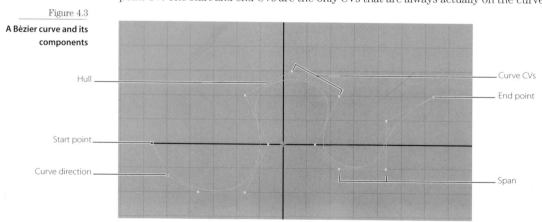

Hull

Start point

Curve direction

Curve CVs

End point

Span

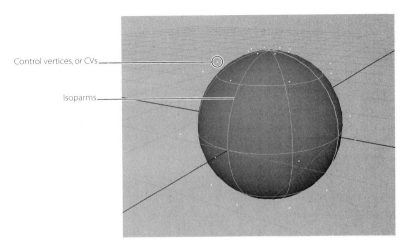

Control vertices, or CVs

Isoparms

Figure 4.4

NURBS surfaces are created between isoparms. You can sculpt them by moving their CVs.

Whereas CVs control the curvature of a Bèzier spline, NURBS surfaces are defined by curves called *isoparms* that are created with CVs. The surface is created between these isoparms to form *spans* that follow the surface curvature defined by the isoparms, as in Figure 4.4. The more spans, the greater the detail and control over the surface; but this added detail makes greater demands on the computer, especially during rendering.

A NURBS surface deformation is based on the interpolation of curves, unlike a polygonal model, which must interpret a deformation of polygons as a collection of faces created from straight edges. For that reason it is easier to get a smooth deformation on a NURBS surface with very few CVs. To get the same smooth look on a polygon would take much more surface detail.

As you can see in Figure 4.5, NURBS yield a smoother deformation, whereas polygons can become jagged at the edges.

If your model requires smooth curves and organic shapes, use NURBS. When in doubt, however, it is better to begin modeling with NURBS. You can convert NURBS to polygons at any time, but converting back to NURBS can be tricky.

You'll get hands-on practice with NURBS modeling later in this chapter.

TRY THIS:

Open a new scene (**File → New Scene**). In the new scene you'll create a few curves on the ground plane grid in the perspective panel (*persp*). Maximize the perspective view by moving your cursor to it and pressing the spacebar. Select Create → CV Curve Tool. Your cursor will turn to a cross. On the grid, lay down a series of points to define a curved line. Notice how the actual Bèzier curve is created between the points (CVs) as they are laid down.

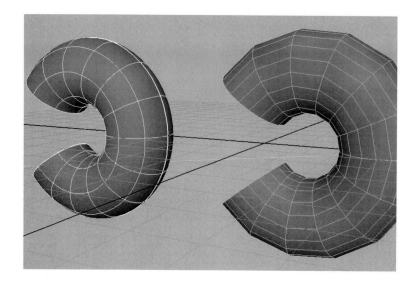

Subdivision Surfaces

Subdivision surfaces incorporate the best of polygons and NURBS modeling to give you the ease of polygon creation with the smoothness and organic forms of NURBS geometry.

Subdivision surfaces usually start as polygonal surfaces. You then use NURBS math to smooth the rough polygon surfaces by subdividing them according to how the model needs to look. For example, you can easily turn a poly cube into a sphere by using subdivisions to subdivide the faces into smaller and smaller faces that are rearranged to form the sphere along smooth curves used to define this new surface.

With this technique, you can create simple poly models quickly and then overlay them with levels of detail to define the new smooth surface. At any time you can go back to the original poly model to make large-scale changes quickly and efficiently.

Furthermore, with subdivision surfaces you have the added advantage in that your surface will not tend to crease or tear at the seams, as NURBS models made of patches of surfaces are prone to do. This leads to better models with which to animate organics.

The disadvantage of subdivision surfaces is that they require even more computation than NURBS. You'll get hands-on practice with subdivision surface modeling in Chapter 6.

Choosing a Method

Maya provides highly effective tools for all three types of modeling, so you can make a model with any type, and it can be as detailed as necessary. The choice depends on how you prefer to model.

A clay sculptor might prefer NURBS. Pushing and pulling CVs to create subtle curves on the surface is like working soft clay with your fingertips; you are nurturing something into shape with the eloquent art of pressure.

Polygons are like a welder's or even a carpenter's tool. Polygon modeling involves tearing and extruding from larger pieces and welding several surfaces together to form a desired whole. Orthogonal models, models with straight lines and sharp corners, are more easily created with polys.

Subdivision surfaces combine the best of both worlds. An artist can begin with a rough shape, chiseled out coarsely, and then switch to finely detailed sculpting by adding levels of detail to the sculpture only when and where needed. Subdivision surface modeling excels at creating organic shapes out of single surfaces.

Using Primitives

Primitives are the simplest objects that you can generate in Maya (or indeed in any 3D application). Primitives are simple geometric shapes, which can be polygons, subdivisions, or NURBS, and are typically used to sculpt out models, as you saw in Chapter 3 with our solar system project.

Primitives offer amazing sculpting versatility (through vertex or CV manipulation) because you can define how detailed the primitive's surface will be. You can create polygonal primitives with practically any level of subdivisions to define the number of vertices and faces. NURBS primitives can be created with almost any number of *sections* and *spans* to define the number of isoparms and CVs.

> Spans are isoparms that run horizontally in a NURBS surface; sections are isoparms that run vertically in the object.

Starting with primitives, a modeler can often create highly complex and detailed models. You may find it easier to analyze your modeling subjects into forms and shapes that fit in with Maya primitives to get a better sense of how to begin a modeling assignment. Figure 4.6 shows all of Maya's primitives, NURBS, polygons, and subdivisions.

Modeling with NURBS

NURBS models can be made of a single surface molded to fit or can be a collection of *patches* connected together like a quilt. In any event, you'll find ample power for creating smooth surfaces for your models.

Figure 4.6

The Maya primitives

NURBS modeling depends on surfaces that are created using curves. Just as CVs are connected together to form curved lines, NURBS surfaces are created by connecting (or *spanning*) curves. Therefore, typical NURBS modeling pipelines first involve the creation of curves that will define the edges, outline, paths, and/or boundaries of surfaces.

Once a surface is created, its shape is defined and governed by its isoparms. These surface curves—curves that solely reside on a surface—show the outline of a surface's shape much like the chicken wire in a wire mesh sculpture does. CVs on the isoparms define and govern the shape of these isoparms just as they would regular curves. So, in short, adjusting a NURBS surface involves manipulating the CVs of the object somewhat like sculpting.

Different Ways to Make NURBS

You can create a NURBS surface in several ways. The easiest way is to create a NURBS primitive. You can sculpt the primitive surface moving its CVs, but you can also cut it apart to create different surface swatches or patches to use as needed. A primitive need not retain its original shape. Using surfacing tools, you can detach, cut, and attach pieces into and out of a primitive to get the shapes you need.

You can also make surfaces in several ways without using a primitive. All these methods involve first creating or using existing NURBS curves (or curves on another surface) to define a part or parts of the surface and then using one of the following surfacing methods to create the surfaces.

The Lofting Method

The most common surfacing method is lofting, which takes at least two curves and creates a surface span between each selected curve, *in the order in which they are selected*. Figure 4.7 shows the result of lofting two curves together.

To create a loft, follow these steps:

1. Draw the two curves.

2. Select the curves in the order in which you want the surface generated.

3. Choose **Surfaces → Loft** in the Modeling menu set (press F3) or click the Loft icon ( ) in the default shelf.

Figure 4.7

A simple loft created between two curves

When you define more curves for the loft, Maya can create more complex shapes. The more CVs for each curve, the more isoparms you have, and the more detail in the surface. Figure 4.8 shows how four curves can be lofted together to form a more complex surface. Indeed, you can use almost any number of curves for a lofted surface.

Lofting works best when curves are drawn as cross-sectional slices of the object to be modeled. It is used to make a variety of surfaces, which may be as simple as table tops or as complex as human faces.

Figure 4.8

A loft created with four curves that are selected in order from left to right

Revolved Surface

A *revolved* surface requires only one curve that is turned about a point in space to create a surface, like a woodworker shaping a candlestick on a lathe. First you draw a *profile curve* to create a profile of the desired object and then revolve this curve (anywhere from 0° to 360°) around a single point in the scene (usually the object's pivot point) to create the surface. The profile will revolve around the object's pivot point, which is typically placed at the origin but can be moved (as seen in the solar system exercise in Chapter 3), and sweeps a new surface along its way. On the left in Figure 4.9 is the profile curve for a wine glass. On the right is the complete revolved surface once the profile is revolved around the Y-axis.

To create a revolved surface, follow these steps:

1. Draw and select your profile curve

2. Choose **Surfaces → Revolve**.

Figure 4.9

A profile curve is drawn in the outline of a wine glass in the Y-axis. The curve is then revolved around the Y-axis a full 360° to create a wine glass.

A revolved surface is useful for creating objects such as bottles, furniture legs, and base-ball bats—anything that is symmetrical about an axis.

Extruded Surface

An *extruded* surface uses two curves, a profile curve and a path curve. The profile curve is drawn to create the profile shape of the desired surface. It is then swept from one end of the path curve to its other end, creating spans of a surface along its travel. The higher the CV count on each curve, the greater the surface's detail. An extruded surface can also take the profile curve and simply stretch it to a specified distance straight along one direction or axis, doing away with the profile curve. Figure 4.10 shows the profile and path curves, and Figure 4.11 shows the resulting surface once the pro-file is extruded along the path.

Figure 4.10

The profile curve is drawn in the shape of an I, and the path curve comes up and bends toward the camera.

To create an extruded surface, follow these steps:

1. Draw both curves.

2. Select the profile curve.

3. Select the path curve.

4. Choose **Surfaces → Extrude**.

An extruded surface is used to make items such as winding tunnels, a coiled garden hose, springs, or curtains.

Planar Surface

A *planar surface* uses one perfectly flat curve to make a two-dimensional cap in the shape
of that curve. It does this by laying down a NURBS plane (a flat square NURBS primitive)
and carving out the shape of the curve like a cookie-cutter. The resulting surface is a perfectly flat, cut-out shape, also known as a trimmed surface since the "excess" outside the
shape curve is trimmed away.

To create a planar surface, follow these steps:

1. Draw and select the curve.

2. Choose **Surfaces → Planar**.

You can also use multiple curves within each other to create a planar surface with holes
in it. On the left in Figure 4.12 is a simple planar surface. When a second curve is added
inside the original curve and both are selected, the planar surface is created with a hole. On
the right is the result when the outer curve is selected first and then the inner curve before
choosing **Surfaces → Planar**.

A planar surface is great for flat lettering, for pieces of a marionette doll or paper cutout,
or for capping the ends of a hollow extrusion. Planar surfaces are best left as flat pieces,
however, as deforming them may not give the best results.

Figure 4.12

(left) A planar surface based on a single curve. (right) A planar surface based on a curve within a curve to create the cutout.

Beveled Surface

The *bevel surface* function takes an open or closed curve and extrudes its outline to create a side surface. It creates a bevel on one or both corners of the resulting surface to create an edge that can be made smooth or sharp (see Figure 4.13). The many options in the bevel tool allow you to control the size of the bevel and depth of extrusion, giving you great flexibility. Once a bevel is created, you can easily cap the bevel with planar surfaces.

Figure 4.13

A curve before and after it is beveled. The beveled surface is given a planar cap.

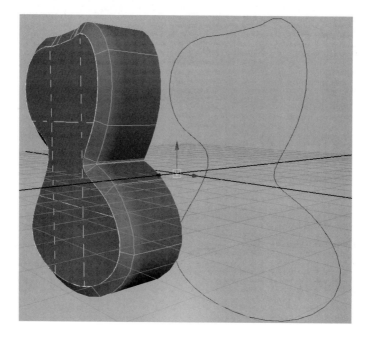

To create a bevel, follow these steps:

1. Draw and select your curve.

2. Choose **Surfaces → Bevel**.

Maya also offers a Bevel Plus surface, which has many more creation options for more advanced bevels.

A beveled surface is great for creating 3D lettering, for creating items such as bottle caps or buttons, or for rounding out an object's edges.

Boundary Surface

A *boundary surface* is so named because it is created within the boundaries of three or four surrounding curves. For example, two vertical curves are drawn opposite each other to define the two side edges of the surface. Then two horizontal curves are drawn to define the upper and lower edges. These curves can have depth to them; they need not be flat for the boundary surface to work, unlike the planar surface. Although you can select the curves in any order, it is best to select them in opposing pairs. In Figure 4.14, four curves are created and arranged to form the edges of a surface to be created. First, select the vertical pair of curves, as they are opposing pairs, and then select the second two horizontal curves before choosing **Surfaces → Boundary**.

A boundary surface is useful for creating shapes like car hoods/fenders and other formed panels.

Figure 4.14

(left) Four curves are arranged to create the edges for a surface. (right) The resulting boundary surface from the four curves.

Combining Techniques

You can use some surfacing techniques in conjunction with each other to create intricate models. For example, whenever a curve is required for a surface, you can use an isoparm instead to create a surface between two existing surfaces.

Try This: Let's take a couple of lofted surfaces and connect them with a third surface. Figure 4.15 shows two surfaces with two intermediate curves in between them. (Notice that the view panel's option **Shading → Shade Options → X-ray** is turned on so you can see through the shaded surfaces.) You will select an isoparm from the first surface (on the left), then the curve on the left, the curve on the right, and finally an isoparm on the second surface.

1. Either create two lofted surfaces and curves as shown in Figure 4.15, or load the Lofting_Exercise_1.ma file from the Lofting_Exercise project on the CD.

2. To select the first isoparm, press F8 for component selection mode and click the Lines Selection Filter button ( ) in the Status line to allow you to select isoparms.

3. Select an isoparm close to the left edge. Press F8 to return to object selection mode and Shift+select the first curve and then the second curve. Press F8 again for component mode, and Shift+select an isoparm toward the left edge on the second surface, as in Figure 4.16.

4. Choose **Surfaces → Loft** to create the intermediate surface between the existing lofts. Figure 4.17 shows how the new surface snakes from the first loft to the second loft by way of the two curves.

Figure 4.15

Two lofted surfaces with two curves in between

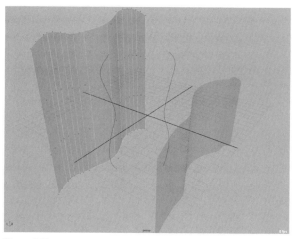

Figure 4.16

Selecting the isoparm

Surface History

In Chapter 2 you learned that the History icon (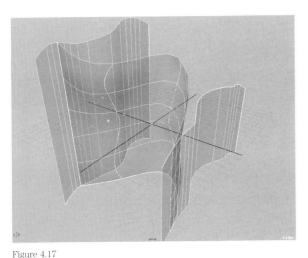) toggles history on and off. History has to do with how objects react to change. Leaving history on when creating primitives, as you did in Chapter 2, gives access to the object's original parameters.

Leaving history on when creating NURBS surfaces allows the surface to update as any of its creation pieces changes. For example, the loft you just created will update whenever the two original surfaces or curves you used to create the loft move or change shape. If you were to move the original loft on the left and rotate it back a bit, the new loft would adjust to keep its one side attached to the same isoparm. If one or more of the input curves were to change, the loft would bend to fit.

> You must toggle history on before you create the object(s) if you want history to be on the object(s).

By lofting using isoparms and with history toggled on, you can keep the new surface permanently attached to the original loft, no matter how the isoparms move, as in Figure 4.18. This technique works with all surface techniques, not just with lofting, as long as history is turned on. History is useful for making adjustments and fine-tuning a surface and can be handy in animation if several surfaces need to deform but stay attached.

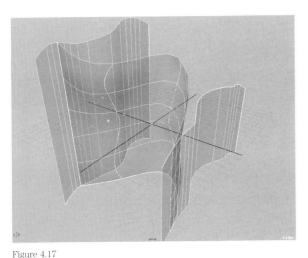

Figure 4.17

The spanning loft between the existing surfaces snakes from the first isoparm to the curves to the second isoparm.

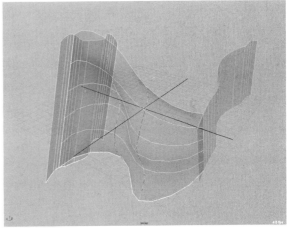

Figure 4.18

History will update the newly created loft to keep it attached to the isoparms and curves used to create it, even when they've been moved or altered.

Why wouldn't you want history turned on for everything? After a long day modeling, having history on every single object can slow down your scene file, adding unnecessary bloat to your workflow. But it is not typically a problem on most surface types unless the scene is huge, so you should leave it on while you're still modeling.

If you decide that you no longer want a surface or an object to retain its history, you can selectively delete it from the surface. Select the surface and choose **Edit → Delete by Type → History**. You can also rid the entire scene of history by choosing **Edit → Delete All by Type → History**. Just don't get them mixed up!

Creating an Axe Using NURBS

The exercise in this section will take you through the following NURBS modeling techniques:

- Image planes
- Lofting
- Revolves
- Boundary surfaces
- Trims
- Curve and surface attachment/detachment
- Object and curve duplication

In this exercise, you will model an axe using NURBS geometry. Instead of replicating in 3D a fully finished design, you will design the axe on the fly. But even when you're using Maya as a design tool, you'll need a good starting point. That involves research and some sketching to give you a good idea of where to start and which direction to head.

Getting Started

Create a new project called axe_model. In a real project, you would now gather any reference information, stills, and images on which to base your axe design. Typically, those reference images are placed in the sourceimages folder of your project. For this exercise, you will find all the source files in the axe_model project on the CD.

For this example, you will use a sketch of a simple axe design as a template for the model. Copy the file `Axe_outline_1.tif` in the sourceimages folder of the Axe_model project from the CD into your project's sourceimages folder.

CREATING AN AXE USING NURBS ∎ **95**

It is unwise to work on files directly from the CD. As a matter of fact, you shouldn't work from or on files stored on any removable medium. Always copy files to the project folders set up on a local or network hard drive.

1. Choose **File → New Scene**. Open the Modeling menu set either by selecting it in the menu or by pressing the default hot key F3.

2. Import the sketch of the axe into Maya. You will need to import it as an *image plane*. In your front window, choose **View → Image Plane → Import Image**.

An image plane is a bitmap picture, such as a TIFF or JPEG, that is displayed in one or all of your work panels as a reference guide. Image planes are extremely useful for modeling alone, but a sequence of files can be brought in to track motion as well. More on that later.

3. Point to `Axe_outline_1.tif` in your sourceimages folder and load it. The sketch will now display full screen in your front window and as a plane in the perspective window (see Figure 4.19).

Figure 4.19

An image plane loaded into the front panel

Figure 4.20

The Attribute Editor for the image plane settings for placement

Placing the Plane behind the Grid

In the next steps, you'll adjust the image plane settings to place the plane behind the grid. As it is now, the image plane should have loaded at the origin and on top of the grid in the front window. Move it back a few units to view the grid.

1. Choose **View → Image Plane → Image Plane Attributes→ image-Plane1** to open the Attribute Editor for the image plane.

2. Under Placement Extras, change the Center's Z value to –2.0. This will push the image plane back in the Z-axis and reveal the grid once again. This will also allow you to create curves on the origin plane without losing site of them behind the image plane. Figure 4.20 shows the proper settings.

3. If the clutter of seeing the image plane in the other windows bothers you, under Display at the top of the Attribute Editor, change the radio button selection from In All Views to Looking Through Camera. This setting will remove the image plane from the other windows.

Tracing the Outline

In the front window, trace the outline of the axe using NURBS curves. Start with the axe head to the left of the handle. Also, make sure history is enabled. Follow these steps:

1. Select the CV Curve tool by choosing **Create → CV Curve Tool** or by clicking the tool's icon (🔲) in the shelf.

2. Starting from the top of the axe head, a little bit behind where it meets the handle as shown in Figure 4.21, lay down a series of CVs to create a curve that follows the contours of the axe head counterclockwise. When you reach the top tip, you'll need to lay down three CVs directly on top of each other to make a sharp corner:

   - Lay down the first CV at the corner tip.

   - Turn on point snaps with the Snap to Points icon (🔲).

   - Put down two more CVs, snapping them both on top of the first corner CV.

   - Turn off snaps

MENU SET HOT KEYS

Remember, to toggle between the menu sets, you can use the following hot keys:

F2   Animation

F3   Modeling

F4   Dynamics

F5   Rendering

3. Follow along the axe counterclockwise until you reach the bottom tip of the head. Place three CVs there, using snaps to make a sharp corner.

4. Follow the axe head's curvature into the handle and a little bit beyond where it meets the handle. Place three CVs at that point, and continue the curve up to meet the start of the curve.

It doesn't matter if you don't place the final CV directly on top of the first CV. As a matter of fact, place it just a little below it. You will close the curve using the Open/Close Curve command later.

5. Press Enter to create the curve.

6. With the curve selected, choose **Edit Curves → Open/Close Curves**. This command will complete the curve for you.

7. In component mode (press F8), adjust the CVs to make the curve better fit the sketch of the axe.

8. Save your work now.

9. Load `Axe_model_v1.mb` in the Axe_model project on the CD and compare your work up to this point.

By saving your own scene file before opening the other version, you've made sure you won't lose your work. When you open a new file or new scene, Maya asks you to save your current scene if you have not done so already. It's a good idea to save before opening a new file regardless. As discussed in Chapter 3, Maya 5's incremental save feature makes it easy to back up your work at any time.

Using point snaps, place three CVs to make a sharp corner.

Start your curve here and proceed counterclockwise.

End your curve with a CV here, just below the starting CV.

Figure 4.21

Laying down a curve for the axe head

Figure 4.22

**Positioning the dupli-
cate axe head curve**

Turning off the Image Plane

Now, you can turn off the image plane. Go to the front panel and choose **View → Image Plane → Image Plane Attributes → imagePlane1** to open the Attribute Editor for the image plane. In the Display Mode menu, choose None to turn off the image plane in all views. To turn it back on, change the display mode back to RGB.

Duplicating the Curve

We'll now make a copy of the outline curve to give the axe head depth. Follow these steps:

1. To duplicate the curve you've drawn, select it and choose **Edit → Duplicate**. The duplicate curve is now selected.

2. Move the curve back in the Z-axis a little bit to give the axe head some depth. Figure 4.22 shows a good depth for the axe head's curves. Notice that the pivot point for both the original and duplicate curves are at the origin.

3. To quickly center their pivots (and to also center their manipulators), select them both and choose **Modify → Center Pivot**. You'll find this function useful.

> If you get strange results from Duplicate (or any other menu command), open its option box and reset its settings by choosing **Edit → Reset Settings**.

Creating the Axe's Edge

To create the axe's edge, follow these steps:

1. Select the original axe curve and duplicate it. Move the new curve in between the two curves.

2. Select the original curve again, toggle into component mode (F8), and move the CVs on the front edge in about a halfway toward the middle curve. Do the same with the third curve to get its CVs closer in to the middle.

3. Select the CVs on the front edge of the middle curve *except* for the corners, and move them out in the X-axis away from the edge just a little bit, as in Figure 4.23. This will give a nice crisp edge for the axe when you loft the three curves together to form the sides of the axe head.

4. You're going to create a groove in the top and bottom sides of the axe head for a nice detail. Select the top and bottom CVs of the middle curve *without* the corners and bring them down and in by scaling them down in the Y-axis and moving them to the left in X as shown in Figure 4.24.

Figure 4.23

Positioning the middle curve CVs for the edge

Figure 4.24

Creating a groove on the sides

Breakpoint

This is a perfect time to save a version of your work. You have finished the preparation work and are now ready to move on to creating the NURBS surfaces themselves. It might also be a good time to go back to the beginning to redo the procedures in a new file to practice the prep work in the exercise up to this point. You'll find that with practice, these procedures become almost second nature.

Creating the Surfaces

Now on to create the surfaces. You'll create a boundary surface for the faces of the axe head and lofts for its sides. You cannot use the planar surface for the axe's two faces because the curves you created are no longer flat. They push in slightly at the cutting edge to make the axe sharp. Planar surfaces must be perfectly flat.

First, to make the axe faces, you have to create four curves to make the boundary surface work properly. Instead of re-creating them all, you can detach the current curve into four separate curves instead. Follow these steps:

1. Select the top curve and toggle into component mode. You will need to pick curve points instead of CVs to cut apart the curve. Turn off the Points Filter (■) and turn on the Parm Points Filter (●) on the Status line. The curve will turn cyan, and little Xs called *edit points* will appear on the curve. You can select any point on the surface; it does not need to fall on an X.

Curve points are points that actually make up the curve, as opposed to CVs, which control the shape of the curve. Choosing a curve point is choosing a location on the curve. Edit points are much like CVs in that they change the shape of the curve, but unlike CVs, they lie on the curve itself.

2. Click somewhere on the curve, and drag the little orange box that appears to the bottom corner of the cutting edge. Shift+click again, and drag that new point to the top cutting-edge corner. You now have two curve points selected at the top and bottom of the cutting edge. Shift+select/drag points for the remaining two corners of the axe, as shown in Figure 4.25. These points locate the exact position where you want to detach the curve into four new sections.

3. Choose **Edit Curves → Detach Curves** to cut the curves apart at the selected points. This will generate four separate curves so that you can make the boundary surfaces. The detached curves will be displayed as new curves in the Outliner and Hypergraph.

4. Let's hide these curves to make the work area more manageable:

   - In the Layer box right under the Channel box, choose **Layers → Create Layer**. Do this three times to create three layers.

   - Select the four new curves from the first axe profile curve and assign them to layer1 by choosing **Layers → Add Selected Objects to Current Layer**.

   - To toggle visibility of this layer, click the V to the left of the layer1 name. This will take those curves off your screen to make it easier to work.

   - Select the middle curve and assign it to layer2, and then assign the third curve to layer3.

5. Turn off visibility for the first and second curves to work on the third profile curve. Repeat the curve detach procedure to cut apart the remaining outside axe profile curve. Repeat for the middle curve as well.

Once you detach the curves, Maya will place three of the detached curves into the default layer. You will have to select them and place them back in layer3.

6. Turn off layer3, and turn layer1 back on. Select the four curves and make a boundary surface by choosing **Surfaces → Boundary**.

The surface at this point does not fit in the boundaries, because the spans on each curve don't line up. Some curves have more CVs than other curves. Since surfacing relies on the CVs on the input curves, you'll need to rearrange the axe profile curves to match up with each other first.

7. Select all four curves and choose **Edit Curve → Rebuild Curve** ❐ In the window, leave Rebuild Type to Uniform and change the number of spans to 10. This will rebuild the curves to each have the same number of CVs so the surface will build properly. You might notice that some of the new CVs on the rebuilt curve are out of place though, and the curve is now slightly misshapen.

8. In component mode, position those CVs to regain the original curve shape.

9. Select these rebuilt curves in opposite pairs, and create the boundary surface seen in Figure 4.26. If necessary, refer to the "Boundary Surface" section in this chapter. Once created, this surface will be your axe's front face. Assign it to layer1.

10. Turn off layer1 and turn on layer3. Rebuild these curves with the same settings as before.

11. Create a boundary surface to make the back face for the axe head.

Figure 4.25

Selecting the corner curve points

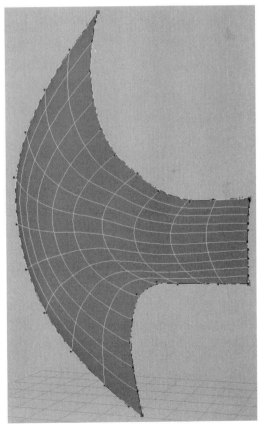

Figure 4.26

The front axe face surface

Connecting the Axe Faces

Now that you have the faces for the axe, you'll need to connect them to create the side edges of the axe. Follow these steps:

1. Turn on layer2. You'll use these curves as the middle input curves for a loft between the two faces you've just made. This will give the sharp edge and the grooves on the sides.

> You can clean up your work window so that selecting is easier. In the *persp* panel, choose **Show → NURBS Surfaces** to toggle off NURBS surface display in this window. That will leave you with just the curves.

2. Rebuild these middle curves as you did the face curves.

3. Turn back on NURBS Surfaces display in the panel by choosing **Show → NURBS Surfaces** if you've turned them off previously.

4. Select the top curves from front to back and choose **Surfaces → Loft** to make the top side edge. Do the same for the bottom side curves. You should end up with something like Figure 4.27.

5. To create a nice sharp edge, you'll make a slightly different version of a loft. Select the cutting edge curves from front to back and choose **Surfaces → Loft** ❑. In the window, change the Surface Degree option from Cubic to Linear. Click the Loft button to create the surface.

> NURBS can calculate at different level degrees. Cubic NURBS curves and surfaces are standard and create the smooth curves you've already seen. Linear degree will create direct, straight spans between CVs, creating sharp corners.

6. To adjust the cutting edge, select the middle curve in this new loft, and move it away from the axe a bit more. Surface history will stretch the cutting edge surface and make it sharper. Be sure you turn on history before you make these surfaces, though.

Figure 4.27

The axe's top and bottom grooved edges

Fine-Tuning the Axe

Now it's time to make a few adjustments to the new surfaces. You'll notice that the top and bottom tips of the cutting edge flare out. Taper them by moving the CVs on the original curves in together. Follow these steps:

1. Select the bottom tip CVs for all four curves as shown here:

2. With CVs selected, go to Scale and scale them in toward each other in the Z-axis to taper the bottom tip.

3. Select pairs of CVs up the edge and sides of the axe and scale them in Z (the blue locator handle) a bit to taper them in as well.

Breakpoint

This is another good time to take a break and save your work.

Once you've saved, use the CD file `axe_model_v2.mb` to check your work up to this point. Make sure you understand the techniques used thus far. You have been exposed to a number of procedures, and it's a good idea to make sure they make sense before continuing. Although the process of creating this axe, and most CG, may seem daunting, taken one step at a time, creating CG is not as complex as it might seem.

> You can either choose to manually save a filename with a new version number of your axe scene to better keep track of your progress, or rest assured that Maya will make a backup for you through Incremental Save (make sure the option is turned on through **File → Save ❑**).

Building the Back of the Axe Head

What remains now is the right side of the full axe head. Follow these steps:

1. Turn the image plane back on in the front view panel.

> An easy way to toggle the image plane view on and off in a work panel is to toggle camera display. As long as the image plane's display is set to RGB, choose **Show → Cameras** to toggle the image plane on and off.

Figure 4.28

Select corner curve points to detach the curves.

2. In the same way you created the edge of the cutting side of the axe, create a curve to trace around the image plane, starting where the back of the axe head meets the handle up top and proceeding clockwise around the shape.

3. Close the curve by choosing **Edit Curves → Open/Close Curves**.

4. Duplicate the curve and move it to create a thickness to match the front of the axe head.

5. Pick the corner curve points and cut apart the curve into four parts by choosing **Edit Curves → Detach Curves**. (See Figure 4.28.)

6. Rebuild the curves by choosing **Edit Curves → Rebuild Curve**, and use 20 spans. You'll lose some definition, so you'll have to go in and adjust the CVs manually.

7. Create a boundary surface to make the faces, and use lofts to create the sides.

8. Now you'll try something different. Delete the original curves to leave behind the two faces of the axe head.

To create the sides without curves to loft with, you'll need to use isoparms.

9. Switch to component mode and enable isoparm selection. Select an isoparm at the top edge of both faces and choose **Surfaces → Loft**.

10. Repeat with the remaining three sides. Figure 4.29 shows the completed surface.

Modeling with Deformers

Deformers are tools in Maya that allow you to easily change the shape of an object. As opposed to using CVs to manually distort or bend an object, you can use a deformer to affect the entire object. Popular deformers such as Bend or Flare can be powerful tools for adjusting your models quickly and evenly. For more on modeling with deformers, see Chapter 6.

To alter the shape of the axe head using a Flare deformer, follow these steps:

1. Select the two faces. Since the lofted edges have history, they will be affected when the faces are deformed.

2. Switch to the Animation menu set (press F2).

3. Create a Flare deformer by choosing **Deform → Create NonLinear → Flare**. The Flare deformer appears as a cylindrical object.

Figure 4.29

The back end of the axe head

Figure 4.30

The back of the axe head with a Flare deformer attached

4. Rotate the deformer 90° in the Z-axis.

5. Open the Attribute Editor (press Ctrl+A), click the flare1 tab to access the Flare controls, and enter the following values:

Attribute	Value
Start Flare Z	0.020
High Bound	0.50

Deformers use history to distort the geometry to which they're attached. You can animate any of the attributes that control the deformer shapes, but in this case you're using this deformer as a means to adjust a model. Once you get the desired shape as seen in Figure 4.30, you can discard the deformer. But simply selecting and deleting the deformer will reset the geometry to its original shape. You'll need to pick the geometry (not the deformer) and delete its history by choosing **Edit → Delete by Type → History**.

Now that we're done with the axe head, let's move on to the handle. Follow these steps:

1. Turn the image plane back on in the front view panel.

2. Create a curve to outline just the left *half* of the handle in the image plane. You'll revolve this surface to create the handle itself. Start at the top and work down to the middle of the bottom.

3. Once you make the curve, move its pivot point (toggle pivot mode with the Insert key) to the end CV at the bottom using Snap to Point ( ).

4. Select the curve and choose **Surfaces → Revolve ❐**. In the options, make sure that Axis is set to Y and that Pivot is set to Object (the default settings). Make sure that Start Sweep is set to 0, that End Sweep is set to 360, that Segments is set to 8, and that you're outputting a NURBS surface. Click Revolve to create your handle surface as in Figure 4.31.

Save again and use the file axe_model_v3.mb on the CD to check your work.

See Chapter 6 for more on modeling with deformers, particularly the lattice deformer.

Figure 4.31

The revolved surface handle completes the axe model.

Cleaning Up

Open the Outliner, and you'll see the long, unorganized list of curves and surfaces shown in Figure 4.32. Cleanup is probably the most overlooked part of the modeling process, but vital. Go though the nodes and group objects, and name everything in a consistent and straightforward manner, if you haven't been keeping track of items as you went along. With time, this will be routine.

Once you're done with the axe, all the original input curves will no longer be needed. You can delete them and the history on the surfaces you used them to make. Search through and select these curves from the Outliner to delete them, as shown in Figure 4.33. While in wire-frame mode in the view panels, you will notice some of the surfaces turning magenta. That means the selected object has an output connection to that magenta object, most usually history. If that surface or object is final, you can safely delete the input. If you made a mistake, use the undo function (press Z or Ctrl+Z).

Axe Conclusion

Surfacing techniques can yield powerful results. Using curves and isoparms, you can create intricately connected surfaces to model very detailed organic shapes with NURBS. History plays a huge part in modeling as it allows you to make easy adjustments to keep surfaces in certain harmony with each other.

In the end you should have an axe similar to Figure 4.34. Feel free to adjust the design of the axe to try out a few more axes to brush up on NURBS techniques.

Editing NURBS Surfaces

Maya provides numerous NURBS editing tools you'll find useful in editing your surfaces. Besides tools for moving CVs, there are some important functions and tools that allow you to add realism to your model. This section gives you a quick preview of these tools; you'll need to try them for yourself.

Open and tear off the Edit NURBS menu and follow along here. The following functions are all accessed through it.

Figure 4.32

The Outliner full of nodes

Figure 4.33

The cleaner Outliner

Figure 4.34

The finished axe

Project Curve on Surface

The ability to project a curve onto a surface allows you to cut out holes in the surface using the Trim Surfaces tool (choose **Edit NURBS → Trim Surfaces** to use the Trim tool). It also allows you to create, using history, another surface that is attached, following the outline of your projected curve, as seen in the "Combining Techniques" section earlier in this chapter.

Projected curves are also useful for tracing animation paths for objects to follow. For example, you can project a curve around a hilly landscape surface and assign a car to animate (drive) along that projected curve. The car will stick to the surface of the road with ease.

To use Project Curve on Surface, select the surface and the curve to project and choose **Edit NURBS → Project Curve on Surface**.

Trim and Untrim Surfaces

Trimming a surface (choose **Edit NURBS → Trim Tool**) allows you to create holes in your surface, using curves that are either drawn or projected onto the surface.

If you have a surface that's already been trimmed, and it's too late to undo the function with Undo, you can use Untrim Surfaces to remove either the last trim performed or all trims the surface has by selecting **Edit NURBS → Untrim Surfaces**.

Attach Surfaces

Attach Surfaces will do exactly that—attach two contiguous NURBS surfaces together along two selected isoparms. Select an isoparm on the edge of the first surface, Shift+select an edge isoparm on a second surface, and choose **Edit NURBS → Attach Surfaces** to create a new surface of the two. As shown in Figure 4.35, the attach point will be along the selected isoparms.

Figure 4.35

Attach Surfaces connects surfaces along their selected isoparms

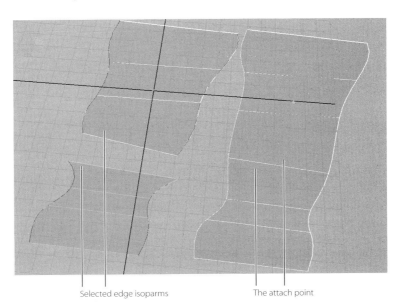

Selected edge isoparms

The attach point

Figure 4.36

Detach Surface cuts a surface at the selected isoparms to create a new surface.

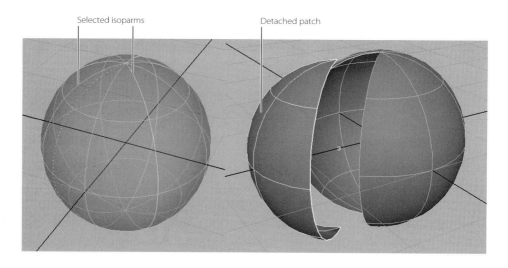

Selected isoparms

Detached patch

Detach Surface

Detach Surface is a highly useful tool for generating specific areas of a NURBS surface, or patches. Select an isoparm to define the line of detachment, choose **Edit NURBS → Detach Surface**, and the surface will be cut along that isoparm to create two distinct surfaces (see Figure 4.36).

> To select an isoparm that is not displayed on the surface, click a viewable isoparm, and drag the mouse to place the isoparm selection elsewhere on the surface. Release the button to make the selection; a dashed isoparm line is now selected. This is a valid surface isoparm, but is not one used to define the number of spans in the surface.

Insert Isoparm

You'll inevitably come upon a modeling assignment for which you'll need extra surface definition (that is, more spans) on a NURBS object. Select an isoparm such as you did for Detach Surface earlier, and choose **Edit NURBS → Insert Isoparm**. This will create an isoparm and redefine the surface to add more spans. This function is used to make extra detailed parts of a NURBS surface to allow for smoother deformations, for example, adding an isoparm or two to the elbow joint of a model to make the arm bend with a cleaner crease (see Figure 4.37). You can either create a new isoparm between two already existing ones or add isoparms to your own defined area.

Using Artisan to Sculpt NURBS

Imagine that you can create a NURBS surface and just sculpt it using your cursor to mold the surface like hands on wet clay. Well, you can with a Maya module called Artisan, without the mess.

Try This: Artisan is basically a 3D painting system that allows you to paint directly onto a surface. By painting on the surface with the Sculpt Surfaces tool, you are moving the CV points in and out to effectively mold the surface.

1. In shaded mode (press 5), maximize the perspective window (press the spacebar) for a nice big view. Create a NURBS sphere and open the A_E. In the sphere's creation node (makeNurbSphere1), set Sections to 24, and set Spans to 12. The greater the surface definition you have here, the more detailed the sculpting can be.

2. Select the sphere and choose **Edit NURBS → Sculpt Surfaces Tool** ❐. Clicking the option box will open the tool settings. You'll need those almost every time you paint with Artisan, to change brush sizes and so forth.

Figure 4.37

Inserting isoparms for a smoother deformation

Figure 4.38

The Sculpt Surfaces Tool allows you to mold your surface by painting on it. Here the brush is set to push in the surface of the sphere as you paint.

Your cursor will now change to the Artisan brush as shown in Figure 4.38. The red circle around the brush cursor and the black lettering display the type of brush you are currently using. When the red lines point outside the circle, and the lettering reads *Ps*, you're using the *push* brush, which will push in the surface as you paint it. The black arrow pointing toward the sphere's center is a measurement of the Max Displacement slider in the tool settings. This sets how far each stroke will push in the surface. The lower the number, the less the brush will affect the surface.

3. Click and drag the cursor across the surface of the sphere to get a feel for how the surface deforms under your tool. Use the Max Displacement slider to control the force of the brush, and use Radius (U) and Radius (L) to set the size of the brush.

> The Opacity slider also controls the force of the brush, but it is subtler than Max Displacement to give you greater control. Since this is after all a 3D painting tool, opacity controls how much *value* you paint onto the surface. The value in this case is not a color, but how far the surface is deformed. You'll see how Artisan comes back into play in other aspects in Maya later in the book. It really is a nice little addition to the software.

4. Switch your brush type to *pull.* Your cursor will change to read *Pl*, and the red lines appear on the inside of the circle. You'll now be able to pull out the surface.

5. *Smooth* will blend the pushed in and pulled out areas of the surface together to get a smoother result. *Erase* will simply erase the deformations on the surface, setting it back to the way it was before.

If you plan to sculpt a finely detailed surface, be sure to create the surface with plenty of surface spans and sections. If you only want to paint a specific area of a NURBS surface, use **Edit NURBS → Insert Isoparm** to add extra detail to that area before you begin painting. Once you begin to sculpt this way, going back into the surface's creation node to increase its sections and spans will ruin your results.

Modeling Suggestions

For further practice, use this chapter as a reference to create some of the following NURBS models.

Bathroom sink Snap a few digital stills of your bathroom sink, or find some on the Internet. A sink will give you a great chance to explore NURBS surfacing, making pristine curves and smooth surfaces. It may be a bit involved, but it's not overwhelming.

Couch or loveseat Cushy furniture is great for NURBS. Use lofting to make plush cushions, or just use a primitive. It's up to you, but try it. You'll only get better with practice.

Disposable lighter Sounds simple, but try to get detailed with it.

Cartoon head Use Maya Artisan and the Sculpt Surfaces tool to turn an ordinary sphere into a cartoonish head. You'll find it fun to use sculpt surfaces to model. Try to make the head only using Artisan.

Summary

Modeling is usually the first step of CG production. It is important to keep in mind the goal of modeling: to represent an object with CG. To that end, simplifying and deconstructing the object to be modeled into its simplest components puts the task of modeling into clearer perspective. For example, a car is not best modeled as a car per se, but as a collection of parts: tires, doors, seats, a hood, side panels, a trunk, and so forth. Learning to see how objects come together is invaluable in creating them in CG.

CHAPTER 5

Modeling with Polygons

Polygon modeling has become popular because its resulting models are usually one piece of geometry with many facets. You can therefore deform polygon models without fear of patches coming apart, as can happen with NURBS. Polygons, however, have a finite detail limitation and can look jagged up close or when scaled up. The solution to this problem in the Maya software is the Smooth tool. Many 3D applications support only this form of modeling, so it is a popular exchange method among platforms as well.

- **Making Polygons**

- **Using NURBS to Create Polygons**

- **Polygon Editing Tools**

- **Using the Tools: Making a Hand**

- **Creating Areas of Detail**

- **Polygon Sculpting**

- **Putting It All to Use: Creating a Complex Model**

Polygon Basics

Polygons are inherently better for orthogonal models, mechanical objects, and the like. Character modeling with polygons, however, is quite powerful once you understand the tools to edit polygons. A popular method of modeling based on polygons involves creating a base object, such as a simple cube, and pulling and pushing faces to draw out angles to create more faces. Whereas NURBS typically need the creation of curves to start, complex polygons are typically created from more basic shaped polygons such as primitives.

Another method for creating poly surfaces is based on the same curves that NURBS surfaces use. A third method is to create poly surfaces directly with the Polygon tool, which allows you to outline the shape of each face.

Creating Polygonal Primitives

Choosing **Create → Polygon Primitives** gives you access to the poly version of most of the NURBS primitives. Opening the option box for any of them gives you access to their creation options. To see an example, choose Create a Polygonal Sphere and open the option box.

The most notable difference between the options for a NURBS primitive and a poly primitive are the options for surface detail. With a NURBS surface, detail is defined by sections and spans. With a poly surface, detail is defined by *subdivisions*, which are the number of rows and columns of poly faces that are running up and down and across. The more subdivisions, the smoother the surface.

Click **Create** to make the poly sphere. Open the Attribute Editor and switch to its creation node called polySphere1. Make sure that history is turned on first, or there will be no creation node. In the creation node polySphere1, just as in the option box, you'll find sliders for the Subdivisions Axis and Subdivisions Height to retroactively change the surface detail.

Figure 5.1

Polygon faces created with the Polygon tool

The Polygon Tool

You use the Polygon tool (choose **Polygon → Create Polygon Tool**) to create a single polygon face by laying down its vertices. When you select this tool, you can draw a polygon face in any shape by just clicking down the position of each point or vertex. Aside from creating a polygon primitive by choosing **Create → Polygon Primitives**, this is the simplest way to create a polygon shape. Figure 5.1 shows some simple and complex single faces you can create with the Polygon tool.

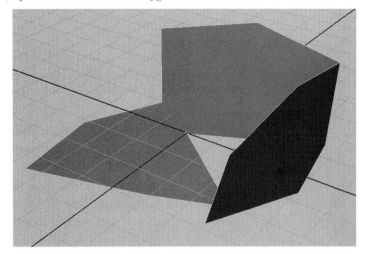

Once you've laid down all your vertices, press Enter to create the poly face and exit the tool. On complex shapes, you might want to create more than just the single face so that you can manipulate the shape. For example, you might want to fold it.

Try This The following poly was created with the Polygon tool and has only one face. Thus, adjusting or deforming the surface is impossible. For example, to fold this object, you need more faces and the edges between them. Make your own intricate poly shape with the Polygon tool by clicking vertices down in all the different views to get vertices in all three axes. With the surface selected, choose **Polygons → Triangulate**. The surface will now have more faces and edges and can be edited easier, but it was still simple to create first as a single face. If you need a uniquely shaped poly, start with this tool, and then triangulate it into several faces.

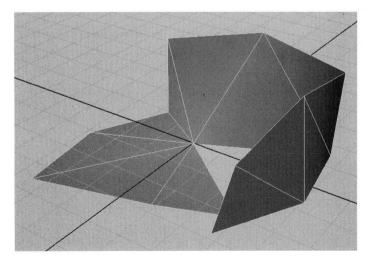

Using NURBS Surfacing to Create Polygons

You can create swatches of polygon surfaces, just as you did with NURBS in Chapter 4. The tools are similar. Any of the surfaces can just as easily be produced as polygons; they do not have to remain NURBS.

To create a polygonal surface with any of the surfacing techniques, open the option box for the particular tool. For example, create two simple curves. Choose **Surfaces → Loft** ❐. In the options for **Output Geometry**, click the Polygons button to display the options for creating the polygon surface and its detail level.

History for the surface will adjust the new polygonal surface just as if it were NURBS. The detail of the surface will try to adjust as changes to the input curves are made. But if you anticipate significant changes to the input curves, make sure to create the poly surface with a high poly count to accommodate major changes. This is probably the best way to create a single poly surface, especially if you prefer NURBS workflow.

Try This Draw two CV curves with the same number of CVs each. Open the Loft option box and click the Polygons option for the Output Geometry. The creation options that appear at the bottom of the window affect the tessellation of the resulting surface; that is, you use them to specify the level of detail and the number of faces with which the surface is created. Generally speaking, the more faces, the more detail. But that doesn't mean a detailed surface can't be efficient, with areas of high tessellation only where needed.

The default tessellation method Standard Fit will yield the fewest faces to achieve the surface without losing overall integrity. The sliders adjust the resulting number of faces to try to fit the finer curvature of the input curves.

The lower the fractional tolerance, the smoother the surface and the greater the number of faces. The Chord Height Ratio determines the amount of curve in a particular region and calculates how many more faces to use to give an adequate representation of that curved area with polygons. This option would be best used with surfaces that have multiple curves, or very intense curves.

It is not uncommon to create a surface, undo it, change slider settings, and re-create it again and again to get just the right tessellation. That's why you should click the Apply button, to keep the window open, as opposed to the Loft button (which closes the window after applying the settings).

TESSELLATION

In the rendering phase, all 3D objects are broken into polygonal triangles that form the surfaces that shape your objects. This process—called *tessellation*—happens on all rendered surfaces, whether polygonal, subdivided, or NURBS.

The computer calculates the position of each significant point on your surface and connects the points to form a skin representing your surface.

The General tessellation method creates a specific number of lines, evenly dividing the horizontal (U) and vertical (V) into rows of polygon faces. The Control Points method tessellates the surface according to the number of points on the input curves. The more CVs and spans on the curves, the more divisions of polygons. The Count method simply relies on how many faces you tell it to make. The higher the count, the higher the tessellation on the surface. Experiment with the different options to get the best poly surface results.

Converting NURBS to Polygons

Some people prefer to model on NURBS curves and either create poly surfaces or just convert to polygons after the entire model is done with NURBS surfaces. Ultimately you will find your own workflow preference, but it helps greatly that you can use all surfacing methods. Most modelers choose one way or another, but are familiar with both methodologies.

Try This Convert the NURBS axe into a poly model, as it might be needed in a game. Open your latest scene file from the axe_model project (or load `axe_model_C.mb` from the CD). The toughest part of this simple process is getting the poly model to follow all the different curves in the axe with fidelity; so you'll have to convert parts of the axe differently. Follow these steps:

1. Grab the handle and choose **Modify → Convert → NURBS to Polygons** ❏. Use the default presets (if need be, reset your settings by choosing **Edit → Reset Settings**), and the handle will convert well to polygons. Click Apply, and a poly version of the axe handle will appear on top of the NURBS version. Move it 8 units to the left to get it out of the way. You'll move the other parts 8 units as well to properly assemble the poly axe.

2. Select the back part of the axe head. Hopefully you should have all the surfaces grouped together to make selection easy as in the file on the CD; otherwise, select all the surfaces that make it up. The default settings will work for this part as well, so click Apply, and move it 8 units to the left.

3. The front of the axe head holds a lot of different arcs, so you'll have to create it with finer controls. Change Fractional Tolerance from 0.01 to 0.0005. This will yield more polygons, but finer curved surfaces. Figure 5.2 shows the result.

Figure 5.2

A faithful high-poly conversion (on the left) of the original NURBS axe

If you were following this process for a conventional game engine, you would be restricted to a low number of polygons, and your axe design would be different to better handle a low poly count.

Poly Editing Tools

Here's a brief preview of what to expect in the world of poly editing. You should experiment with using each tool on a primitive sphere as each tool is introduced; then you'll take the new skills into two different poly models. As you've learned, you can easily create complex models by adjusting existing, simpler poly objects with some of the poly editing tools Maya provides.

Open the Edit Polygons menu and tear it off to get a good look at the tools and functions. You can access all the following tools from that menu.

The Extrusion Tool

The most often used poly editing tool is Extrusion. You can use this tool to pull out a face or an edge of a polygon surface to create additions to that surface. Follow these steps:

1. Select a face or multiple faces of a polygon, and choose **Edit Polygons → Extrude Face**. The regular manipulator will change to a special manipulator as shown (below left).

2. Grab the Z-axis move handle (the blue arrow) and drag it away from the sphere (below center.

    The face(s) you selected pull out from the sphere, and new faces are created on the sides of the extrusion(s). This is an exceptionally powerful tool in that it allows you to easily create additions to any poly surface in any direction. It is particularly useful in modeling characters and creatures. Later in this chapter you'll use it to make a simple human hand.

3. Using the scale handles (the boxes) will scale the faces of the extrusion. The cyan circle will rotate the face (below right).

  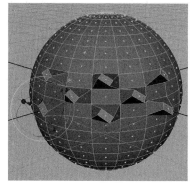

4. Choosing the **Extrude Faces** command again without deselecting the faces will let you extrude even farther, keeping the original extrusion shape and building on top of that.

5. Selecting the edges of the poly surface instead of the faces and choosing **Edit Polygons** → **Extrude Faces** will extrude flat surfaces from the edges selected. The special manipulator works the same way as **Extrude Faces**.

The Wedge Faces Toll

Similar to **Extrude Faces**, Wedge Faces pulls out a poly face, but in an arc instead of a straight line. For this tool you need to select a face and an edge of that face for the pivot point of the corner. Follow this step:

- Select a face, Shift+select one of its edges, and choose **Edit Polygons** → **Wedge Faces** ❑.

In the option box, you can select the degree of turn (90° is the default) as well as the number of faces used to create the wedge (by moving the Wedge Divisions slider).

To more easily access selection filters, you can right-click an object to display a marking menu. Drag the cursor in the direction of the selection type you want and release the mouse button. Then click or Shift+click your selection.

The Wedge Faces tool is useful for items such as elbows, knees, building archways, tunnel curves, and so on.

The Poke Faces Tool

You use the Poke Faces tool to easily add detail to a face. Follow this step:

- Select a face, and then choose **Edit Polygons** → **Poke Faces**.

A vertex is added to the middle of the face, and a move manipulator appears on the screen which lets you move the point to where you need it on the face. This lets you add bumps and depressions to your surface as well as create regions of extra detail. By selectively adding detail, you can subdivide specific areas of a polygon for extra detailed work, leaving lower poly counts in less-detailed areas for an efficient model.

Poke Faces is great for creating detailed sections of a mesh (poly surface) and bumps or indentations.

The Bevel Tool

The Bevel tool used for editing polygons is similar to the NURBS version, but only where it is used to round sharp corners. The Bevel tool requires that you select an edge or multiple edges and then use them to create multiple new faces to round that edge or corner.

Select an edge or edges, and choose **Edit Polygons → Bevel ❏**. In the option box you can adjust your bevel. Move the Offset slider to set the distance from the edge to the center of

where the new face will be. This basically determines the size of the rounded corner.

The Roundness setting specifies how round the corner is. Setting the number too high will make the beveled edge stick out, as shown in Figure 5.3, which can be a valid design choice. You can allow Maya to automatically set the roundness based on the size of the geometry being beveled. Check the Auto Fit check box to disable the Roundness slider. Move the Segments slider to set the number of new faces that are created on the bevel: the higher the segments, the smoother the bevel.

You can use the Bevel tool to round polygonal edges and even, in some cases, to add extra surface detail, since Bevel creates more faces on the surface.

Putting the Tools to Use: Making a Simple Hand

Starting with a simple polygonal cube, you will create a basic human hand. This choice of subject allows you to skip the research stage described in Chapter 4 and go right into the modeling.

Now either create a new project called Poly_Hand, or copy the entire project from the CD and use that. Follow these steps:

1. Begin by creating a polygonal cube. Open the Attribute Editor, and in the Polycube1 tab set Subdivisions Width to 4, Subdivisions Height to 1, and Subdivisions Depth to 3. If you don't have that tab in the Attribute Editor, click Undo, turn history on, and re-create the cube.

2. Scale the cube to X 1, Y 0.25, and Z 1.3 so that it looks as shown in Figure 5.4.

3. Enter component mode (press F8) and turn on the Faces filter ◈ in the Status line. You can also right-click the object and choose Face from the marking menu, although it might be easier to use the icons for a little while to become more accustomed to the interface.

4. Select the front face that is in the corner closest to you by clicking its little blue handle box. You will extrude the face to make the first part of the index finger. Before you extrude though, rotate the face a little bit out in the Y axis away from the rest of the hand, to make the extrusion angled out toward where the thumb would be.

5. Choose **Edit Polygons → Extrude Face**, and use the Z-axis translate handle to pull out the face to a distance of 0.4 in the **Local Translate Z** attribute in the Channel box. This is the first segment of the index finger. Select the Extrude Face command for a new extrusion. Extrude the second segment of the finger out to 0.4 in **Local Translate Z**. Use Extrude Face again for the tip of the index finger, pulling that out to 0.3. Figure 5.5 shows the full index finger with the slight rotation away from the hand.

Figure 5.3

A poly bevel's round-ness set too high

Figure 5.4

The poly cube in position to make the hand

Save your work and compare it to the scene file `poly_hand_v1.mb` in the Poly_Hand project on the CD.

6. Repeat steps 4 and 5 for the remaining three fingers. Remember, if you rotate the initial face of each finger a little bit away from the previous finger, the extrusions will have small gaps in between them, as shown in Figure 5.6. Otherwise, the fingers will extrude right next to each other, like a mitt. Use the following guide for the extrusion lengths:

Finger	1st	2nd	Tip
Middle	0.45	0.45	0.3
Ring	0.45	0.4	0.3
Pinkie	0.35	0.3	0.3

 The scene `poly_hand_v2.mb` shows the hand with the four fingers created.

7. Now for the thumb. First you'll need to move a couple of edges to make room for where the thumb attaches to the hand. Select the three edges on the index finger side of the hand, and move them up toward the tip of the hand, as shown in Figure 5.7. This will create an elongated face to start the thumb.

Figure 5.5

The index finger

Figure 5.6

Four fingers

8. You will use the Wedge Faces tool to start the thumb. Select the elongated face. Right-click the object to display the marking menu, and choose Edge. Shift+select the edge on the left side of that face. (See Figure 5.8.)

9. Choose **Edit Polygons → Wedge Faces** ❐. In the option box, set Wedge Angle to 65, and set Wedge Divisions to 5. Click Wedge Face. With that wedged face still selected, scale it down in the X axis to just under half its width to make it less broad, and rotate it toward the hand a bit (below left).

10. To make the thumb itself, extrude that face first to 0.5 and then to 0.4 in **Local Translate Z**. The hand looks a bit awkward right now, especially the thumb area (below right).

11. Select the faces along the meat part of the thumb, and move and rotate them to round out the hand. While you're at it, squeeze in the tips of the fingers a bit to point them all by selecting and scaling the very top face of each finger.

Figure 5.7

Creating an elongated face for the thumb

Select these three edges.

12. Select the pinkie finger edges (not faces), and scale them in to narrow the pinkie.

13. Select the edges that make up the knuckle of each finger (one by one), and scale them out in the X axis to fatten the knuckles a bit. Your results should be similar to Figure 5.9.

Figure 5.8

Select the face and edge for the Wedge Faces function

Select this edge.

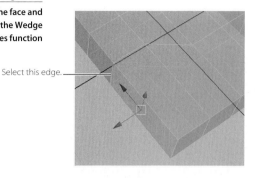

14. Now to add a bit more detail to the hand, you'll raise the knuckles. You'll have to create new vertices for the knuckles where each finger meets the hand. For this, the Split Polygon tool is perfect. Go back into object mode (press F8) and select the hand. Choose **Edit Polygons → Split Polygon Tool**. Your cursor will change to a sharp triangle. Use it to select a point on the hand where the index finger starts. Click the

Figure 5.9

Better proportioned fingers and knuckles

Scale these edge pairs out for bigger knuckles.

opposite edge on that face along the back of the hand. A line will be drawn between the two points (below left).

15. If you press Enter, now that line becomes a single new edge on that face. But, while you have the Split Polygon tool active, select three more points along the back of the hand as shown (below right.)

16. Press Enter to add four new edges and, hence, four new faces along the back of the hand for the knuckles. Select each of those new faces, and choose **Edit Polygons ➔ Poke Faces** to subdivide them into four triangles, with a vertex in the center. A special manipulator will appear. Use the Z translate handle to pull those middle vertices up to make knuckles. (See Figure 5.10.)

17. Now that you have a simple hand, you'll want to smooth out the mesh to make it less boxy. In object mode, select the hand and choose **Polygons ➔ Smooth ❐**. In the option box, set Subdivision Levels to 2 and leave the rest at their defaults.

18. Click Smooth, and your hand should take on a smoother, rounder look, more like a real hand. Notice in Figure 5.11 all the nodes listed under INPUTS in the Channel box. This is because history has been on for the entire duration of this exercise. At any time, you could select one of those nodes and edit the extrusion of the pinkie, for example. You won't be needing any of that, so with the hand selected, choose **Edit ➔ Delete by Type ➔ History** to get rid of them all. Feel free to edit any of those nodes through the Attribute Editor if you'd like.

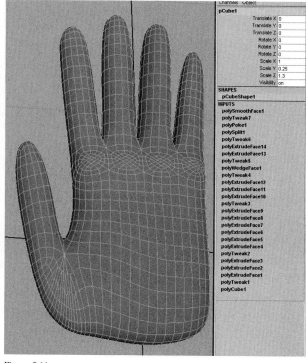

Figure 5.10
_____

Use the Poke Faces tool to raise the knuckles.

Figure 5.11
_____

The smoothed hand with all its history nodes

Save your file again. To verify that you've been working correctly, you can load the finished hand (with its history intact) `poly_hand_v3.mb` from the CD.

Creating Areas of Detail on a Poly Mesh (Surface)

As you've seen with the hand, it became necessary to add more faces to parts of the surface to create various details. The hand takes on better form when more time is devoted to detailing it after its initial creation. The hand shown below was created through the above steps, but was further detailed by creating faces using the tools outlined below and moving vertices, in addition to adding fingernails. The most intricate of objects need only begin from the simplest models.

Maya provides several ways to add surface detail or increase a poly's subdivisions.

The Subdivide Tool

You can use the Subdivide tool to increase the number of faces of a poly surface by evenly dividing either all faces or just those selected. Select the poly surface, face, or faces, and choose **Edit Polygons → Subdivide**. In the option box, you can adjust the number of times the faces are divided by moving the Subdivisions Levels slider. The Mode drop-down menu gives you the choice to subdivide your faces into quads (four-sided faces, as on the left below) and triangles (three-sided faces, as on the right).

You can also select a poly edge to subdivide. Running this tool on edges divides the edges into separate edges along the same face. It will not divide the face; rather you use it to change the shape of the face by moving the subdivided edges as shown here.

You use the Subdivide tool to create regions of detail on a poly surface. It is a broader approach than using the Poke Faces tool, which adds detail for more pinpoint areas.

The Split Polygon Tool

Another way to create detail is to use the Split Polygon tool, which does exactly what its name implies. As you've seen, when you choose **Edit Polygons → Split Polygon Tool**, your cursor changes to a triangle. Use this cursor to select two points along two edges of a face. That creates a straight line from the first to the second point, which serves as a new edge to divide the face into two halves. Press Enter to create the new edge and faces, or continue to select new points for more edges.

Using the Split Polygon tool is a more flexible way to create surface subdivisions for your model.

The Cut Faces Tool

Known as a poly knife in other 3D applications, the Cut Faces tool lets you cut across a poly surface to create a series of edges for subdivisions, to pull off a section of the poly, or to simply delete a section. (See Figure 5.12.) Select the poly object, and choose **Edit Polygons → Cut Faces Tool**. Click the option box if you want the section to be extracted or deleted.

Figure 5.12

You can use the Cut Faces tool to create the edges, to pull apart the poly object, or to cut off a whole section.

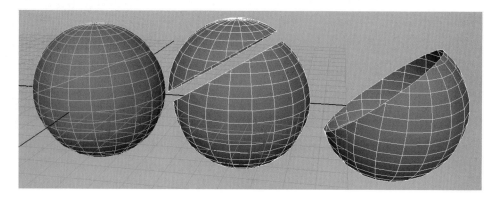

You can use the Cut Faces tool to create extra surface detail, to slice portions off the surface, or to create a straight edge on the model by trimming off the excess.

The Duplicate Face Tool

Select one or more faces, and choose **Edit Polygons → Duplicate Face** to create a copy of the selected face(s). You can use the manipulator that appears to move, scale, or rotate your copied face(s).

The Extract Tool

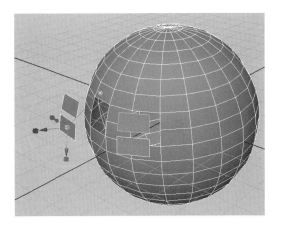

The Extract tool is similar to the Extrude tool, but it does not create the extra faces. Select the face(s), and choose **Edit Polygons → Extract** to pull the faces off the surface. With the Separate Extracted Faces option on, the extracted face will be a separate poly object; otherwise, it will remain as a part of the original.

You can use the Extract tool to create a hole in an object and still keep the original face(s). When you use this tool with the Split Polygon tool to make custom edges, you can create cutouts of almost any shape.

The Smooth Tool

The Smooth tool (choose **Polygons → Smooth**) evenly subdivides the poly surface or selected faces, creating several more faces to smooth and round out the original poly object.

The Sculpt Polygons Tool

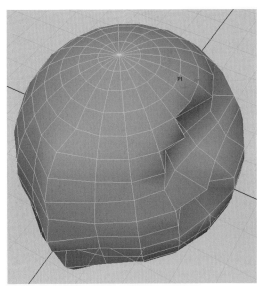

You can use Artisan to sculpt polygonal surfaces. The method is the same as with NURBS. Select your poly object, and choose **Edit Polygons → Sculpt Polygons Tool ❑**. You'll see the same tool cursors and settings. The only difference with sculpting polygons is that the surface will behave slightly differently when sculpted. Whereas with the NURBS sphere the brush strokes give smooth curves in and out, a polygon surface is more jagged. Of course, if you create the poly with a large number of subdivisions, you'll have a smoother result when using the Sculpt Polygons tool. (See Figure 5.13.)

Figure 5.13

The Sculpt Polygons tool

Modeling Complex Objects: The Polygon Catapult

This exercise will demonstrate the following polygonal modeling techniques:

- Extrusion
- Object duplication
- Pivot placement
- Revolved surfaces
- Complex model hierarchy

You're going to create a rather complex looking object, a catapult, using nothing but polygons. You'll use some sketches as a reference for the model. Since this is a fairly complex object, it's much better to start with good plans. This, of course, involves some research, some web surfing, some image gathering, or some sketching to get a feel for what it truly is you're trying to make.

To begin, create a new project for all the files called Catapult, or copy the Catapult project from the CD to your hard drive. If you do not create a new project, set your current project to the copied Catapult project on your drive. Choose **File → Project → Set** and select the Catapult. If you forget, your rendered images and scene files will be saved into your last project, axe_model. When you create a new project, Maya automatically sets it as the current project. Remember that you can enable incremental save to make backups at any point in the exercise.

Now on to model a design already sketched and modeled. To begin with, study the design sketches included in the sourceimages folder of the project. These sketches set up the intent rather easily.

In Chapter 8, you'll animate the catapult. When building any model, it's important to keep animation in mind, especially for grouping related objects in the scene hierarchy so that they will move as you intend. Creating a good scene hierarchy will be crucial to a smooth animation workflow; so throughout this exercise you'll use the Outliner to keep the catapult's component pieces organized as you create them.

The Production Process

The trick with a complex object model is to approach it part by part. Deconstruct the major elements of the original into distinct shapes that you can approach one by one. The catapult can be broken down to six distinct objects, each with their own sub-objects:

- Base
- Wheels
- Fulcrum assembly
- Winch assembly
- Arm assembly

You will model each part separately based on the sketch in Figure 5.14 and the detailed schematic in Figure 5.15.

Fulcrum assembly　　Arm assembly

Winch assembly

Wheels

Base

Figure 5.14

**A sketch of the catapult
to model**

Figure 5.15

**A schematic diagram of
the finished model**

The Base

The base is made of simple polygonal cubes representing timber and arranged to connect to each other. Follow these steps:

1. Choose **Create → Polygon Primitives → Cube** to lay down your first cube. This will be for the two long, broad boards running along side.

2. Scale the cube to 2.0 in X, 0.8 in Y, and 19.5 in Z. Move it off the center of the grid about 2 units to the right.

3. You will now create a copy of one side of the base to create the other side. Select the cube and choose **Edit → Duplicate**. This will place a copy of the cube exactly where the original is in the scene, but it will be already selected for you. Move the copy about 4 units to the left. You should now have something similar to the picture here.

4. Now for the cross braces. Create a poly cube and scale it 7.25 in X, 0.6 in Y, and 3.25 in Z. Place this platform on top of the two beams, at the end of the catapult's base.

5. Create a cube for the first of the top two cross braces and scale it 6.5 in X, 0.6 in Y, and 1.2 in Z. Place it on top of the beams at the head of the base, with a little room for the two beams to stick out a bit. Duplicate the cube, and move the copy about a third of the way down toward the end.

You're going to add some detail as you go along; namely the bolts that hold the timber together. You'll learn two ways of doing it, to give you exposure to two different workflows for this simple task. The bolts will merely be the tops of spheres placed at the intersection of the pieces. Figure 5.16 shows the bolt positions.

Save your file now and compare it to `catapult_v1.mb` in the Catapult project on the CD to see what the completed base should look like.

- Create a poly sphere. In the front view panel, select the bottom two-thirds of the sphere's individual faces in component mode (press F8) and simply delete them. Duplicate and place the hemisphere at the intersections of the wood pieces.

- Or you can use the Cut Faces tool to define a cut line straight across the top third of the sphere in the front view. Select the sphere and choose **Edit Polygons** → **Cut Faces Tool** ❐. Set the option box to delete the cut faces. Duplicate the hemisphere and place the copies at the intersections.

6. Grab the pieces and their bolts, and group them into a logical order or as shown in the Outliner.

Again, the time you spend keeping your scene objects organized now will pay off later when you animate the catapult in Chapter 8.

Figure 5.16

The base with bolts

The Winch Baseboards

Next are the bars that hold the winch assembly to the base. Follow these steps:

1. Create two long narrow poly cubes for the base boards of the winch, and position them across the top two side braces.

2. For the brackets that hold the winch down, create a small poly cube. Scale X to 0.5, Y to 0.32, and Z to 0.44. Select the side face and extrude it to about 0.75 in **Local Translate Z**.

3. Select the top face and extrude it to about 1.54 in **Local Translate Z** to take it up to an L shape. Select the two inside vertices on the top of the L, and move them up to create a 45° angle at the tip.

4. Select that angled face, and open the option box for Extrude Face. Enter –1.55 for the **Translate Z** attribute in the Global Values section. This will pull out the face in a straight line across, as opposed to up at an angle if you were to drag the manipulator to extrude it. Then, using the special manipulator, rotate that face to angle it down.

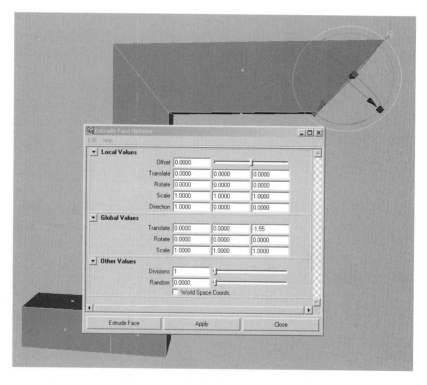

5. Open the Extrude Face option box again with the new angled face selected. Enter –1.54 for the **Y Translate** attribute in the Global Values section, and reset the **Translate Z** value to zero to bring the bracket piece straight down. That segment will have an angled end, so grab the two outside vertices and move them down to even out the end. Rotating the face will flare out the end; moving the vertices is much cleaner.

6. Select that end's face and open the Extrude Face option box again. Choose **Edit → Reset Settings** to clear the options in the Global Values section. Click the Extrude Face button and pull down the face to extrude it about 0.315 to line it up with the bottom of the cube you originally created for the bracket.

7. Select the outside face of that new extrusion and pull it out about 0.75 to create the second flange and to finish the bracket. Move the bracket on top of one of the baseboards for the winch, and place a duplicated and properly sized bolt head on the flanges. Duplicate the flange and the bolt head, and move the copies to the other baseboard, as shown in Figure 5.17.

Figure 5.17

The winch's base completed

Figure 5.18

MM dragging a node to another location in the Outliner regroups the move node.

8. Group the pieces of the brackets together by selecting them and choosing **Edit → Group**. Call the object Bracket. Repeat this procedure for the duplicated bracket and bolt. Then select the top node of the bracket and its baseboard, and make a new group for them called Winch_baseboard. Repeat this procedure for the other baseboard and bracket.

The Ground Spikes

The last items you need for the base are the spikes that secure the base into the ground at the foot of the catapult. Follow these steps:

1. Copy a bracket group and remove it from its current hierarchy (the baseboard group) by MM dragging it to another location in the Outliner. (See Figure 5.18.)

2. Move, scale, and rotate the bracket to fit it to the side of the base at the foot of the catapult. Create a poly cube, and scale it to fit through the bracket. Elongate it to about 3.75 in Y-axis scale, and create a pointed tip by extruding the bottom face and scaling it down. If you don't extrude that face and merely scale it, the spike will look more like a long pyramid than a spiked stake. Group the bracket and spike together, and call the new group Stake. Duplicate that group and move it to the other side of the base. Group all these groups together into a parent Catapult group (see Figure 5.19) and save.

 The scene file `catapult_v2.mb` on the CD has the completed base for comparison.

Figure 5.19

The completed base

The Wheels

You will now create the wheels. Follow these steps:

1. First is the axle. Create a poly cylinder with end caps by choosing **Create → Polygon Primitives → Cylinder**. Scale and position the axle as shown, and place two duplicated brackets at each end. Remember to move the duplicated brackets out of their current hierarchy.

2. To model a wheel, you'll use NURBS curves first to lay out a profile to revolve. Choose **Create → CV Curve Tool** ❐, and select 1 Linear for Curve Degree. Since the wheel's profile will have no smooth curves, you can create a linear CV curve like that in Figure 5.20. It's important for the design to create three spans for the top part of the curve. Place the pivot point (Ins key) about ¾ of a unit below the curve.

3. Select the curve and revolve it by choosing **Surfaces → Revolve** ❐. In the option box, set Axis Preset to X to make it revolve correctly. Change Segments from the default 8 to 20 to give a smoother wheel. Set Output Geometry to Polygons, and set Tessellation Method to Control Points. This will create the edges

Figure 5.20

The profile curve for the wheel

of the faces along the CV points on the curve. Click Revolve, and there it is. Delete the history and the original NURBS curve since you won't need either again. Center the wheel's pivot point by choosing **Modify → Center Pivot**.

4. Next, add some detail to the wheel. Duplicate a bolt head, and remove the copy from whatever group it was in. Arrange a few of the bolt heads around the front face of the wheel.

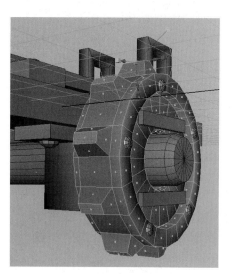

5. Add a couple of braces on the front of the wheel above and below the wheel's middle hole with two thin, stretched poly cubes. Group them together by selecting them and pressing Ctrl+G. That is the hot key for **Edit → Group**. Name that group node Wheel. Move the group to fit it around the axle.

6. Adding studs to the wheel makes for better traction when moving the catapult through mud and also for a more realistic catapult. Because you created the wheel with subdivisions along the tread of the wheel, this step will be easy. To create all the studs at once, grab *every other middle face* along the outside of the wheel and extrude it out about ¼ of a unit. Then scale the face with the special manipulator in both the X and the Z axes.

7. Copy the wheel node and rotate it 180° in the Y axis to create the other rear wheel. Position it on the other side of the rear axle. Group the two wheels together with the axle and call the new node Rear_Wheel. Later, you will animate this node to make the wheels turn.

8. Select the Rear_Wheel node and the two brackets, and duplicate them by choosing **Edit → Duplicate** or by pressing the hot key Ctrl+D. Move the objects to the foot of the catapult for the front wheels. Rename the nodes to reflect the change.

9. Add the new axle bracket and wheel nodes to the Catapult node by MM dragging them onto the Catapult node in the Outliner and save your scene.

The file `catapult_v3.mb` on the CD reflects the finished wheels and base.

The Winch Assembly

To be able to pull the catapult arm down to cock it, you'll need the winch assembly to wind a rope that connects to the arm to wind it down into firing position. Since animating a rope can be a rather involved and advanced technique, the catapult will not actually be built with a rope.

To build the winch assembly, follow these steps:

1. The first part of the winch will be the pulley around which the rope winds. Create a profile curve for extrusion as you did with the wheel. Place the pivot point of the curve at the first CV. Revolve the curve around the X axis with only 12 segments (as opposed to the wheel's 20). Center its pivot.

2. Position the pulley at the head of the catapult, placing the brackets in the grooves.

3. Now you'll need some sort of geared wheel and handle to crank the pulley:

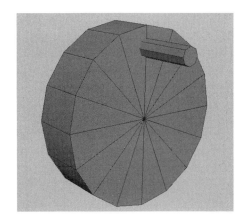

   - Create a poly cylinder, and rotate it so it's on its side. Scale it to a squat wheel with scale values of 1.4 in the X and Z axes and 0.4 in the Y axis.

   - Create another poly cylinder and rotate it to its side. Scale it to be a long thin stick. You'll use this as the first of eight gear teeth for the wheel. Position it at the top of the wheel as shown. Now move its pivot to the center of the wheel. Click the Snap to Points icon in the Status line (the magnet with the black dot).

- Instead of duplicating the gear tooth and positioning it seven more times, you'll use the array capabilities of the Duplicate tool. Select the tooth and choose **Edit →
Duplicate ❑**. In the option box, set Rotate to 45 in the X axis, and set Number of Copies to 7. Since the pivot for the tooth is at the center of the wheel, as soon as you click the Duplicate button in the option box, Maya places seven copies around the wheel at 45° intervals.

Make sure you reset the Duplicate settings (choose **Edit → Reset Settings**) before you use the command again; otherwise, you will get a circle of seven of whatever you're copying in 45° intervals.

- Now for the handle, create a poly cube with enough segments for you to adjust vertices and faces to match the handle shown. Create cylinders for the crank axle and handle and place them as shown (below left).

- Group the geometry together, and call the object Turn_Wheel, and center its pivot. Place it at the end of the pulley. Place a copy (rotate 180° around) on the other side of the pulley(below right).

Figure 5.21

The assembled winch

4. Now you'll need gear teeth on the pulley. Create a poly cylinder and position it at the end of the pulley and in between two of the turning wheel teeth. Place the pivot at the center of the pulley using snaps. (You may have to temporarily move the turning wheel aside to get to the pulley's center point.)

5. Duplicate the new tooth seven times around the pulley at 45° intervals. Make a single copy of all those teeth, and move the copies to the other side of the pulley. (Remember to reset your Duplicate settings!) Group the pulley and turning wheels together and name the object Winch. Center the pivot.

6. Using a couple of poly cubes, make a winch arm on either side to hold the winch on the catapult. Place the arm between the hand crank and the turning wheel, and bolt it to the catapult's base, as shown in Figure 5.21. Save your scene file.

To verify your work up to this point, compare it to `catapult_v4.mb` on the CD.

The Arm

Now, try creating the arm (see Figure 5.22) on your own, using all the techniques you've already used and the following hints and diagrams.

- Create the intricate-looking arm with face extrusions. That's all you'll need for the arm geometry. Follow Figure 5.23 for subdivision positions to make the extrusions work correctly.

- Duplicate and place bolt heads around the basket assembly.

- Create the straps for the basket with poly cubes. It's easier than it looks. You'll just need to create and extrude the cubes with enough subdivisions to allow you to bend them to weave them together as shown in Figure 5.24. The ends of the straps wrap around the arm's basket with extrusions and wedges.

- Create the hinge for the arm with a couple of duplicated brackets and a cylinder.

- Create the arm's stand with multiple extrusions from a cube. Follow the subdivisions in Figure 5.25 for reference.

- Group the objects together and add their groups to the Catapult node.

Figure 5.22

The catapult arm assembly

Figure 5.23

Follow the subdivisions on your model.

Figure 5.24

Basket straps

Figure 5.25

Follow the subdivisions on the arm stand.

When you're finished, save your scene file and compare it to `catapult_v5.mb` on the CD. Figure 5.26 shows the finished catapult.

Suggestions for Modeling Polygons

Poly modeling lends itself nicely to a wide range of objects. Try modeling the following objects to fine-tune your skills and explore the toolset.

Dining room table and chairs An easy place to start. A good amount of leeway in the design gives you as much a challenge as you feel you can handle.

Computer monitor With all the angles and overall surface details, modeling a monitor makes for a great extrusion and face-editing exercise.

Desk lamp, floor lamp This can be a quick exercise, so try to keep it highly detailed.

Car This exercise can be a real challenge, so keep it simple at first and increase the amount of detail the next time you try a poly car. Try to keep your model to the overall shape of the car, and don't worry about doors and windows that actually operate. Try to model the faces such that different parts of the car have different faces. Use NURBS surface tools to create poly patches to form the body of the car.

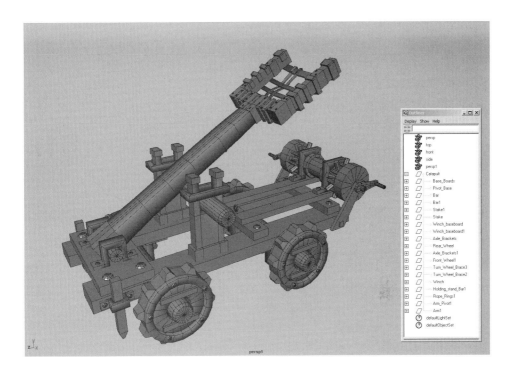

Figure 5.26

The completed catapult

Summary

Complex models become much easier to create once you recognize how to deconstruct them into their base components. You can divide even simple objects into more easily managed segments from which you can create a model.

The art of modeling with polygons is like anything else in Maya. The technique and workflow enhance with age and time. It is less important to know *all* the tricks of the trade than it is to know *how* to approach a model and interpret it into a wireframe mesh.

Above all have fun with it.

CHAPTER 6

Further Modeling Topics

Once you've learned the basics of creating and editing NURBS and poly models, more advanced modeling techniques will easily become part of your toolbox. This chapter shows how to use deformations to adjust a model, as opposed to editing the geometry directly as you did with the previous methods, and introduces you to subdivision surface modeling, which fully incorporates this concept.

- **Modeling with Deformers: The Lattice**
- **Subdivision Surfaces**
- **Creating a Starfish**
- **Building a Teakettle**

Modeling with Deformers: The Lattice

As you have seen in the chapters that deal with NURBS and polygonal modeling, deformers can be handy when creating and editing modeled shapes. Nonlinear deformers such as Bend and Flare create a simple shape adjustment for the attached geometry, like bending it. But when a model requires more intricate editing, you will need to use a *lattice*.

A lattice is a scaffold of sorts that fits around your geometry. The lattice object controls the shape of the geometry. Once you adjust the Lattice deformer, the geometry deforms to match. When a lattice point is moved, the lattice smoothly deforms the underlying geometry.

Lattices become useful when you need to edit a relatively complex poly mesh or NURBS surface that is too dense to efficiently edit directly with control vertices. You assign a lattice and use it to create changes without having to move the surface's individual surface points.

Lattices can work on any surface type, and a single lattice can affect multiple surfaces at the same time.

Creating a Lattice

Make sure you are in the Animation menu set. To begin adjusting an existing model or surface, select the model(s) or applicable groups to deform and choose **Deform → Create Lattice**. Figure 6.1 shows the detailed polygonal hand model from Chapter 5 with a default lattice applied. The top node of the hand was selected, and the lattice applied.

Figure 6.1

A lattice is applied to the polygonal hand model.

To experience how this works, you will remodel the detailed poly hand with a few different lattices. Your objective is to create an alien hand by thinning and elongating the hand and each of the fingers. Since it will take more time and effort to move the vertices of the poly mesh to achieve this, lattices are ideal.

To elongate and thin the entire hand, load the scene file `detailed_poly_hand.ma` from the Poly_Hand project on the CD and follow these steps:

1. Select the top node of the hand (poly_hand), and choose **Deform → Create Lattice**. This will create a default lattice that will affect the entire hand, fingernails and all, as seen in Figure 6.1. Although you can change the lattice settings in the options window upon creation, you will edit the lattice after it is applied to the hand.

2. The lattice will be selected once it's created. Open the Attribute Editor, and click the ffd1LatticeShape tab. The three attributes of interest here are the **S Divisions, T Divisions,** and **U Divisions.** These sliders control how many divisions the lattice uses to deform its geometry. Set S Divisions to 3, set T Divisions to 2, and set U Divisions to 3 for the result shown in Figure 6.2. A $3 \times 2 \times 3$ lattice refers to the number of division lines in the lattice as opposed to the number of sections; otherwise this would be a $2 \times 1 \times 2$ lattice!

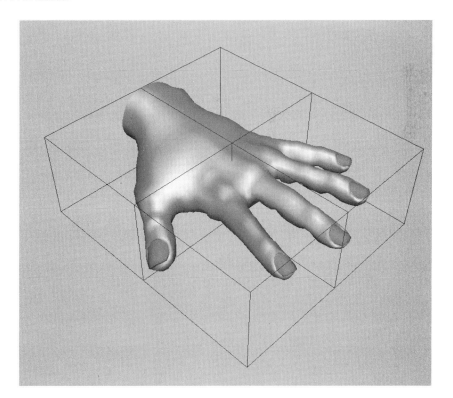

Figure 6.2

Changing the number of divisions for the lattice

3. With the lattice selected, switch to Component mode (press F8) to display the lattice's points. These points act just like the vertices on a polygonal shape. You will use them to change the overall shape of the hand, without resorting to moving the vertices of the hand themselves. Select the vertices on the thumb side of the hand, and move them to squeeze in that half of the hand. Notice how only that zone of the model is affected by that part of the lattice.

4. Switch back to Object mode (press F8), and scale the entire lattice to be thinner in the Z axis and longer in the X axis. Now the entire hand is deformed as the lattice is scaled.

Now that you have altered the hand, you have no need for this lattice. If you delete the lattice, the hand will snap back to its original shape. Instead, to get rid of the lattice you need to delete construction history on the hand itself, as you did with the NURBS axe exercise in Chapter 4.

5. Select the top node of the hand, and choose **Edit → Delete by Type → History**.

The next step is to elongate the individual fingers and widen the knuckles. To begin with the index finger, follow these steps:

1. Select the top node of the hand, and create a new lattice as before. It will form around the entire hand.

   Although you can divide the lattice so that its divisions line up with the fingers, it is easier and more interactive to scale and position the entire lattice to fit around just the index finger.

2. Since transforming the currently selected lattice will deform the geometry, you will need to select the lattice and its base node as well to change the lattice without affecting the hand. In the Outliner, select both the ffd1Lattice and ffd1Base nodes as shown in the graphic on the top of the next page.

3. With both nodes selected, scale, rotate, and transform the lattice to fit around the index finger as shown in Figure 6.3. Set S Divisions to 7, set T Divisions to 2, and set U Divisions to 3.

4. Deselect the base and adjust the lattice to lengthen the finger by pulling the lattice points. Pick the lattice points around each of the knuckles individually, and scale them up to widen them.

5. To delete the lattice and keep the changes to the finger, select the top node of the hand and delete its history. Repeat this entire procedure to adjust the other fingers to finish your alien hand.

> Before you delete the last of your lattices, play with moving the hand geometry through the lattice while it's still applied to one of the fingers. Notice how parts of the geometry of the hand deform as the hand travels through the lattice, and think of ways you can use this warping effect in an animation. You can create an effect like a balloon being squeezed through a pipe by animating the balloon geometry through a lattice.

The alien hand in Figure 6.4 was created by adjusting the polygonal hand from this exercise using only lattices.

As you can see, lattices afford you powerful editing capabilities without the complication of dealing with surface points directly. They can help reshape an entire complex model quickly or adjust minor details on parts of a larger whole.

Figure 6.3

Position the lattice and its base to fit around the index finger.

Figure 6.4

The human hand model is adjusted to be an alien hand using lattices to deform the geometry

Lattices not only work on polygons as you've seen here, they can be used on any geometry in Maya, at any stage in your workflow to create or adjust models as well as create animated effects.

Subdivision Surfaces

Subdivision surfaces combine the best features of NURBS and polygonal modeling for intricate surfaces such as faces. Using subdivision surfaces, you can model complex characters and create models from single primitives as in polygonal modeling, but with perfectly smooth surfaces as in NURBS modeling.

Like lattices, subdivision surfaces rely on varying levels of editing detail that allow you to adjust a surface from a global level, where large parts of the model are modified, to a microlevel, where you have control over the most dense of surface points.

Typical subdivision workflow begins when you create a simple polygonal mesh of your model. The polygon is converted to a subdivision surface that you can edit using any number of subdivision detail levels. More often than not, the resulting subdivision surface is then converted back to a polygonal object for use in the production. Subdivision surfaces can also be converted to NURBS patches.

Creating a Starfish

You will create a starfish model starting with polygons, like the models you created in Chapter 5. You will then convert the polygon mesh to a subdivision surface to mold it into a proper starfish. Follow these steps:

1. Create a new scene. Create a polygon cube and scale it to be 8 wide, 8 deep, and 1.2 high.

2. Use the Split Polygon tool (choose **Edit Polygons → Split Polygon Tool**) to split one side of the box into half as shown.

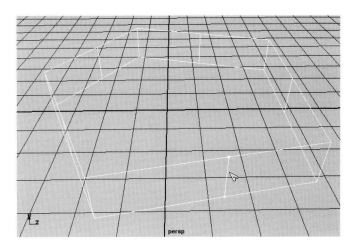

Figure 6.5

Once the pentagon is created, split each face into two.

3. Reshape the box into an irregular pentagon as shown in Figure 6.5 by selecting the polygonal edges of the box in component mode (press F8) and moving them one by one. You needn't make sure each of the five sides are perfectly the same size. Starfish are irregular themselves, but be careful not to move any of the edges up or down in the Y axis. You'll want the pentagon to be flat.

4. Use the Split Polygon tool again to cut all five sides in half as shown in Figure 6.5. You will be using these edges to create a polygonal star, from which you will convert to the subdivision surface.

5. Use the newly created edges to shape the pentagon into a star by moving the edges in toward the center as shown. This will be the basis for your starfish subdivision surface.

6. Save your work and compare it to the scene file `Starfish_v01.ma` in the Starfish project on the CD.

Converting to a Subdivision Surface

Now that you have the basic polygonal shape for the starfish, convert it to a subdivision surface. Follow these steps:

1. Select the star, and then choose **Modify → Convert → Polygons to Subdiv**. The star will turn into a smooth subdivision surface, as shown in Figure 6.6.

2. Although you have all but lost the points of the star in converting it to smooth subdivisions, you now have far greater control. Press the 3 key to increase the display resolution of the surface. As they do with NURBS objects, the keys 1, 2, and 3 set the display resolution of a subdivision surface.

3. With the starfish still selected, choose **Subdiv Surfaces → Polygon Proxy Mode**. This will switch you to a low-level editing mode and restore the shape of the star as seen here. The star here is not the surface of the starfish, but a proxy that will shape the subdivision surface much like a lattice. Switch to component mode (press F8), and you'll see vertices on the polygon proxy that you can move to shape the starfish.

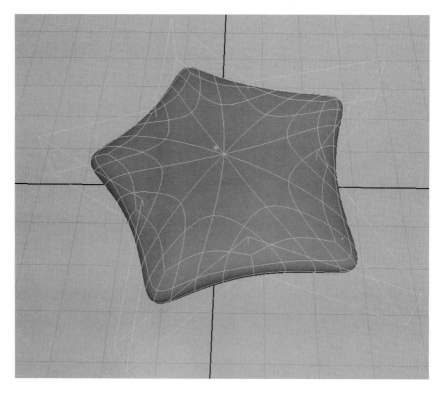

4. Using the polygon proxy to shape the starfish is good for creating "broad strokes" when creating your final model, but will not yield good results by itself, so hit F8 to go back to the object selection mode to select the starfish and not its vertices, and then switch back to Standard mode (choose **Subdiv Surfaces → Standard Mode**). With the starfish still selected, enter component mode to select vertices. The vertices of the starfish will appear in the same location as the points on the polygon proxy and are represented with zeros as in Figure 6.7.

5. Right-click the starfish to open a marking menu, and choose **Display Level → 1**. It is at this level of detail that you will define the arms of the fish. Select the vertices (now represented with 1's) between each point, and pull them in toward the center of the fish as shown. This level of detail is automatically generated when you convert the poly starfish to a subdivision surface. As a matter of fact, you also have another level of detail (**Display Level → 2**), which you'll use later.

If by chance you do not see a **Display Level → 2** as an option and **Display Level → 1** is the highest detail level you have, you can create this higher level of display by selecting all the Level 1 vertices on the starfish in component mode and choosing **Subdiv Surfaces → Refine Selected Components** to create level 2 vertices. You will then be able to choose **Display Level → 2** when needed.

Figure 6.6

Converting the star shape to a subdivision

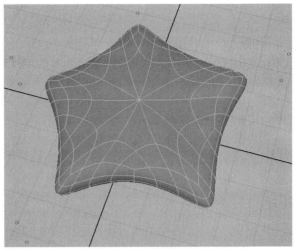

Figure 6.7

The zeros represent the zero-level of detail on this subdivision starfish and correspond to the vertices on its polygon proxy.

6. Save your file now and compare your work to the scene file `Starfish_v02.ma` in the Starfish project on the CD.

7. Right-click the starfish, and choose **Display Level → 2**. The vertices on the next higher detail level appear and are represented by 2's. With this level of detail, you can move these vertices to give your starfish more character. Try making the areas between the points on the star smoother, as shown in Figure 6.8. Also try to flatten the bottom of the starfish using either level 1 or 2 vertices.

8. You may need to further detail your starfish in some areas to achieve the look seen in Figure 6.8, though. As it stands now, the starfish can be edited up to level 2. To create another level of detail, select the areas you want to refine by selecting the level 2 vertices along the outside of each star point, as shown in Figure 6.9.

9. With those vertices selected, right-click the selection and choose **Refine** from the marking menu. Maya will add another level of detail to that area of the starfish with vertices marked as 3's. This will allow you to make more detailed adjustments to the surface to

mold it to your liking. Work the vertices at all levels to sculpt your starfish close to the one in Figure 6.8.

RM clicking the starfish and choosing **Refine** is the same as selecting the vertices and choosing **Subdiv Surfaces → Refine Selected Components**. Choosing vertices in an area of your model and refining them beyond a display level of 2 will create more vertices for that area only. You may continue to refine your selection as needed. At any time you may go back to polygon proxy mode to access the lowest level of detail to adjust the broad strokes of the model.

10. Save again, and load the scene file `Starfish_v03.ma` in the Starfish project on the CD to compare your work.

You can use these same techniques to re-create the polygon hand from Chapter 5 with subdivision surfaces.

Figure 6.8

A molded starfish

Figure 6.9

Select the area to be refined.

Building a Teakettle

Now that you have been exposed to the mechanics of subdivision surface modeling and editing, you're ready for another model. The next subdivision exercise is to create a teakettle that you will later animate in Chapter 12 to blow steam from its spout. You'll first fashion the kettle from simple polygon shapes and then refine it using subdivisions.

Creating the Base Polygon Model

To create the base poly mesh for the kettle, follow these steps:

1. The main body of the kettle will begin as a poly cylinder. Choose **Create → Polygon Primitives → Cylinder** ❏ to open the options window. Set Subdivisions Around Axis to 8, and set Subdivisions Around Height to 4.

2. To create the lid, create another poly cylinder with 8 subdivisions around the axis and only 2 for the height. Scale it to fit as a lid for the first cylinder.

3. Select the upper row of poly edges on the lid, and scale them all in to create a bevel, as shown in Figure 6.10. Then select every other edge on the top surface and delete them, as shown in Figure 6.11.

4. Select the poly edges of the main cylinder, and scale them out increasingly larger as you work your way down. Delete every other edge of the top surface as you did with the lid. Your kettle should look as shown here.

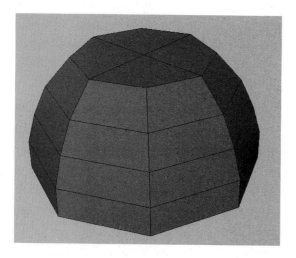

5. You are going to create a simple handle for the lid. Select the lid's top four faces. You will create the handle by extruding these faces and scaling them in. But if you were to choose **Edit Polygon → Extrude Face** and use the special scale handles as shown in Figure 6.12, your faces would all separate.

Instead, you need to first choose **Polygons → Tool Options → Keep Faces Together**. This option lets you extrude these faces properly. Now select the four faces again and choose **Edit Polygon → Extrude Face**. Use the scale handles to scale the extruded faces in, as shown in Figure 6.13. The tool option you set keeps the poly faces together during the extrude operation.

Figure 6.10

Scale the outer edges inward.

Figure 6.11

Delete every other edge of the top surface.

Figure 6.12

By default, faces will extrude separately.

Figure 6.13

The Keep Faces Together allows you to extrude the faces in together.

Figure 6.14

**Round out the handle
by moving the edges.**

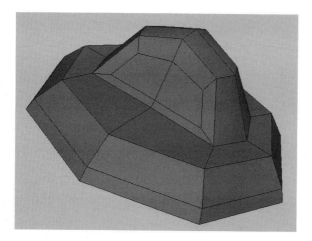

6. With those four faces still selected, extrude faces again, but this time pull them up and scale them in a bit as shown (below left).

7. Select the side faces of the lid's new handle, and extrude the faces inward using the scale handle to create detail on the handle as shown (below right).

8. Select the edges that make up the lid handle, and move them to round out the handle, as shown in Figure 6.14

9. Select the four faces on the top of the kettle and extrude faces. Scale the faces in, and pull them up to round the top of the kettle as shown here.

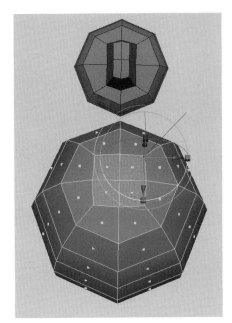

10. Select the kettle and apply a lattice to it by choosing **Deform →** **Create Lattice** (in the Animation menu set). Set S Divisions to 2, set T Divisions to 3, and set U Divisions to 2. Adjust the lattice to bend the kettle back to create the front. Figure 6.15 shows the lattice's final position. Once you have the proper shape, select the kettle and delete its history to delete the lattice.

11. Just before you convert the kettle to a subdivision surface, you need to create more detail at the bottom of the kettle so that the subdivision surface won't round out and you will still have a flat bottom. In the side or front view panel, select the kettle. Choose **Edit Polygons → Cut Faces** (make sure to reset the tool options so as not to delete any of the face), and use the Cut Faces tool to create a new division along the bottom of the kettle, as shown in Figure 6.16.

12. Select all the new faces along the bottom, and extrude them out to create a lip that runs around the kettle's bottom as shown here. Be sure that **Polygons → Tool Options → Keep Faces Together** is still turned on; otherwise, the faces will separate.

13. Save your scene file and load the `Kettle_Model_v01.ma` file from the Tea_Kettle project on the CD to compare your work up to this point.

Figure 6.15

Use the lattice to bend the kettle.

Converting to Subdivisions

Once you complete the base polygon model for the kettle, you can convert it to a subdivision surface to round it out and make it smooth. To convert the kettle, follow these steps:

1. Select the kettle, and choose **Modify → Convert → Polygons to Subdiv**. Then select the lid and convert it as well.

2. Select the converted kettle and the lid, and press 3 to view them in high-resolution mode. Position the lid to go on top of the kettle, and your model should be similar to that in Figure 6.17.

Figure 6.17

**The subdivision
kettle and lid**

3. The only items that remain are the spout and a handle. For the handle, create a subdivision torus (choose **Create → Subdiv Primitives → Torus**). Scale, rotate, and place the torus above and around the lid, on top of the kettle.

4. With the handle selected, choose **Subdiv Surfaces → Polygon Proxy Mode**. Using the vertices on the polygon proxy, make the handle thinner and elongate it up, as shown in Figure 6.18.

5. Return to standard mode with the handle selected (choose **Subdiv Surfaces → Standard Mode**). To make the handle smoother, you will refine it and add more subdivisions. Switch to component mode, and the vertices of the handle will display as zeros. Right-click the handle and choose **Refine** from the marking menu. New vertices will appear, and they will all read as 1's. The handle will be much smoother. Make any modeling adjustments to your liking, switching between level 0 and level 1 display as needed, using the right mouse button and the marking menu's Display Level command.

6. To create the spout, create a subdivision cylinder. Switch to component mode to select faces (not vertices). Right-click the cylinder, and choose display level 2. Select the inside circle of faces on the top of the cylinder, as shown in Figure 6.19. Move them down into the cylinder to hollow it out, but creating a thickness to the spout at the same time, also shown in Figure 6.19.

Figure 6.18

The kettle's handle

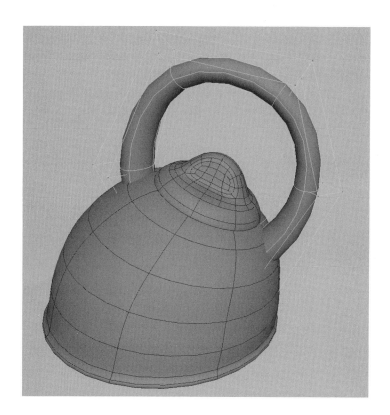

7. Position the spout on the kettle. Move vertices to flare out at the bottom of the spout where it meets the kettle. Figure 6.20 shows the completed kettle.

    Save your file. You will be using it for an exercise in creating steam in Chapter 12.

Figure 6.19

Hollow out the spout.

Figure 6.20

The completed subdivision teakettle

Converting Back to Polygons

Most models created with subdivision surfaces are converted back to polygons once the modeling is finished. Since subdivisions are a more intricate surface type than polygons, it usually makes for improved performance while animating to work with a polygonal model instead of a subdivision. Professionals frequently use subdivision tools and surfaces to create their models, but convert back to polygons once they are finished.

This is a simple procedure, similar to the Chapter 5 exercise in which you converted NURBS surfaces to polygons. Here you will convert the kettle back to polygons.

1. Select the subdivision kettle and its handle, spout, and lid, and choose **Modify → Convert → Subdiv to Polygons** ❏ to open the options window shown in Figure 6.21.

2. Next to Tessellation Method, select Adaptive. This will yield the best results more often than not.

3. The Divisions Per Face slider controls how smoothly the object is converted to polys. At a division factor of 1, your kettle will look jagged. Turn it up to 2, and you will notice a faithful conversion to polygons.

Figure 6.21

The Convert Subdiv to Polygons Options window

4. For best results, however, select each piece of the kettle separately, and convert the pieces one by one, adjusting the Divisions Per Face value appropriately. You will find that a division value of 2 will work for everything but the handle, which requires a division value of at least 3 to remain fairly smooth.

Taking the Kettle Further

Try to create more detail for the kettle, or even experiment with your own designs. Some of the easy additions you can work on include a whistle cap for the spout. Or even try to create a matching set of tea cups and saucers using subdivision surfaces. With the exposure you have gained here, you should feel confident to tackle an entire kitchen full of models!

Also, try your hand at creating the models suggested at the end of Chapter 4 using subdivision techniques instead of NURBS.

Summary

Modeling is perhaps the most visible aspect of CG, since essentially every CG project will need some form of modeling. It is typically the first CG procedure students try to get good at before moving on to other aspects of CG, and it is usually the first aspect of CG to be taught in depth.

As you can see, you can accomplish a modeling task in several ways. Different workflows give you great flexibility to choose your own modeling style. But to make such a choice, you'll need to practice. Good modelers have a good eye for detail and a high tolerance for work that can often be repetitive. But they also love assembling a complex object, and seeing a great result, and they are thrilled by the eventual outcome.

Keep at it; model everything you get your hands and eyes on. Try the same model a few different ways; switch between NURBS, polygons, and subdivisions to get comfortable with Maya's toolset. As you're doing that, keep on top of how you organize your nodes, and keep everything named and organized.

CHAPTER 7

Maya Shading and Texturing

Shading is the term in Maya for applying colors and textures, known as *shaders*. After you model your objects, Maya assigns a default shader to them with a neutral gray color. This is to allow them to render and display properly. Without any shader attached to a surface, the object cannot be seen.

Simply put, a shader is defines an object's look: its color, tactile texture, transparency, luminescence, glow, and so forth.

Topics include:

- **Shader Types**
- **Shader Attributes**
- **Texturing the Axe**
- **Textures and Surfaces**

Shading is the proper term for applying a renderable color, surface bumps, transparency, reflection, shine, or similar attributes to an object in Maya. It is closely related to, but distinct from, the term *texturing,* which is formally used when you apply a map or other node to an attribute of a shader to create some sort of surface detail. For example, adding a scanned photo of a brick wall to the color attribute of a shader that you then assign to a model in Maya is considered applying texture. Adding another scanned photo of the bumps and contours of the same brick wall to the **Bump Mapping** attribute is also applying a texture. Nevertheless, since textures are often applied to shaders, the entire process of shading is sometimes informally referred to as texturing. Applying textures to shaders is also called *texture mapping* or simply *mapping*. You map a texture to the color node of a shader, which is then assigned or applied to a Maya object.

Shaders are based on nodes. Each node holds the attributes that define the shader. With shaders, akin to the hierarchies and groups of models, you create shader networks of interconnected nodes. These networks can be simple, and they can be intricate and involved, when several render nodes are used to create complex shading effects.

Each shader, also known as a shading group, comprises a set of material nodes. Material nodes are the Maya nodes that hold all the pertinent rendering information about the object to which they are assigned, such as the color, opacity, or shininess. The shading groups are the nodes that allow the connection between the surface and the material you've created. When you edit the shader through the Attribute Editor, as you will do later in this chapter, you edit its material node.

As you learn about shading in this chapter, you will deal primarily with the Hypershade and perhaps the Multilister. See Chapter 3, "Your First Maya Animation," for an introduction to both windows. You can access either window by choosing **Window → Rendering Editors**. Through either of these windows you can create and edit your shaders.

Shading in Maya is almost always done hand in hand with lighting, which is the subject of Chapter 10, "Maya Lighting." At the very least, textures are tweaked and edited when in the lighting stage of production. Since the appearance of an object depends on light, in this chapter's exercise you'll create some lights as you create textures; then you'll learn more about lighting in Chapter 10.

Shader Types

Open the Hypershade through **Window → Rendering Editors → Hypershade**. In the left hand column of that window, you will see a listing of shading nodes. Click the Create bar at the top of this list and select Create Materials if it is currently set to something else like Create All Nodes. You will see a listing of the available shader types in Maya.

Of these shader types, you'll find five that are common to other animation packages as well. You'll use two of those later in this chapter. To understand a bit more about shaders, take a look at what makes objects look as they do in the real world.

The short answer is light. The way light bounces off an object and reflects into your eyes defines how you see that object. The surface of the object may have pigments that affect the frequency of light once it reflects off it, giving the object color. Other features of that object's surface also dictate how light is reflected.

Shader types address the differences in how light bounces off surfaces and how you perceive that reflection of light. Most light, once it hits a surface, diffuses across an area of that surface. It may also reflect a hot spot called a specular highlight. The shaders in Maya differ in how they deal with specular and diffuse parameters. As you learn about the shader types, think of the things around you and what shader type would best fit them.

The Lambert Shader Type

The most common shader type is Lambert, an evenly diffused shading type found in dull or matte surfaces. A sheet of paper, for example, is a Lambert surface.

A Lambert surface diffuses and scatters light evenly across its surface, in all directions (bottom left).

The Phong Shader Type

Phong shading, named after its developer Bui Tuong-Phong in 1975, brings to a surface's rendering the notions of specular highlight and reflectivity. You'll find glossy objects such as plastics, glass, and most metals take well to Phong shading.

A Phong surface reflects light with a sharp hot spot, creating a highlight called specular that drops off sharply (bottom right).

The Blinn Shader Type

Also named after its developer (James Blinn), this shading method brings to the surface a highly accurate specular lighting model with increased control over the specular's appearance. This creates a shader that is good for use on shiny surfaces and metallic surfaces.

A Blinn surface reflects light with a hot spot, creating a specular that diffuses somewhat more gradually than a Phong (top left).

The Phong E Shader Type

With this type, the Phong shading model is expanded to include more control over the specular highlight. This creates a Phong surface whose specular drops off more gradually and yet remains sharper than a Blinn. Phong E also has greater color control over the specular than does Phong and Blinn, giving you some more options for metallic reflections.

A Phong E surface reflects light much like a regular Phong, but has more detailed control over the specular settings, to adjust the glossiness of the surface (center left).

The Anisotropic Shader Type

The Anistropic shader is good to use on surfaces that are deformed, such as on a foil wrapper or warped plastic. *Anisotropic* is defined as having properties that differ according to direction. This creates a specular highlight that is uneven across the surface, changing according to the direction you specify on the surface. By contrast, with Blinn and Phong types, the specular highlight is evenly distributed to make a circular highlight on the surface.

An Anisotropic surface reflects light unevenly and creates an irregular shaped specular highlight that are good for representing surfaces with directional grooves like CDs (bottom left).

The Layered Shader Type

A Layered shader allows the stacking of shaders to create more complex shading effects. It is useful for creating objects composed of multiple materials. By using the layered shader to texture parts of the object different materials, you can avoid using excess geometry.

You control Layered shaders by using transparency maps to define which areas show which layers of the shader. You drag material nodes into the top area of the Attribute Editor and stack them from left to right, the left being the topmost layer assigned to the surface.

Layered shaders are valuable resources to control simple compound to even complex shaders. They're perfect for putting labels or stickers on objects or adding dirt to surfaces that need to look aged. You will use a Layered shader in the exercise in this chapter (top right).

The Ramp Shader Type

A *ramp texture* is a gradient that can be attached to almost any attribute of a shader as a texture node. Ramps can create smooth transitions between colors and can even be used to control particles. (See Chapter 12, "Maya Dynamics," for information about how a ramp is used to control particles.) When used as a texture, a ramp can be connected to any attribute of a shader to create graduating color scales, transparency effects, increasing glow effects, and so on. You will use Ramp textures later in this chapter.

The *Ramp shader* is a self-contained shader node, on the other hand, that automatically has several shader nodes attached to its attributes. In addition, all these ramps are attached from within the shader itself; so there is no need to connect external ramp texture nodes. This makes for a simplified editing environment for the shader because all the colors and handles are accessible through the Ramp shader's own Attribute Editor, as shown in Figure 7.1.

To create a new color in any one of the horizontal ramps, click in the swatch to create a new ramp position. Edit its color through its Selected Color swatch. You can move the position by grabbing the area right above the ramp and dragging left or right. To delete a color, click the box beneath it.

Ramp textures are automatically attached to the **Color, Transparency, Incandescence, Specular Color, Reflectivity,** and **Environment** attributes of a Ramp shader. In addition, a special curve ramp is attached to the **Specular Roll Off** to allow for more precise control over how the specular highlight diminishes over the surface.

Before the Ramp shader (added in Maya 4.5), you had to create ramp texture nodes for every attribute to which you wanted to connect. You may still want to follow that rule. However, you might find it easier to deal with the larger, vertical ramp layout of the ramp texture when adjusting colors and positions instead of editing them in the smaller horizontal layouts in the Ramp shader's Attribute Editor.

Figure 7.1

A ramp shader in its Attribute Editor

Shader Attributes

Shaders are composed of nodes just like other Maya objects. Within these nodes, attributes define what shaders do. Here is a brief rundown of the common shader attributes you'll be working with.

Color An RGB or HSV value that defines what color the shader is when it receives a neutral color light. For more on RGB and HSV, see Chapter 2, "The Maya Interface."

Transparency The higher the transparency value, the less opaque and more "see-through" the object becomes.

Although usually expressed in a black to white gradient, with black being opaque or solid and white being totally clear, transparency can have color. In a color transparency, the shader's color shifts as only certain of its RGB values are now transparent as opposed to the whole.

Ambient Color This color affects the **Color** attribute of the shader as more ambient light is created in the scene. Ambient color tends to flatten an object, as **Ambient Color** tends to evenly color the object. This attribute is primarily used to create flat areas and should be used with care. The default is black, to keep the darker areas of a surface dark. The lighter the ambient color, the lighter those areas.

Ambient Color = Black   Ambient Color = Medium Gray   Ambient Color = White

Incandescence This is the ability to self-illuminate. Objects that seem to give off their own light, such as an office's fluorescent light fixture, can be given an incandescence value. It will not, however, light objects around it, nor will it create a glow. It will also serve to flatten the object into a pure color.

Incandecence = 0   Incandecence = 0.5   Incandecence = 1

Bump Mapping This attribute creates a textured feel to the surface by adding highlights and shadows to the render. It will not actually alter the surface of the geometry, though it will make the surface seem to have ridges, marks, scratches, and so forth. The **Bump Map** has to be a texture node such as a ramp, a fractal noise, or an image file. The more intense the variation in tones of that map, the greater the bump. **Bump Maps** are frequently used to make surfaces look more real, as nothing in reality has a perfectly smooth surface.

No Bump Map   Fractal Texture Bump Map   Grid Texture Bump Map

Diffuse This value governs how much light is reflected from the surface in all directions. When light strikes a surface, light disperses across the surface and helps to illuminate it. The higher this value, the brighter an object when lit. The lower the diffuse value, the more directly light will be reflected from the surface. Metals have very low diffuse values.

Diffuse = 0.8 (default)   Diffuse = 0.3   Diffuse = 1

Translucence and Translucence Focus The **Translucence** and **Translucence Focus** attributes give the material the ability to transmit light through its surface, like a piece of canvas in front of a light. At a value of 1 for **Translucence**, all light shines through the object; at 0, none does. The **Translucence Focus** attribute specifies how much of that light is scattered. A light material such as paper would have a high translucence focus, and thicker surfaces should have low focus rates.

Glow Intensity In the Special Effects section, the **Glow Intensity** attribute adds a glow to the object, as if it were emitting light into a foggy area.

Glow = 0   Glow = 0.5   Glow = 1

Matte Opacity Mode and slider Objects rendered through Maya generate a solid matte. Where there is an object, the matte is white; where there is nothing, the matte is black. This helps compositing programs separate rendered CG from their background to composite into a scene. Turning the slider down decreases the brightness of the object's matte, making it appear more transparent. This is usually used for compositing tricks or to make an object render in RGB but not appear in any composites. For more information about mattes, see "Image Mattes" in this chapter as well as Chapter 11, "Maya Rendering."

Raytrace Options This subset of attributes allow you to set the raytracing abilities of the shader. With raytracing you can achieve true reflections and refractions in your scene. See Chapter 11, "Maya Rendering," for more on raytracing.

Some attributes are available with only certain shader types. Here are the attributes you'll see for the Phong, Phong E, and Blinn shaders.

Specular Color The color of the highlights on a shiny surface. Black produces no specular, and white creates a bright one.

IMAGE MATTES

As you learned in Chapter 1 (and will explore further in Chapter 11), image files are stored in channels. Every image has a red, a green, and a blue channel that store the amount of each color in each pixel of the image. Some image formats, including TIFF and TARGA, also have what's called an Alpha channel, also known as a matte channel or image matte. This is a grayscale channel that controls the opacity of an image. Completely white parts of the matte make those parts of the image opaque (solid), while black parts make those parts of the image fully transparent. Gray in the matte channel makes those parts of the image partly transparent. These mattes are used in compositing—bringing together elements created separately into a single composite scene—so that parts of a render, like the black background of a rendered sphere, are clear and only the sphere is visible in the final composited image. See Chapter 11's "Image Channels" section and see Figure 11.3 for an example of how an alpha channel works.

Reflectivity The amount of reflection that is visible in the surface. The higher the value, the more reflective the object will render. Increasing this value increases the visibility of the **Reflected Color** attribute or true reflections in the scene when raytraced.

Reflected Color Gives the surface a reflection. Texture maps are generally assigned to this attribute to give the object a reflective surface without having to generate time-consuming true reflections in a raytrace render. Adding a texture or an image map to a **Reflected Color** attribute is not the same as getting true reflections of other objects in the scene but does not require raytracing.

Cosine Power Only available with a Phong shader. This attribute governs the size of the shiny highlights on the surface. The higher the number, the smaller the highlight will look.

Roughness, Highlight Size, and Whiteness Control the specular highlight on a Phong E surface only. They control specular focus, amount of specular, and highlight color, respectively.

Texturing the Axe

In this section, you will add some shaders to your NURBS axe to make it look real, and in the next chapter, you'll import it into an animation exercise. This is actually a fairly common practice, starting animation on a project and then replacing it with a finished and textured model.

Load `axe_texture_A.mb` from the axe_model project on the CD, or load the NURBS axe you modeled in Chapter 4, "Introduction to Maya Modeling and NURBS."

You'll start by texturing the metal parts of the axe. Metal is one of the toughest materials to create and light since the look of real metals is greatly affected by their surroundings, that is, by the reflections of the environment.

Alias' website lists several premade shaders for your use. Maya also includes a shader library on its installation CD. Even though you can find a good metal to use for your axe head in one of these libraries, you will make it from scratch.

The Metal Axe Head

First, you'll set up your render parameters so that you can render out your axe as you tweak the metal shader to get it right.

1. Choose **Window → Rendering Editors → Render Globals**, or click ( ) in the menu bar to open the Render Globals window.

2. In the Resolution section, set Preset to 640 × 480. In the Anti-Aliasing Quality section, use the Intermediate Quality Preset. This will give you a good idea of the look of the final render with a short render time.

3. You can create the Metal shader in two ways:

    • Open the Hypershade window, and click Phong in the Create Materials section. A new Phong shader will show up in both the top and the bottom parts of the Hypershade window.

    • Open the Multilister, and choose **Edit → Create** to open the Create Render Node window. Click Phong to create a Phong shader type. A new Phong shader will appear in the Multilister.

4. Double-click the phong1 shader node in either the Hypershade or the Multilister window to open the Attribute Editor.

5. Click the gray swatch next to the **Color** attribute to open the Color Chooser. Select a light blue gray for the color. In the Slider section, the HSV values should be something like H:207, S: 0.085, and V: 0.80. Click Accept.

6. Back in the Attribute Editor for the shader, click the gray swatch for the **Specular Color**. By changing this color, you can control the hue and brightness of the highlights on this surface. You'll use a bright faded blue with HSV values of: H: 208, S: 0.20, and V: 0.90.

7. Increase the spread of the specular highlights by changing the **Cosine Power** from the default of 20 to 2.0. This will create a large area for the bright highlights, implying a polished reflective surface.

8. To assign the shader to the surfaces, select both sides of the axe head. In the Hypershade, RM click the shader node (in either the upper or lower window), and choose

Figure 7.2

The Metal shader's material node as shown in the Hypershade and the Multilister

Assign Material to Selection from the context menu; or in the Multilister, choose **Edit → Assign**. Figure 7.2 shows show the shader in both windows.

Figure 7.3

You can add a texture to a shader's attribute by clicking the checkered Map button.

9. Make sure your perspective view is active, and click the Render the Current Frame (🎬) button in the menu bar. Check out different angles of the axe, and render them to see how the metal axe head responds to the default lights Maya inserts into the scene for your render.

This creates a simple Metal shader that will work well overall. To create a more polished look for the axe head, you can add a reflection to it using an environment texture node. This node creates a 3D texture node in the scene that will project its contents onto the material attribute to which it has been connected. As an object animates through the scene, different parts of the texture will be reflected on its surface.

10. In the Metal shader's Attribute Editor, click the Map button next to the **Reflected Color** attribute, as in Figure 7.3. This attaches a new node to create a reflection, and the Create Render Node window opens. Click the Environment Textures section and select Env Chrome. An environment texture will provide a more interesting reflection than a solid color.

11. Move the **Reflectivity** slider from 0.50 to 0.85. The higher this number, the more prominent the **Reflected Color** will reflect in the surface. Figure 7.4 shows the axe before and after a reflection. The Env Chrome reflection texture makes the axe look more polished by reflecting a grid representing the ground and a bright blue sky.

MULTILISTER VERSUS HYPERSHADE DISPLAYS

The Multilister and Hypergraph can accomplish the same shading tasks, although their methodologies are very different, and that is apparent in their layouts. The Multilister lists shading nodes in tabbed pages, while the Hypergraph gives you more options to lay out shaders and work with their connections and input/output nodes. You'll notice in the layout differences that the Multilister's round shader icons shown in the General tab are shader's shading group node. The Hypershade's round shader icons show the material node of the shader.

The shading group is the node that is required to assign a shader to a surface, while the material node is the node that carries all the pertinent shader information like Color, Transparency, Specular, and so forth. The Hypershade by default shows only the material nodes since little editing is actually done to shading group nodes (to display a shading group node, you need to select the material node and display its output connections). To see the material node of a shader in the Multilister however, you must either click the Materials tab, or in the General tab click the small arrow in the lower right of the Shading Group icon to expand the material node.

Figure 7.4

The axe head before and after a reflection is added

After you create the Env Chrome texture, you'll see a green object in the modeling windows at the origin, as in Figure 7.5. This is the Env Chrome's placement node. You can manipulate this node just as you manipulate other Maya objects; you can move it, rotate it, and scale it.

Altering this object will change how the environment chrome will project itself in the scene. For example, if you increase the size of this placement node, you'll notice that the grid showing in the reflection in the axe will get larger. You'll find more on projections and placement nodes in the "Texture Nodes" section later in this chapter.

Figure 7.5

Use placement nodes in the scene to scale and position textures.

The Wooden Handle

A nice, glossy, cherry wood would look good for the handle, so a Phong shader would be best.

1. In the Hypershade, choose **Create → Materials → Phong**. Set Diffuse to 0.70, **Specular Color** to a light gray, and **Cosine Power** to 50.

2. Click the Map button for the color. In the Create Render Node window, in the 3D Textures section, select Wood. Figure 7.6 shows this texture in the Attribute Editor.

3. In the Wood's Attribute Editor, adjust **Filler Color** to a nice red brown with an HSV of (8.5,0.85,0.43). Change **Vein Color** to a darker version of the filler with an HSV of (8.5,0.75,0.08).

4. Change **Vein Spread** to 0.70, change **Layer Size** to 0.119, and darken **Grain Color** a bit by pulling the slider to the left, but not all the way. This will give you a nice dark cherry wood.

The Wood texture is a projected 3D texture; it's projected from a source onto the object using a 3D placement node, just like the Env Chrome you applied to the reflection of the axe head. To assign the Wood texture from the Hypershade, select the handle and RM click the shader to select Assign Material to Selection, or you can simply MM drag the icon to the handle in the viewport. For more on projected textures, see the "Texture Nodes" section later in this chapter.

> You can assign a shader to any object by MM dragging its icon from the Multilister or Hypershade to the object in the viewport.

5. To see this dark texture on your object, create a new light in the scene. In the main menu, choose **Create → Lights → Ambient Light**. (For more on lights, see Chapter 10). Open the Attribute Editor for the light by pressing Ctrl+A or by double-clicking its icon on the Lights tab in the Multilister or Hypershade. Increase Intensity to 2.5.

6. Render a frame of the axe handle up close, as shown in Figure 7.7. Notice how the wood repeats on the handle and makes for an undesirable texture. Adjust the wood's texture placement.

7. To get to the Wood texture's placement node, open the Hypershade. Drag the Wood shader to the Hypershade work area (bottom half). RM click the wood and choose Graph Network from the context menu. You could also select it and click the Input Connections button (⊡) at the top of the Hypershade. Figure 7.8 shows the shader nodes for the wood shader network in the Hypershade work area. The place3dTexture2 node connects to the wood2 node and gives it position information. The wood2 node then connects to the phong3 material node as a color texture map.

Figure 7.6

The Wood texture in its Attribute Editor

8. Double-click on the place3dTexture node to open its Attribute Editor.

9. Click the Fit to Group Box button to automatically position the placement node for the wood around the handle. In your viewport, you'll see the green placement node around the handle, as in Figure 7.9.

10. Rendering a frame would reveal that the wood still does not look quite right. Select the placement node in the viewport, and rotate it in Z to 90. Click the Fit to Group Box button again to rescale it to fit the handle. This will not rotate it back to the way it was; it will only scale it to fit the extents of the object to which it's assigned.

11. Render another frame, and you'll see the wood veins are running the length of the handle. It looks more like wood now, but it still repeats too much.

Now instead of moving and scaling the texture placement node and rendering multiple times to get the wood placement just right, you can use Maya's Interactive Photorealistic Renderer (IPR) to see your changes in real time. Click the IPR Render the Current Frame button (![IPR]) in the Status line, or choose **Render → IPR Render Current Frame**.

The Render View window will show a lower quality render of the axe. It will prompt you to select a region to begin tuning. Drag a marquee selection in the Render View window around the handle. IPR will refresh that part of the window. Every change you make to the texture placement node will prompt IPR to update that section of the render, giving a fast update on the positioning and scale of the wood texture.

12. Select the texture placement node and scale it up in the three axes until you get a good-looking grain. Figure 7.10 shows a well-spaced wood grain.

Figure 7.7
_____

The Wood texture repeats too much by default.

Figure 7.8
_____

The wood shader network

The scene file `axe_texture_B.mb` in the axe_model project on the CD will bring you up to this point.

The Metal Spike

Currently, the entire length of the handle is shaded as wood, including the top spike. The spike on the axe head should be metal like the axe head.

You can approach this in two ways: with geometry and with shaders. If you manipulate geometry, you can select a horizontal isoparm and detach the spike portion of the handle to make it a separate surface. You would then assign a Metal shader to the new tip surface.

Figure 7.9

The wood's placement mode

Using a shader instead of cutting up or creating more geometry can be more desirable in many instances. For example, you won't be able to detach surfaces like this all the time

The Layered shader is a normal surface shader that allows you to stack materials on top of each other to assign to a surface. You control which layer of material is exposed and by how much by assigning transparency values or textures to each layer. You'll use a Ramp texture to specify where on the handle the wood stops and the metal starts.

To create a Layered shader to make the handle wood with a metal tip, follow these steps:

1. Select the axe handle, and choose **Lighting/ Shading → Assign New Material → Layered Shader** to open the Attribute Editor, as in Figure 7.11. By default, the Layered shader will contain a green layer in the top of the Attribute Editor window. The layers display from left to right the order of layers from top to bottom that are assigned to the surface. So the leftmost shader in the Layered shader will be on top of all the others.

Figure 7.10

The wood handle after the texture has been scaled and placed

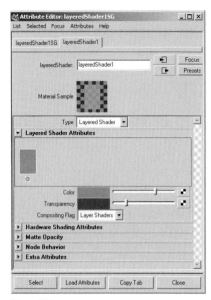

Figure 7.11

The Layered shader in the Attribute Editor

Figure 7.12

The Layered shader with the wood on top of the metal

> Choosing **Lighting/Shading → Assign New Material** is an easy way to create and assign a material without having to open the Hypershade or Multilister.

2. Using the Hypershade, MM drag the metal material you've made into the top region of the Layered shader's Attribute Editor window. To delete the default green material, click the X'ed square beneath it. The Material Sample icon in the Attribute Editor turns into the metal.

3. MM drag the wood material into the Layered shader's Attribute Editor. Make sure it is placed to the left of the metal material. If the materials are already in place, you can rearrange their order by MM dragging them left or right of the other materials in the Attribute Editor. Notice in Figure 7.12 that the Material Sample icon changed to the wood material. The wood is now the top layer, so only it will show until you give it some transparency to reveal some metal at the tip.

> You can see the names of the materials in the Layered shader by pointing to the icons.

4. Click the wood shader icon in the Layered shader's Attribute Editor to highlight it. Notice that the **Transparency Map** button (as well as Color) is now a square with an arrow ( ) as opposed to the checkerboard you've seen before. Click this button to open the Attribute Editor for the wood material.

When an attribute is already mapped, its Map button turns from a checkerboard to an input connection icon. Clicking it opens the Attribute Editor for whatever node is attached to that attribute. In this case, clicking the Map button opens its Attribute Editor since the wood material was assigned to this layer. Here you need to attach a transparency ramp to control where the metal tip starts and the wood handle ends.

5. Click the Map button for the wood's **Transparency** attribute. Create a ramp texture node. Make sure the Normal radio button is checked and not the As Projection or As Stencil radio button.

6. In the ramp's Attribute Editor, change **Interpolation** to None, and change **Type** to U Ramp.

7. Delete the middle (green) color by clicking the square to the right of green's position. Select the bottom (red) color by clicking its round handle on the left of the ramp. Change the **Selected Color** attribute to white. Drag it all the way to the bottom of the ramp.

Figure 7.13

The ramp texture set on the metal's Transparency attribute controls where the wood and metal meet.

8. Select the top color (blue) and change it to black. Drag the handle down the ramp to a **Selected Position** of 0.185. Figure 7.13 shows the ramp position and the axe. If you're in texture display mode in the perspective view (press the 6 key), you'll see that the tip of the model is a blue-gray color (the metal) and the bottom of the handle is a reddish brown (the wood). As you adjust the position of the white color on the ramp, notice how the spike and handle change.

9. In the Hypershade, choose **Edit → Delete Unused Nodes** to purge all unused shading nodes from your scene. Make sure your Layered shader and Metal shader are assigned, of course.

10. Render out a frame of the axe. Save this frame in the render buffer by clicking Keep Image ( ) in the Render View. This will keep the image so that you can scroll back to it for reference. A scroll bar will appear at the bottom of the Render View.

11. Select the axe's top node and rotate it about 45° in Z to angle it. Render a frame at this point. Notice how the grain of the wood has changed. Use the scroll bar to toggle back and forth and compare these two images, as in Figure 7.14.

When a projected texture such as the wood does not "stick" to an object, and the object seems to move through the texture, the object is said to be swimming through the projection. Since the wood is being projected by the 3D placement node you scaled and positioned to get the grain just right, you'll need to group the texture node under the axe's top node. When the axe moves, the texture will stick with it, maintaining its orientation with the axe.

12. Rotate the axe back to 0 in Z. Select the place3dTexture2 node from either the viewport (it's the green texture you scaled to fit the handle) or the Outliner. Be careful not to use the Env Cube's 3D placement node you used for the axe head reflection. In the Outliner, MM drag it under the axe's topmost node.

The file `axe_texture_C.mb` in the axe_model project on the CD has the final textured axe for your reference.

Now you have a fully textured axe. By using a Layered shader, you did not need to build another piece of geometry to represent a metal tip. You can embellish a model a lot at the texturing level. Although you may first consider using geometry, you can be accomplished a number of tasks by using simple texturing tricks such as the axe handle and its metal spike. The more you explore and experience shaders and modeling, the better you'll be at how to juggle modeling with texturing to get the best, easiest, and most effective solution.

Try loading the catapult model from Chapter 5, "Modeling with Polygons," and texturing it from top to bottom. A great deal of independent geometry needs textures, some to be carefully placed with 3D placement nodes. Experiment with as many different ways of shading the catapult as you can.

Figure 7.14

The wood grain changes as the axe moves.

Textures and Surfaces

Texture nodes generate maps to connect to an attribute of a shader. There are two types of textures: procedural and bitmapped (or simply maps). Procedural textures use Maya's own nodes' attributes to generate an effect, such as ramp, checkerboard, or fractal noise textures. You can adjust each of these procedural textures by changing their attribute values.

BAKING A TEXTURE PROJECTION

In the axe handle texturing exercise, you grouped the 3dplacement node for the wood grain to the handle of the axe, to make the texture stick to the handle. But you can also "bake" the texture onto the axe handle by converting the texture projection to a file node. By baking the texture node, you are converting the 3dplacement node into an image file that is then mapped to the color channel of the material, discarding the projection node altogether so you needn't group it with the handle as you did above.

Take these steps to bake that wood grain texture to the axe:

1. Open the Hypershade.

2. Click to select the axe handle's layered shader node and MMB drag it to the work area of the Hypershade.

3. RM click on it and select **Graph Network** to see all the nodes of the layered shader (bottom left).

4. Select the axe handle geometry and then shift + select the *wood2* node in the Hypershade.

5. Choose **Edit → Convert to File Texture (Maya Software)** ❑. In the option box, select an **X Resolution** and a **Y Resolution** of 512 each and click Convert and Close. If you get an error when you convert, you can choose **Edit → Delete Unused Nodes** and try again. The shader will rebuild itself to create a texture file, material, and a shading group node that is automatically assigned to the selected geometry. Delete all unused nodes again to clean up the Hypershade window and your new shader network should look as pictured here (bottom right).

Notice that the 3dplacement node is removed from the scene as well as the Hypershade view. Your axe handle's texture will now stick to the handle as a mapped file texture.

A map, on the other hand, is a saved image file that is imported into the scene through a file texture node. These files are pregenerated through whatever imaging programs you have and include digital pictures and scanned photos.

You need to place all texture nodes onto their surfaces through the shader. You can map them directly onto the surfaces' UV values, or project them.

UV Mapping

Just as 3D space is based on coordinates in XYZ, surfaces have coordinates denoted by U and V values along a 2D coordinate system, width and height. The UV value helps a texture position itself on the surface. The U and V values range from 0 to 1, with (0,0) UV being the origin point of the surface.

Maya creates UVs for primitive surfaces automatically, but frequently you may need to edit UVs for proper texture placement, particularly on polygonal meshes. In some instances, placing textures on a poly mesh will require projecting the textures onto the mesh, since the poly UVs may not line up as expected once the mesh has been edited. See the following section on Using Projections.

If you find that the placement of your texture or image is not quite right, simply use the 2D placement node of the texture node to position it properly. See the "Texture Nodes" section later in this chapter for more information.

Simply put, UV mapping places the texture directly on the surface and uses the surface coordinates for its positioning.

Using Projections

You need to place textures on the surface. You can often do so using UV placement, but some textures need to be projected on to the surface. It is common to project textures when texturing polys for example.

A projection is what it sounds like. The file image, ramp, or other texture being used can be "beamed" onto the object in several ways. This allows you to position textures in a new way.

You can create any texture node as either a normal UV map or a projected texture. In the Create Render Node window, select the method—Normal (for UV mapping) or As Projection—by clicking the appropriate radio button before you create the texture.

When you create a projected texture, a new node is attached to the texture node. This projection node controls the method of projection with an attached 3D placement node, which you saw in the axe exercise. Select the projection node to set the type of projection in the Attribute Editor (see Figure 7.15).

Setting the projection type will allow you to project an image or texture without having it warp and distort, depending on the model you are mapping. For example, a planar projection on a sphere will warp the edges of the image as they stretch into infinity on the sides of the sphere.

Try This In a new scene, create a NURBS sphere and a NURBS cone and place them side by side. Create a Blinn shader and assign it to both the objects. In the Blinn shader's Attribute Editor, set its **Color** attribute to a checkerboard pattern. Make sure Normal is checked to create a UV-mapped checker texture (see image on the bottom left).

Now try removing the color map from the Blinn shader. In the Blinn shader's Attribute Editor, right-click and hold the attribute's title word "**Color**," and then choose Break Connection from the context menu. This will sever the connection to the checker and reset the color to gray. Now re-create a new checker map for the color, but this time create it as a projection. In the illustration on the right, you see the perspective view in texture mode (press the 6 key) with the two objects and the planar projection placement node. Try moving the planar placement object around in the scene to see how the texture maps itself to the objects. On the left are the rendered objects (see images on the bottom center and right).

Try the other projection types to see how they affect the texture being mapped. It takes experimentation to figure out what is the best projection method for a model.

Projection placement nodes control how the projection maps its image or texture onto the surface. Using a NURBS sphere with a spherical projected checker, with U and V wrap turned off on the checker texture, you can see how manipulating the place3dTexture node will affect the texture.

In addition to the Move, Rotate, and Scale tools, you can use the Special Manipulator tool (press T to activate or click the Show Manipulator Tool icon in the toolbar) to adjust the placement. Figure 7.16 shows this tool for a spherical projection.

Figure 7.15

The projection node in the Attribute Editor

Figure 7.16

The spherical Projection's Manipulator tool

Figure 7.17

The manipulator wrap-
ping the checker tex-
ture around the sphere:
left, perspective view;
right, rendered view

Drag the handles on the special manipulator to change the coverage of the projection, orientation, size, and so forth. All projection types have special manipulators. Figure 7.17 shows
the special manipulator wrapping the checker in a thin band all the way around the sphere.

To summarize, projection textures depend on a projector node to position the texture
onto the geometry.

Texture Nodes

You can create a number of texture nodes in Maya. This section covers the most important.
All texture nodes, however, have common attributes that affect their final look. Open the
Attribute Editor for any texture node. The two top sections affect the
color balance of the texture. The Color Balance and the Effects section are
described here.

Color Balance This set of attributes adjusts the overall brightness and
color balance of your texture. Use these attributes to tint or brighten a
texture without having to change all the individual attributes of the shader
itself.

Effects You can invert the texture's color space by clicking the Invert
check box. This changes black to white and white to black in addition to
inverting the RGB values of colors.

You can map textures to almost any shader attribute to give surface
detail. Even the tiniest amount of texture on a surface's bump, specular,
and color will greatly increase its reality.

Place2dTexture Nodes

2D texture nodes come with a 2D placement node that controls their repetition, rotation, size, offset, and so on. Adjust the setting in this node of your 2D texture in the Attribute Editor, as shown in Figure 7.18, to position it within the shader network. You used a similar approach when dealing with the wood's 3D placement node in the axe exercise earlier this chapter.

The **Repeat UV** setting controls how many times the texture is repeated on whatever shader attribute it is connected to, such as color. The higher the wrap values, the smaller the texture will appear, but the more times it will appear on the surface.

The **Wrap U** and **Wrap V** check boxes allow the texture to wrap around the edges of their limits to repeat. When these are turned off, the texture will only appear once, and the rest of the surface will be the color of the **Default Color** attribute found in the texture node itself.

The **Mirror U** and **Mirror V** settings allow the texture to mirror itself when it repeats. The **Coverage**, **Translate Frame**, and **Rotate Frame** settings control where the image is mapped. These are particularly useful for positioning a digital image or a scanned picture.

Figure 7.18

A 2D placement node in the Attribute Editor

Ramp Texture

A ramp is a gradient in which one color transitions into the next color. You've already seen how useful it can be in positioning materials in a Layered shader. It's also perfect for making color gradients, as shown in Figure 7.19.

Use the round handles to select the color and to move it up and down the ramp. The square handle to the right deletes the color. To create a new color, click inside the ramp itself.

> The ramp texture is different from the Ramp shader. The Ramp shader automatically has several ramp textures mapped to some of its attributes.

The **Type** setting allows you to create a gradient running along the U or V direction of the surface as well as make circular, radial, diagonal, and other types of gradients. The **Interpolation** setting controls how the colors grade from one to the next.

The **U Wave** and **V Wave** attributes let you add a squiggle to the U or V coordinate of the ramp, and the **Noise** and **Noise Frequency** attributes specify a randomness to the placement of the ramp colors throughout the surface.

Using the **HSV Color Noise** attributes, you can specify random noise patterns of Hue, Saturation, and Value to add some interest to your texture. The HSV Noise options are great for making your shader just a bit different, since adding some variation to an otherwise solid color object will enhance its look. It's common practice to use a ramp texture with only a single color in the ramp. That color has a little bit of HSV noise added to it to make the surface seem less perfect than if you assigned a solid color to it.

Figure 7.19

The Ramp shader

Fractal, Noise, and Mountain Texture

These textures are used to create a random noise pattern to add to an object's **Color**, **Transparency**, or any other shader attribute. For example, when creating a surface, you'll almost always want to add a little dirt or surface blemishes to the shader to make the object look less CG. These textures are commonly used for creating bump maps.

Bulge, Cloth, Checker, Grid, and Water Textures

These textures help create surface features when used on a shader's **Bump Map** attribute. Each creates an interesting pattern to add to a surface to create tactile detail, but you can also use them to create color or specular irregularities.

When used as a texture for a bump, grid is useful for creating the spacing between tiles, cloth is perfect for clothing, and checker is good for rubber grips. Placing a water texture on a slight reflection makes for a nice pool-side reflection in patio furniture.

The File Node

You use the file node to import image files into Maya for texturing. For instance, if you want to texture a CG face with a digital picture of your own face, you can use the file node to import a Maya-supported image file.

Importing an Image File as a Texture

To attach an image to the color attribute of a Lambert shader (for example), follow these steps:

1. Create the Lambert shader. (Phong, Blinn, or any of the shaders will do.)

2. Click the Map button to map a texture on the **Color** attribute of the new Lambert shader. Select the file node as a normal texture. (You can also use a projected texture with an image file.) The Attribute Editor will show the attribute for the file node.

3. Next to the **Image Name** attribute, click the folder icon to open the file browser. Find the image file of choice on your computer. (It's best to put such images to use as textures in the source images folder of the project. As a matter of fact, the file browser will default directly to the source images folder of your current project.) Double-click the file to load it.

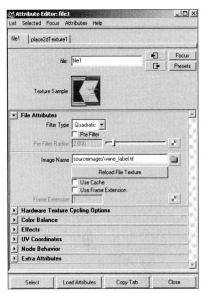

4. After you import the image file, it will connect to the **Color** attribute of that shader. You can position it as you please by using its Place2dTexture node or by manipulating the projection node if you created the file texture node as a projection.

You can attach an image file to any attribute of a shader that is map-able, meaning it can accept a texture node. Frequently, image files are used for the color of a shader as well as for bump and transparency maps. You can replace the image file by double-clicking the file texture node in the Hypershade and choosing another image file with the file browser. Maya will disconnect the current image file and connect the newly selected file in its stead.

3D and Environment Textures

As you've seen earlier with the axe, 3D textures are projected within a 3D space. These textures are great for objects that need to reflect an environment, for example.

Instead of simply applying the texture to the plane of the surface as 2D textures do, 3D textures create an area in which the shader is affected. If an object moves through a scene with a 3D placement node, its shader looks as if it swims, unless that placement node is parented or constrained to that object, as you saw with the wood handle of the axe. (For more on constraints, see Chapter 9, "Further Animation Topics.)

Disconnecting a Texture

You will find that sometimes the texture you've applied to an object is not what you want and you need to remove it from the shader. To do so, double-click the shader in the Hypershade to open its Attribute Editor.

You can then disconnect an image file or any other texture node from the shader's attribute by RM clicking on the attribute's name in the Attribute Editor and choosing Break Connection from the marking menu.

Summary

Texturing a scene is never an isolated process. As you've seen, making textures work can involve render settings, lighting, and even geometry manipulation and creation. Your work so far in this chapter will be expanded on in Chapters 10 and 11 with discussions on lighting and rendering.

Just like everything else in Maya, it's all collaboration, and the more experience you gain, the more you'll see how everything intertwines.

But for Maya to be an effective tool for you, it's important to have a clear understanding of the look you want for your CG. This involves plenty of clear research into your project, downloading heaps of images to use as reference, and a good measure of trial and error.

The single best weapon in your arsenal in texturing and indeed in all aspects of CG art is your eye, your observations of the world around you and how it relates to the one you're creating in CG.

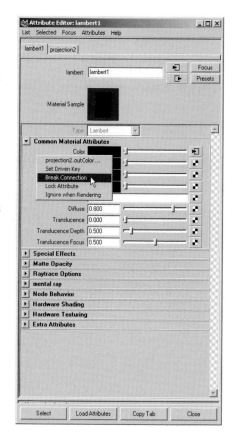

CHAPTER 8

Introduction to Animation

The best way to start learning about animation is to start animating, so you'll begin this chapter with the classic exercise of bouncing a ball. You'll then take a closer look at the animation tools Maya software provides and how they work for your scene. You'll do that by throwing the axe you created earlier, and finally you'll tackle animating a more complex system of parts when you bring your catapult to life.

Topics include:

- **Keyframe Animation—Bouncing a Ball**
- **Throwing an Axe**
- **Object Replacement**
- **Animating the Catapult**

Keyframe Animation—Bouncing a Ball

A classic exercise for all animators is to create a bouncing ball. Creating and animating a ball is simple, you would think, but you can imbue so much character into the ball that the possibilities are almost endless. Animating a bouncing ball is a good exercise in physics as well as cartoon movement. You'll first create a rubber ball, and then you'll add cartoonish movement to accentuate some principles of the animation techniques discussed in Chapter 1.

Creating the Cartoon Ball

First you need to create the ball, as well as the project for this exercise. Follow these steps:

1. In a new scene, begin with a NURBS sphere, create a poly plane, and scale it up to be the ground plane.

2. Press 5 for shaded mode. Select the ball, and press 3 for a smooth view of the sphere.

3. Move the sphere 1.0 unit up in the Y axis so it's resting on the ground, as shown here, and not halfway through it.

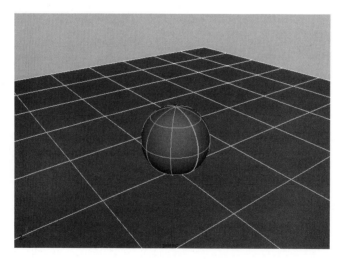

4. Choose **Modify → Freeze Transforms** to set the ball's resting height to 0 as opposed to 1. This action will set the ball's **Translate** attribute back to 0, effectively "resetting" the object. This is called *freezing the transforms*. This is useful when you position, scale, and orient an object and need to set its new location, orientation, and size as its beginning state.

5. Choose **File → Project → New** to create a new project. Call the project bouncing_ball, and place it in the same folder as the solar system project. Click the Use Defaults button to create the necessary folders in your project, and then click Accept. Now save the scene file into that project.

Animating the Ball

Your next step is to keyframe the positions of the ball. As introduced in Chapter 1, keyframing is the process—borrowed from traditional animation—of setting positions and values at particular frames of the animation. The computer can interpolate between these keyframes to fill in the other frames to complete a smooth animation.

You'll start with the "gross animation," or the overall movements. First, you'll move the ball up and down to begin its choreography. Follow these steps to set up the scene and animate the ball:

1. Press W to open the Translate tool, select the sphere, and move it up to the top of the frame, say about 10 units up in the Y axis. Place the camera so that you'll have some room to work in the frame. Next you'll set keyframes.

2. Instead of selecting the **Translate** attributes in the Channel box and pressing S as you did in Chapter 3 to set keyframes on the planets, you'll set keyframes for translation in an easier way:

   Press Shift+W to set keyframes on **Translate X**, **Translate Y**, and **Translate Z** at frame 1. To make sure your scene is set up properly, set your animation speed to 30fps by choosing **Window → Settings/Preferences → Preferences** to open the Preferences window, or by clicking the Animation Preferences button next to the Auto-Key button ⬚ . In the Settings category of the Preferences window, set **Time** to NTSC (30 fps). A frame range of 1–120 is good for now.

3. Click the Auto Keyframe button (⬚) to turn it on; when on, it will be red. Auto Keyframe automatically sets a keyframe at the current time for any attribute that has changed since its last keyframe for the selected object.

   > For the Auto Keyframe feature to work, you have to manually set the initial keyframe for any of the attributes you want to animate.

4. Now you need to set down gross animation keyframes to choreograph the overall movement. Disregarding any specific timing, go to frame 10, and move the ball down in the Y axis until it is about ¼ through the ground plane. Since you'll be creating squash and stretch (see Chapter 1 for a brief explanation) for this cartoon ball, you'll need to send the ball through the ground a little bit. The Auto Keyframe feature sets a keyframe in the Y axis at frame 10.

5. Move to frame 20, and raise the ball back up to about ¾ of its original height (about 7.5 units in the Y axis). Auto Keyframe sets a Y Translation keyframe at frame 20 and will continue to set keyframes for the ball as you animate.

6. At frame 30, place the ball back down a little bit less than ¼ of the way through the ground.

7. At frame 40, place the ball back up in the air in the Y axis at about ½ its original height (5 in Y).

8. Repeat this procedure until you have bounced the ball a few more times. Make sure you are decreasing the ball's height at the crest with each successive bounce and decreasing how much it passes through the ground with every landing. Open the Graph Editor for a peek into the ball's animation curves. (Choose **Window → Animation Editors → Graph Editor**.) You'll pick up this exercise after a look at the Graph Editor.

By holding down Shift as you pressed W in step 2, you set a keyframe for **Translate**; and you can also keyframe **Rotation** or **Scale**. Here's a summary of the keystrokes for setting keyframes:

Shift+W	Sets a keyframe for the selection's position in all three axes at the current time
Shift+E	Sets a keyframe for the selection's rotation in all three axes at the current time
Shift+R	Sets a keyframe for the selection's scale in all three axes at the current time

The Graph Editor

The Graph Editor is a critical tool for an animator. You provide most of an animation's finesse through work in this window. As a matter of fact, you can animate a number of objects solely through this window. (See Chapter 2 for an introduction to the Graph Editor.) Using its graphlike view of where in space and time each keyframe lies, you can conveniently control your animation. Move a keyframe in time to the right, for example, to slow the action. Move the keyframe to the left in time to speed up the action.

Reading the Curves in the Graph Editor

Understanding what curves do in the Graph Editor is crucial to getting your animation right. Using the Graph Editor, you can judge an object's direction, speed, acceleration, and timing.

As you will see next in this chapter with the axe-throwing tutorial, you will invariably come across problems and issues with your animation that require a careful review of their curves. Being able to see a curve and translate it into what your object is doing comes with time and practice, so be patient, and don't be afraid to open the Graph Editor and animate through it as much as you can.

First, the curves in the Graph Editor are like the NURBS curves you've modeled with so far. Instead of CVs on a NURBS curve controlling the curvature, points directly on an animation curve represent keyframes and control the curvature with their tangency handles. By grabbing one end of a key's handle and dragging it up or down, you adjust the curve.

Second, the graph is a representation of an object attribute's position (vertical) over time (horizontal). Every place on the curve represents where the object is in that axis; there needn't be a keyframe on the curve. Not only does the placement of the keys on the curve make a big difference, so does the shape of the curve itself. Here then is a quick primer on how to read a curve in the Graph Editor and, hence, how to edit it.

In Figure 8.1, the object's **Translate Z** attribute is being animated. At the beginning, the curve begins quickly to move positively (that is, to the right) in the Z axis. The object shoots off to the right and comes to an *ease-out*, where it decelerates to a stop. The stop is signified by the flat part of the curve at the first keyframe at frame 41. The object then quickly accelerates in the negative Z direction (left) and maintains a fairly even speed until it hits frame 62, where it suddenly changes direction and goes back right for about 45 frames. It then slowly decelerates to a full stop in an ease-out.

Consider a single object in motion. The shape of the curve in the Graph Editor defines how the object moves. The object shown animated in Figure 8.2 is moving in a steady manner in one direction.

Figure 8.3 shows the object slowly accelerating toward frame 30, where it suddenly comes to a stop. If there is nothing beyond the end of the curve, there is no motion. The one exception deals with the *infinity* of curves, which is discussed shortly.

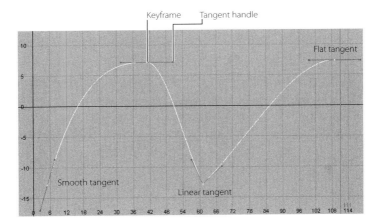

Figure 8.1

An animation curve

Figure 8.2

Linear movement

The object in Figure 8.4 begins moving immediately and comes to a slow stop by frame 27, where the curve first becomes flat.

Cartoon Ball

Now let's apply what you've learned about the Graph Editor to the bouncing ball. Follow these steps:

1. Open the Graph Editor and take a look at the ball's animation curves. They should be similar to the curves in Figure 8.5.

2. Notice how only the Y-axis translate has a curve, and yet the **Translate X**, **Translate Y**, and **Translate Y** attributes have keyframes in the left column. This is from the initial position keyframe you set at frame 1. And since you've only moved the sphere in the Y axis, Auto-Key has only set Y keys. If you don't have animation on something, it is better not to set keyframes on those attributes. Keep your scene clean.

Figure 8.3

Acceleration (ease-in)

Figure 8.4

Deceleration (ease-out)

3. Playback the animation and see how it feels. Be sure to open the Animation Preferences window (click the Animation Preferences icon (▣) to set the playback speed to real time [30fps]). You'll find this icon in the Playback section in the Timeline category.

4. Timing is the main issue now, so you're concerned with how fast the ball falls and bounces:

   • The ball is falling too fast initially, although the second and third bounces should look fine.

   • To fix the timing, move the keyframes in the Graph Editor. Select the keyframe at frame 10 and all the others beyond it. Move them all back two frames. (See Figure 8.6.)

> To move a key in the Graph Editor, press W to open the Move tool and MM move the key as you drag the cursor in the Graph Editor window. Press the Shift key and drag the cursor left and right or up and down to lock the movement to either horizontal or vertical to make it easier to control.

Figure 8.5

The ball's animation curves. Note how the height decays over time.

Figure 8.6

Move all the keyframes to the right to slow the initial fall by two frames, but to leave the timing the same for the rest.

- As the ball's bounce decays over time, it goes up less, but still takes the same amount of time (10 frames) to go up the lesser distance. For better timing, adjust the last few bounces to occur faster. Select the keys on the last three bounces and move them, one by one, a frame or two to the left to decrease the time on the last short bounces. (See Figure 8.7.)

Understanding Timing

In animation, timing is all about getting keyframes in proper order. Judging the speed of an object in animation is critical to getting it to look right, and that comes down to timing. The more you animate, the better your timing, which is why the bouncing ball is such a popular exercise.

 Load the file `ball_v02.mp` from the bouncing_ball project on the CD to get to this point.

When you playback the animation, it should look more natural. But it still looks like CG animation, as if it were rising and falling on a wave as opposed to really bouncing. You still need to edit the timing of the ball. The problem with the animation is that the ball eases in and out as it rises and falls. By default, setting a key in Maya sets the keyframes to have an ease-in and ease-out in their curves, meaning their curves will be smooth like a NURBS curve.

Because of the smooth animation curve, the ball does not look natural in its timing. You need to accelerate the ball as it falls with a sharp valley in the curve, and you need to decelerate it as it rises, with smooth peaks. Follow these steps:

1. In the Graph Editor, select all the landing keyframes (the ones in the valleys of the curve) and change their *interpolation* from smooth to linear by clicking the Linear Tangents button (∧).

2. Likewise, select all the peak keyframes at the ball's rise, and change their tangents to flat by clicking the Flat Tangents icon (—) to make the animation curve like the one shown in Figure 8.8.

Figure 8.7

Move the keys to the left to make the final short bounces quicker.

Figure 8.8

The adjusted timing of the bounce

3. When you playback the animation, you'll see that the ball seems like it's moving much more realistically. Adjust the keys a bit more to get the timing feeling right if you need to before you move on to squash and stretch.

Squash and Stretch

The idea of squash and stretch has been an animation staple for as long as there has been animation. It is a way to convey the weight of an object by deforming it to react (usually in an exaggerated way) to gravity and motion.

In Maya, you use the Scale tool to squash and stretch your object, in this case, your ball. Follow these steps:

Load the file `ball_v03.mb` from the bouncing_ball project on the CD to get to this point.

1. To initiate squash and stretch, go to frame 12, the first time the ball hits the floor. Press R to open the Scale tool, and scale the ball down in the Y axis until it no longer goes through the floor (about 0.6). Set a keyframe for all the scale axes by pressing Shift+R.

2. Move ahead in the animation about 3 frames to frame 15, and scale the ball up in the Y axis slightly past normal to stretch it up (about 1.3) right after its bounce. Three frames later at frame 18, set the Y-axis scale back to 1.

3. Scrub your animation. Notice how the ball stays squashed at the beginning of the animation; that's because you didn't set a key before it hit the ground. Back up to frame 9, and reset the Y-axis scale to 1 in the Channel box. Scrub your animation again, and you'll notice that the ball begins stretching even before it hits the ground. That's a bit too much exaggeration, so open the Graph Editor and move the Y-axis scale key from 9 to 11. Now the ball will squash when it hits the floor and stretch up as it bounces up.

4. Repeat this procedure for the remaining bounces, squashing the ball as it hits the floor and stretching it as it bounces up. Remember to decay the scale factor as the ball's bouncing decays to a stop. The final bounce or two should have very little squash and stretch, if any.

Load the file `ball_v04.mb` from the bouncing_ball project on the CD to see an example. Although the bouncing of this ball looks okay, it could definitely use some finesse, a little timing change, and so on. Open the file, open the Graph Editor, and edit the file to get a feel for how the ball bounces.

Throwing an Axe

This next project will exercise your use of hierarchies and introduce you to creating and refining motion to achieve proper animation for a more complex scene than the bouncing ball. The workflow is simple, but standard for properly setting up a scene for animation. First, you'll model an axe and a target, and then you'll set up the grouping and pivots for how you want to animate. Then you throw!

Why not use the NURBS axe you've already created and textured? Because you'll use that for a later exercise in this chapter in importing and replacing an object in Maya, while keeping the animation intact.

The Preproduction Process

To begin the animation right away, you'll create a basic axe, focusing on the animation and the technique. To this end, connect to the Internet if you can, and look up axes and the art of axe throwing to get more familiar with the task at hand. You will also need to create a simple bull's-eye target at which to throw your axe, so look for some references for a target as well.

Create a new project; choose **File → Project → New**. Place this project in the same folder as your other projects, and call it axe_anim so as not to confuse it with your earlier axe_model project. Click the Defaults button to fill in the rest. Click the Animation Preferences button, and set the frames per second to 30 fps. Later, you'll replace this simple axe with the NURBS axe you modeled in Chapter 4 and textured in Chapter 7 to learn how to properly replace objects and transfer animation in Maya.

Setting up the Scene

To get started, model the axe and target from primitives and set up their grouping and pivots. Once your scene is set up properly, you will animate. It's important to a healthy workflow to make sure the scene is set up well before you begin animating.

Making the Axe

The axe will be made of two primitives, a cylinder and a cube. You will model it with polygons. Follow these steps:

1. Choose **Create → Polygon Primitives → Cube ❑**. Set Subdivisions Along Width to 4, and click Create.

2. Call this axe_head.

3. Choose **Create → Polygon Primitives → Cylinder** to create a cylinder to be the handle for your axe, and call it handle.

4. Scale the cylinder so that it's about ½ unit across and about 14 units tall.

5. Move the cube to the top of the cylinder, leaving just a little of the tip showing, and scale it so that it's about 3 units high and 4 units wide in the front view. (See Figure 8.9.)

6. Scale the cube in the Z axis so that it's just a little thicker than the handle.

7. To put a sharp edge on the axe, go into component mode (press F8) and select the four vertices on the very end of the cube.

   - Press R to activate the Scale tool

   - Scale the vertices down in the Z axis to a sharp edge, and scale them slightly up in the Y axis.

   - Select the next four vertices in from the edge. Scale them down in the X axis about halfway, and scale them slightly up in the Y axis. (See Figure 8.10.)

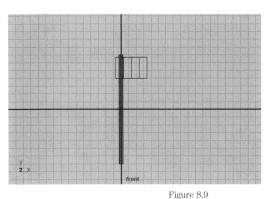

Figure 8.9

Placing the axe's head on the handle

Most animation work does not depend on precise measurements. The key is using proportions and relative sizes. You can almost always use Maya's generic units (which are set to centimeters by default). The scope of your project will determine if greater precision is necessary.

Figure 8.10

Creating a sharp edge for the axe

8. Press F8 to get back into object mode, and select both pieces.

9. Choose **Edit → Group** to group the pieces into one hierarchy, and call it axe.

Now, you need to identify the center of balance for this axe. Doing so gives you the place for your pivot point. Since the heaviest part of this axe is the head, the center of balance will be toward the top of the handle. In addition, your axe head protrudes in only one direction; so the balance point is a unit or two away from the handle.

10. Press Insert to activate the pivot manipulator, and move the pivot just under the axe head and about 1 unit from the handle, as in Figure 8.11.

Your scene should now look like the file `axe_v1.mb` in the scenes folder of the axe_anim project on the CD.

Making the Target

Move the axe about 40 units in the negative X axis away from the origin to make some room for the throw, and move it about 15 units up in the Y axis. Now you need to create a simple target for your axe to hit. Follow these steps:

1. Start with a polygonal cylinder.

2. Scale down the cylinder's height to make it squat, and rotate it just a bit past being perpendicular to the ground, facing toward the sky a little bit.

3. Scale the cylinder up about 7 times its original size.

Now you need to create a simple stand to put the target on. Follow these steps:

1. Choose **Create → Polygon Primitives → Cube** for the base.

2. Scale the cube so that the target fits on the base with some room to spare.

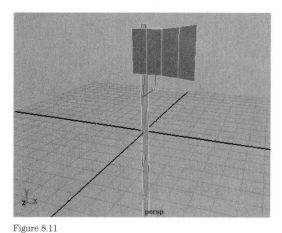

Figure 8.11

Finding the axe's center of balance gives you the proper place for its pivot point.

Figure 8.12

Positioning the cross braces for the target

3. Choose **Create → Polygon Primitives → Cylinder** to create two cylinders to make a cross brace for the back of the target.

4. Scale, rotate, and position the cylinders to fit behind the target and into the back of the base. Figure 8.12 shows the positions of the pieces to make up the target.

5. Once you're happy with the target, group the four objects together and name the group Target.

6. Move the target about 40 units in the positive X axis away from the origin, and move it up in the Y axis so its base is basically on the ground plane.

7. Press Insert to move the target's pivot point to the bottom of the base, right where the cross beams connect to it. Figure 8.13 shows the proper pivot placement.

Figure 8.13

The proper placement of the target's pivot point

You're placing the pivot point at that location because the target will jerk up and back a little bit when the axe hits it. This is the best point for you to rotate around to lift the front of the base up a bit to make it look like the axe is really hitting it. Save your file as your next version number. The scene is now ready for animation!

Preproduction: Keyframes and Motion Study

What separates good animation from bad animation is the feeling of weight that the audience infers from the animation. Since we have all been life-long observers of natural physics, we intimately and instinctively understand how nature works in motion. We see an object in motion, and we see how it moves through its surroundings and how it affects its surroundings as it moves. From that, we immediately feel its essence of true motion; most noticeably its weight makes a distinct, albeit subliminal impression on us. As it pertains to animation, that essence is simply called *weight*, and its observation is called *motion study*.

Unfortunately, merely knowing how something should look while moving is not quite all you'll need to animate it properly. The key element to remember and build on is that giving the axe believable weight is your primary job as an animator. You will need to make the audience feel as if that CG axe is every bit as real as an actual axe flying through the air. Modeling, texturing, and lighting are a small part of it, but motion will make or break the animation. Creating a convincing scene takes compelling motion. And creating compelling motion requires close observation.

A good feeling of weight in animation depends on timing and follow-through, which require practice.

When you want to animate an object or an action, it's a good idea to first try that action for yourself. Take a pen, remove its cap, and lob it across the room a few times like you might an axe. Notice how it arcs through the air, how it spins around its center of balance, and how it hits its mark. Its weight affects itself as well as the objects with which it comes in contact. Now try putting the cap on the pen, lob it again, and notice the subtle, yet monumental differences in motion.

As an animator, this experimentation is part of your preproduction and motion study. It is always important to have as thorough an understanding of your subject matter as is possible, within the resources and time at your disposal.

The perfect axe throw should contain as few spins as possible, depending on distance, and some say a throw should ideally have only one spin. This is good to know, as it will shape your animation.

Animating the Axe: Keyframing Gross Animation

The next step is to keyframe the positions of the axe. You'll start with the gross animation as you did with the bouncing ball. This will be the movement from one end of the axe's trajectory to the other—start to finish, origin to target.

Setting Initial Keyframes

You can start within your current scene, or you can load the unanimated, premade axe and target from the CD (`axe_v2.mb` in the scenes folder of the axe_anim project). Follow these steps:

1. Select the axe's top group node—and not just the pieces. To make selecting groups like this easier, display the object's selection handle. To do so, select the axe's top node and choose **Display → Component Display → Selection Handles**. This will display a small cross at the pivot point of the axe. You need only select this handle to select the top node of the axe.

   > As you will see later in this chapter's catapult exercise, you can use selection handles to select the children of a group as well as the top node.

2. Choose **Display → Component Display → Selection Handles** to turn on a handle or a marker that will allow you to select the group node by only selecting that handle, whether you are in object or hierarchy selection mode.

   Since this node is the parent node of the axe, the selection handle will display as a hollow cross (✛) at the node's current pivot point.

   > You can turn on selection handles for practically any object in Maya, no matter where it is in a group's hierarchy—whether it is a child or a parent. If it is not the top node, like the axe in this example, the selection handle will appear as a regular cross (+).

3. With the axe selected, go to frame 1, and set a keyframe for the rotation and translation.

4. Hold down Shift and press W for the axe's translation keyframe, and press Shift+E for the axe's rotation keyframe. You won't need to set a scale keyframe on the axe by pressing Shift R because you won't be changing its size. Once you're done, you have the initial keyframes for the axe at its start position.

Creating Anticipation

Instead of the axe just flying through the air toward the target, you'll animate the axe moving back a bit first to create *anticipation*, as if an invisible arm were pulling the axe back just before throwing it. Follow these steps:

1. Go to frame 15.

2. Move the axe back in the X axis about 8 units, and rotate it counterclockwise about 45°.

3. The Auto Keyframe feature will set keyframes for the position and new rotation at frame 15.

Since you've only moved the axe back in the X axis and made the rotation on the Z axis, Auto Keyframe sets keyframes only for **Translate X** and **Rotate Z**. The other position and rotation axes were not keyframed since their values did not change.

4. Scrub through the animation, and notice how the axe moves back in anticipation.

> Auto Keyframe inserts a keyframe at the current time for the selected object's changed attributes only.

5. Go to frame 40, and move the axe so that its blade cuts into the center of the target.

Notice that you will have to move the axe in the X and Y axes, whereas before you only had to move it back in the X axis to create anticipation. This is because the axis of motion for the axe rotates along with the axe. This is called the *local axis*. The local axis for any given object shifts according to the object's orientation. Since you angled the axe back about 45°, its local axis rotated back the same amount.

The file `Axe_v3.mb` in the scenes folder of the axe_anim project on the CD will catch you up to this point in the animation.

This last step will reveal a problem with the animation. If you scrub your animation now, you'll notice that the axe's movement back is now different from before, setting a keyframe at frame 40.

This is because of the Auto Keyframe feature. At frame 1, you set an initial keyframe for all axes of translation and rotation. Then, at frame 15, you moved the axe back in the X axis only (in addition to rotating it in the Z axis only).

Auto Keyframe set a keyframe for **Translate X** at frame 15. At frame 40, you moved the axe in *both* the X and Y axes to strike the target. Auto Keyframe set a keyframe at 40 for **Translate X** and **Translate Y**. But since the last keyframe for **Translate Y** was set at 1 and not at 15 as **Translate X** was, there is now a bobble in the Y position of the axe between frames 1 and 15.

With the axe selected, open the Graph Editor (choose **Window → Animation Editors → Graph Editor**) to see what's happening here. As you saw in the bouncing ball exercise, using the Graph Editor is crucial, and the more practice you get with it, the better.

When you open the Graph Editor for this scene, you should see red, green, and blue line segments running up and down, left and right. You will probably have to zoom your view to something more intelligible. You can navigate the Graph Editor much like any of the modeling windows by using the Alt key and mouse button combinations.

The hot keys A and F also work in the Graph Editor. Click anywhere in the Graph Editor window to make sure it's the active window, and press A to zoom all your curves into view. Your window should look something like Figure 8.14.

The curves in the Graph Editor represent the values of the axe's position and rotation at any given time. The three axes are in their representative red, green, or blue color, and the specific attributes are listed much as they are in the Outliner in the left column. Selecting an object or an attribute on the left displays its curves on the right.

Notice that the **Scale** attributes on the axe are not shown in this window; only animated attributes appear here.

Also notice that the curve for **Translate Y** has keyframes only at frames 1 and 40. The animation dips in the first 15 frames because there is no keyframe at frame 15 as there is for **Translate Z**. That dip was not there before you set the end keyframe at frame 40.

Figure 8.14

The Graph Editor displays the axe's animation curves.

6. Move the first keyframe of **Translate Y** from frame 1 to frame 15 to fix the dip.

- Press W to activate the Move tool in Maya, or click the Move Nearest Picked Key icon ( ) in the Graph Editor.

- Click the Time Snap icon ( ) to toggle it on.

- Select the offending **Translate Y** keyframe at frame 1, and MM move it to the right until it's at frame 15.

Scrub your animation, and the backward movement will look as it did before. You might have prevented this problem by manually setting your keyframes for the axe instead of using Auto Keyframe. But the more you work with Maya, the more valuable you'll find Auto Keyframe.

The axe now needs an arc on its way to the target.

7. Go to the middle of the axe's flight, frame 27.

8. Move the axe up in the Y axis a bit using the green handle of the Tool Manipulator.

Auto Keyframe sets a key for both **Translate Y** and **Translate X**, when you were perhaps expecting only a key in **Translate Y**. Since the Move tool is on the axe's local axis, and since the axe was slightly rotated at frame 27, there is a change in the Y and X position in the world space axis, which is the axis represented in the Graph Editor.

9. Select the **Translate X** key at frame 27, and press Delete to delete it.

Now you should add a full spin to the axe to give the animation more reality and life. You can spin it more in one of two ways.

- Go to frame 40, select the axe, and rotate it clockwise a full 360° positive. Auto Keyframe will enter a new rotation value at frame 40, overwriting the old value. You should see the **Rotate Z** curve angle down steeply as soon as you let go of the Rotate Manip.

- In the Graph Editor, make sure you're at frame 40, grab the last keyframe on the **Rotate Z** curve, and MM move it down, probably past the lower limit of the window. If you keep the middle mouse button pressed as you move the mouse, the keyframe will keep moving as you move the mouse, even if the keyframe has left the visible bounds of the Graph Editor.

> If you hold down Shift as you MM drag the keyframe to move it in the Graph Editor, the keyframe will move in only one axis (up or down, left or right).

By moving the keyframe down, you're changing the **Rotate Z** value to a lower number, which will spin the axe clockwise. Before you try that though, move your Graph Editor window so you can see the axe in the perspective window. As you move the **Rotate Z** keyframe down in the Graph Editor, you will see the axe rotate interactively. Move the keyframe down until the axe does a full spin.

Playback the animation. Click the Play button in the playback controls. If your animation looks blazingly fast, Maya's playback speed is probably set to Play Every Frame. Open the Animation Preferences window by clicking its icon ( ), which is next to the Auto Keyframe icon, and set Playback Speed to Real-Time (30 fps).

Changing the playback speed of an animation through the Animation Preferences window does not alter the timing of your animation. It only changes the speed with which Maya plays the animation back to you in its windows. To change the playback speed, choose **Window →** **Setting/Preferences → Preferences** to open the Preferences window, choose **Settings →** **Working Units**, and select the proper setting.

Now when you playback the animation, it should look rather slow. Maya is playing the scene back in real time, as long as your Animation Preferences are set to play back properly at 30fps. Even at 30fps, the scene should playback slowly, and this means that the animation of the axe timing is too slow.

All you need to do is tinker in the Graph Editor a bit to get the right timing. For a good result in timing, move the first set of keyframes from 15 to 13. Then, grab the **Translate Y** keyframe at frame 27 and move it to 19. Finally, grab the keyframes at frame 40 and move them all back to frame 25. Playback the scene.

Adding Follow-Through

Load the Axe_v4.mb file from the axe_anim project on the CD, or continue with your own file.

The axe is missing weight. Nothing much in this scene indicates that this is a heavy axe. You can add some finesse to the scene using follow-through and secondary motion to give more weight to the scene.

SECONDARY MOTION AND FOLLOW-THROUGH

Secondary motion in animation comprises all the little things in a scene that move because something else in the scene is moving. For example, when a character with long hair moves their head around, the hair whips past their face and hits their shoulder. Or when a superhero jumps from a tall building and their cape flutters in the wind, the cape's undulation is secondary motion.

Follow-through is the action in animation that immediately follows an object's or a character's main action. For example, once the superhero lands from their jump, their knees buckle a little, and the superhero bends at the waist, essentially squashing down a bit. That squashing motion is follow-through. The more follow-through, the more cartoon-like the animation appears.

In the axe scene, follow-through motion is the axe blade driving farther into the target a little beyond its initial impact. Secondary motion is the recoil in the target as the momentum of the axe transfers into it. As you increase the amount of follow-through and secondary motion, you increase the axe's implied weight. You must, however, walk a fine line; you don't want to go too far with follow-through or secondary motion. The Graph Editor is great for adding these nuances to the axe. Follow these steps:

1. Select the axe in the scene using its selection handle, and open the Graph Editor.

2. Because you will add three frames to the end of this animation for follow-through, go to frame 28 (25 being the end of the current animation).

3. In the perspective window, rotate the axe another 1.5° in the Z axis.

4. Rotating the axe in step 3 moves the axe's blade down a bit in the Y axis, so move the axe using the **Translate Y** manipulator handle up slightly, to bring the axe back up to about where it was before the extra rotation. This will also dig the axe into the target a little more. You'll see a keyframe for **Translate X** and **Translate Y**, as well as **Rotate Z**.

If you playback the animation, the follow-through doesn't look good. The axe hits the target and then digs into the target as if the action were done in two separate moves by two different animators who never talk to each other. You need to smooth out the transition from the axe strike and its follow-through in the Graph Editor.

5. Highlight the **Rotate Z** attribute in the Graph Editor to get rid of the other curves in the window. Figure 8.15 shows the **Translate Z** curve of the axe after the follow-through animation is added.

6. Focus in on the last three frames of the curve, and zoom into that range only. The curve, as it is now, dips down past where it should and recoils back up a bit.

Figure 8.15

The Translate Z curve of the axe after the follow-through animation

When you set keyframes, you create animation curves in the Graph Editor for the axe. These curves are Bèzier splines, which use a type of mathematics that will keep the curve as smooth as possible from beginning to end, regardless of where its points lie. When you set the new keyframe rotating the axe about 1.5 more degrees for follow-through, the animation curve responds by creating a dip, as seen in Figure 8.15, to keep the whole curve as smooth as possible.

Although keeping animation curves as smooth splines is desirable overall, it is often necessary to adjust the curvature in the Graph Editor at some keyframes to get good motion. The axe needs to hit the target with force and dig its way into the target, slowly coming to a stop.

You will need to adjust the curvature of the keyframes at frame 25 by using the keyframe's *tangents*. Tangents are handles that will change the amount of curvature influence that a point on a bspline (Bèzier spline) has. Selecting the keyframe in question reveals its tangents. (See Figure 8.16.)

7. Select the out tangent for the **Rotate Z** attribute's key at frame 25, and MM move it up to get rid of the dip. Notice that the tangency for the in tangent also changes.

8. Press Z to undo your change. You need to break the tangent handles so that one does not disturb the other.

9. Select the out handle and click the Break Tangents icon ( ) to break the tangent.

10. Move the handle up to get rid of the dip so that the curve segment from frame 25 to frame 28 is a straight line, angled down. Figure 8.17 is zoomed into this segment of the curve after it's been fixed.

Now, to get the axe to slowly stop as it digs into the target, you need to curve that end segment of the **Rotate Z** curve to flatten it out.

11. Grab the last frame to reveal its handles. You can manually move the in handle to make it horizontal, or you can press the Flat Handles icon ( ), which is on the left side of the icon bar under the menus in the Graph Editor.

Figure 8.17

Zoomed into the end segment of the Rotate Z animation curve once the dip is fixed

Figure 8.18

Zoomed into the end segment of the Rotate Z animation curve. Notice how the curve now smoothly comes to a stop by flattening out.

The curve's final segment for **Rotate Z** should now look like Figure 8.18.

12. Adjust the keyframe tangents similarly for the **Translate Y** and **Translate X** curves for the axe. (See Figure 8.19.)

13. Play back the animation, and you should see the axe impact the target and sink into it a bit for its follow-through.

Now you need another bit of finesse.

Adding Secondary Motion

Load `Axe_v5.mb` from the axe_anim project on the CD, or continue with your own scene file. For secondary motion, you will move the target in reaction to the impact from the axe's momentum.

Generally speaking, an object in motion has momentum. This momentum is calculated by multiplying the mass of the object by its velocity. So the heavier and the faster an object is, the more momentum it will have. When two objects collide, some if not all the momentum transfers from one object to the other.

In a game of pool, for example, when the moving cue ball collides with the stationary 8 ball for the last shot of the game, the cue ball transfers some of its momentum into the 8 ball, setting it in motion, and uses the rest of its own momentum to ricochet off into another direction.

In the axe scene's impact, the axe lodges into the target, and its momentum is almost fully transferred to the target. But, since the target is much more massive than the axe, the target moves only a little bit in reaction. The more you make the target recoil, the heavier the axe will seem. Remember, mass multiplied by velocity equals momentum.

First, you need to group the axe's parent node under the target's parent node. The axe would be left behind to float in midair if you were to animate the target's parent node without grouping the axe under it. By grouping the axe under the target, you'll be able to move the target to recoil while keeping the axe lodged in it. The animation on the axe will not change in the slightest when you group the axe and target under a new node.

You'll need to grab the parent node of the target (called Target) and reset its attributes to 0 by freezing its transforms as you did with the ball. This sets the Target node's **Translate** and **Rotate** attributes back to 0 and its **Scale** attributes back to 1.

1. To freeze the transforms, select the Target node, and then choose **Modify → Freeze Transforms**.

2. In the Outliner, MM drag the Axe node to the Target node to group it under. You could also MM drag the nodes in the Hypergraph to group the Axe node under the Target node.

3. Go to frame 25, the moment of impact, and set position and rotation keyframes on Target.

4. Go to frame 28, rotate the Target node in the Z axis about –2.5°, and move it up and back slightly in the Y and X axes, as in Figure 8.20

Figure 8.19

Smoothed translate curves to ease out the motion

Figure 8.20

The front panel display of the target reacting to the impact of the axe

5. Go to frame 31. Rotate the Target node back to 0 in the Z axis, move it down to 0 in the Y axis, and move it back a bit more in the X axis.

6. Go to frame 35 and repeat step 4, but only move it half as much in Rotate Z, Translate X, and Translate Y.

7. Go to frame 40 and repeat step 5, but move Target back only a slight bit in the X axis.

> If you don't freeze the transforms on the target's parent node before grouping the axe under it, the axe's animation will change and yield undesirable results.

The preceding steps should give you an animation similar to `axe_v6.mb` in the axe_anim project on the CD.

Motion Trails

You can see a moving object's trajectory or motion trail—its path of motion. Follow these steps:

1. Select the axe through its selection handle, and then choose **Animate → Create Motion Trail ☐**. (See Figure 8.21.)

2. Select Line for Draw Style, and make sure the Show Frame Numbers check box is checked.

3. Click Apply, and then click Close to close the window.

The motion trail will be useful for fine-tuning your motion. Editing the animation curves in the Graph Editor and watching the motion trail adjust in the work panels will show you the precise trajectory of the axe throughout its movement. Play back your animation a few times to get a good sense for how the scene looks.

4. Select the axe and open the Graph Editor.

5. Try adding some more arc to the axe in the middle of its trajectory to the target.

6. In the Graph Editor, focus on the **Translate Y** curve, and select the keyframe at frame 19.

7. Move the keyframe up about 2 units, and watch the motion trail adjust to show you the higher arc.

8. Replay the animation with the higher arc in the middle.

You'll notice that the axe seems a little more solid than before. The extra height in the trajectory really helps give the axe more substance. Figure 8.22 shows the axe and its motion trail after more height is added to its arc.

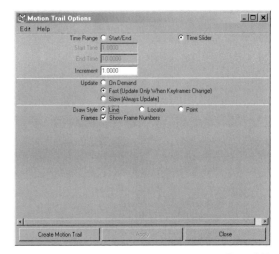

Figure 8.21

The Motion Trail Options window

You can toggle the frame number display on/off and change the display type of the motion trail from curve to points or locators through the motion trail's Attribute Editor. To get rid of the motion trail, select it and press Delete.

Path Animation

As an alternative to keyframing the position of the axe, you can animate it *on a path*. Path animation allows you to assign an object to move along the course of a curve, called a path.

Load `axe_v7.mb` from the axe_anim project on the CD. This is the finished axe animation. You'll delete most of your hard work by removing the translation animation on the axe, but you'll keep the rotation and everything else. You will replace the translation keyframes you set up with a motion path instead. Follow these steps:

1. In the front window and with the motion trails turned on, trace the motion trail with a CV curve (choose **Create → CV Curve Tool**) from the beginning of the trail to the end. Make sure the CV Curve tool is set to make cubic (3) curves.

Figure 8.22

**The axe and its
motion trail**

2. Take note of the frames you set important keyframes on for the axe's position (like when it recoils and releases at frame 10 and when it hits the target at frame 25). Select the axe's top node (axe), and delete its translation animation. Select all three **Translate** attributes in the Channel box, and right-click to display the shortcut menu. Choose Break Connections to delete the animation from those channels. The axe will now spin around, and it and the target will recoil at the moment of impact, but the axe will not actually move.

3. Keep the motion trail in the scene for now to help with the timing you've already created.

4. Select the top axe node, Shift+select the path curve, and click in the Animation menu set. Choose **Animate → Motion Paths → Attach to Motion Path ❑**.

5. In the options window, turn off the Follow check box.

The Follow feature will orient the object on the path so that its front always points in the direction of travel. Because the axe moves backward in anticipation before it's thrown forward, Follow would cause it to turn around twice; so you turn this option off.

Now the axe will follow the curve end to end from frame 1 to frame 60. Of course, you have to adjust the timing to fit it as before.

6. Select the motion trail and move it down in the window to get it out of the way, but do keep it lined up vertically with the path curve so that you can figure out the timing again.

The file `axe_path_v1.mb` in the axe_anim project will bring you up to this point.

7. Select the top axe node, and open the Graph Editor to see the axe's curves. The rotation curve is still intact, but there is now a motionPath1.UValue curve instead of translation curves. On the left side of the Graph Editor, select the motionPath1.UValue curve to display only that. Zoom into it. (Press A for all view.)

8. The curve is an even linear curve from 1 to 60. You need the axe to hit at frame 25, so move the end of the curve to frame 25 from frame 60.

GHOSTING

You can enable *ghosting* in Maya, which let's you see the position of an animated object a few frames before and a few frames after its current position. For example, select the animated axe in your scene, and open the Animation menu set. Choose **Animate → Ghost Selected**. Maya will now display the axe three frames before and after the current time. To turn off ghosting, choose **Animate → Unghost Selected**.

9. Retime the backward movement. Scrub the animation until the axe moves all the way back (frame 4). Using the Insert Key tool ( ), insert a keyframe at frame 4. Select the animation curve, click the tool, and MM click the curve to create a key on it. You can MM drag the cursor to place the key precisely at frame 10 before releasing the mouse button.

10. Move this new keyframe to frame 10 (the frame where backward movement originally ended).

11. Scrub the animation, and the timing is just about right. You'll have to adjust the tangents a bit to make the axe move more like before, but the movement is essentially there with path animation.

The file `axe_path_v2.mb` in the axe_anim project will bring you up to this point.

Path animation is extremely useful for a number of tasks, but particularly for animating an object along a particular course. By adjusting the resulting animation curve in the Graph Editor, you can readjust the timing of the path animation easily.

A good path animation exercise is to create an atom and draw CV curves around the nucleus for the paths of the electrons. Then animate all the electrons orbiting the nucleus with the paths. Also, try reanimating the solar system exercise with paths instead of the keyframes you set on the rotations.

Axe Project Summation

In the axe example, you furthered your use of layered animation by beginning with the gross animation to cover the basic movements of the axe. Once those timings were set, you completed most of the rest of the work in the Graph Editor by moving keyframes here and there to add detail to the motion. You added more keyframes to create follow-through and secondary movement to insinuate weight into the axe and target.

Without secondary movement in the target, the axe would seem to weigh nothing. With too much movement, however, the axe would seem too heavy, and the scene would not look right. Subtle nuances can make stunning differences in the simplest of animations. You also went back into the animation and replaced the animation method entirely with path animation. This illustrates the multiple ways to accomplish a task in Maya; finding your own comfort zone with workflow is one of the goals in learning Maya.

Object Replacement

Aside from the need to model objects and texture them, there is the all-important task of animation setup. Nothing is more frustrating than finding out midway through a day's work that your animation won't work with a particular hierarchy setup or with the way a model has been put together. Check your pivots, your geometry, and your grouping to make sure your scene will hold up. How will you know? Through experience: the more you do it and the more you see things break apart, the better you'll be at figuring out how to prevent that breakage.

It's also common practice in production to animate a *proxy* object—a simple model that you later replace. In production, an object is often replaced when another object is remodeled or retextured. The next exercise will show you how to replace the simple axe you already animated with the fully textured NURBS from the previous chapter and how to copy an animation from one object to another.

Replacing the Axe

Load your completed keyframed axe animation scene (not the one using path animation), or switch to the axe_anim project and load the scene file `axe_v7.mb` from the CD. Now, follow these steps:

1. Choose **File → Import**.

2. Locate and import the final textured axe in your project, or use `axe_texture_C.mb` from the axe_model project on the CD. The new axe appears at the origin in your scene. You will notice that the ambient light is also imported into this scene.

Transferring Animation

To assume all the properties and actions of the original axe requires some setup. Follow these steps:

1. Move the pivot on the new axe to the same relative position as the pivot on the original animated axe (up toward the top and a little out front of the handle, just under the blade). This will ensure that the new axe will have the same spin as the old axe.

2. Rotate the new axe's top node 180 in Y to get it to face the right direction.

3. Use grid snap to place the top node of the new axe at the origin.

4. Freeze transforms on the new axe group to reset all its attributes. However, freezing transforms with the third placement node of the wood grain still grouped in with the axe resets the wood grain. Try it, but make sure to undo the action. As a workaround, MM drag the wood third placement node momentarily out of the axe group. Choose **Modify → Freeze Transformations** on the new axe group. MM drag the third placement node back into the axe's hierarchy.

5. Choose **Display → Component Display → Selection Handles** to turn on the selection handle of the new axe.

6. Go to frame 1. Select the original axe, open the Graph Editor, and choose **Edit → Copy**.

7. Select the new axe to display its curves in the Graph Editor. It has none yet. With the axe_2 node selected in the Graph Editor, choose **Edit → Paste**. As shown in Figure 8.23, the new axe will be slightly offset from the original axe.

Figure 8.23

The new axe placed next to the original

> When you copy and paste curves in the Graph Editor, make sure you're on the first frame of that animation. Pasting curves will place them at the current frame. Since the animation of the original axe started at frame 1, make sure you're at frame 1 when you paste them to the new axe.

8. Move the new axe to match the original. Since it's already animated, move it using the curves in the Graph Editor as opposed to moving it in the viewport. With the new axe selected, in the Graph Editor, select the Translate Y curve and move it up to match the height of the original axe.

9. Select the Translate X curve and move it to match the axe's X position, as in Figure 8.24. You'll want to line up the axe handle as a guide.

Scrub the animation, and you'll notice the new axe has the same animation except at the end when it hits the target. It won't have the same follow-through as the original axe. Remember that you grouped the original axe under the Target node for follow-through animation. Place the new axe under this node as well.

The file `axe_v8` in the axe_anim project on the CD has the new axe imported and all the animation copied and will get you caught up to this point.

10. Once you scrub the animation and make sure the new axe animates properly, select the original axe and delete it.

Animating the Catapult

Now you'll return to the catapult you modeled in Chapter 5 and put your new animation skills to use.

Create a new project called Catapult_Anim, or copy the project on the CD to your hard drive. Load the file `catapult_anim_v01.mb`, which is the completed model of the catapult from the polygon modeling exercise in Chapter 5.

The Scene Setup

As you know, it's important to keep animation in mind as you build a model. In particular, making a good scene hierarchy is crucial to getting a smooth animation workflow going. That's why, when you built the catapult in Chapter 5, you used the Outliner to make sure the objects in your scene were grouped together logically. Now you're merely going to check and refamiliarize yourself with the catapult to make sure everything is ready for animating it.

Figure 8.24

Lining up the two axes

Figure 8.25 shows the organization of the catapult as it stands now. And it's in good shape; all the moving parts of the catapult are named and grouped together.

Figure 8.25

The catapult's Outliner view

If your catapult is in organizational disarray, identify the objects that are part of the same moving mechanism of the catapult, group them together, and give them an appropriate name. If some parts of the catapult are parts of a greater part, group the hierarchy of your modeled pieces in the same manner.

As you did with the solar system exercise in Chapter 3, you will need to make sure the proper objects are not only grouped correctly, but also that every one of these parent groups has a well-positioned pivot point.

For example, the group Arm1 should have its pivot at the end so that the entire arm can swing off its hinge. (See Figure 8.26.) You need to animate three important groups, so check the hierarchies and the pivots on your model.

Figure 8.27 shows the groupings you should have and the pivot placement for each parent for the remaining two groups:

Group each wheel with all the elements that make up that wheel, with a centered pivot. Then make a new group with two opposing wheels and their axle, and center that pivot for the front and rear wheels, as in Figure 8.28.

Figure 8.26

You need to work out the proper pivot placement for the catapult's mechanical pieces during setup or modeling.

Figure 8.27

Pivots of the wheel
groups centered
on the axle

Figure 8.28

The winch pieces
are grouped, and
that group's pivot
is centered on the
winch wheel for
proper rotation.

The winch's pivot needs to be physically centered on the winch since choosing **Modify → Center Pivot** may not work, depending on how you built your winch's handles.

If the pivots are off, you will notice as soon as you begin to animate; things will just not rotate on the correct axis. The wheels, for example, may wobble around their axle.

 For more practice in grouping and hierarchies, you can load `catapult_anim_v01.mb` from the CD, ungroup everything in the scene, and piece it all back together. To ungroup everything, select the top node of the catapult and choose **Edit → Ungroup**. That will ungroup the major parts of the catapult. With those groups selected, ungroup again to flush out individual geometry. You can also load `catapult_anim_v01_B.mb` from the CD; it has all major grouping removed. Then regroup and re-pivot everything.

Selection Handles

As you've seen, using selection handles can make selection easier, so you should turn on selection handles for each of the groups you're animating. Select the winch group in the Outliner, and then choose **Display → Component Display → Selection Handles**. Select the wheel groups and the arm group, and turn on their selection handles as well.

This makes it far easier to select and animate parts of a group quickly without having to go back and forth between the work window and the Outliner or Hypergraph.

How selection handles work depends on Maya's selection order. Selection order, which you can customize, lets you set the priority of one type of object over another when you try to select in a work window. Once the four handles for the catapult's top nodes are turned on, only the handles will be selected and not the whole catapult when you make a marquee selection that covers the entire catapult. Handles have a high selection priority by default, so they are selected above anything else.

Animating the Catapult

It's straightforward to animate most of the catapult. Simple rotations will make the wheels turn. Translating the catapult's top node will move the entire object. Rotating the winch group will turn the winch to pull the catapult arm back into firing position.

But how to animate the catapult arm itself? Get a timing for the winch first, and use that to pull back the arm. Follow these steps:

1. Select the Winch group with its selection handle, and at frame 1, set a keyframe for rotation. To keep it clean as you go along, instead of pressing Shift+E to set a key for all three axes of rotation, select the **Rotate X** attribute in the Channel box, right-click to open the shortcut menu, and choose **Key Selected**.

2. Jump to frame 60.

3. Rotate the winch backward a few times. (Or type **–400** or so for the **Rotate X** attribute.)

4. Open the Graph Editor, ease in the curve a bit, and ease out the curve a lot so that the rotation starts casually but grinds to a stop as the arm gets more difficult to pull back. Now obviously you're missing the rope between the winch and the arm. Since animating a rope is a fairly advanced task, the catapult will be animated without its rope, but the principle of an imaginary rope pulling the arm down to create tension in the arm will drive the animation.

5. To accentuate the more difficult winding at the end, you'll add a key to the X-axis rotation through the Graph Editor. Select the curve, and click the Insert Key Tool icon ( ) in the upper-left corner of the Graph Editor. Your cursor will change to a cross.

6. MM click frame 42 to add a keyframe already on the curve at frame 42. You can drag the key back and forth on the curve to place it directly at frame 42. It may help to turn on key snapping first. (See Figure 8.29.)

7. Move that keyframe down to create a stronger ease-out for the winch. Be careful not to let the curve dip down so that the winch switches directions. Adjust the handles to smooth the curve. You can also add a little recoil to the winch by inserting a new keyframe through the Graph Editor at frame 70. (See Figure 8.30.)

Figure 8.29

Insert a keyframe at frame 42.

Figure 8.30

Creating a greater ease-out and adding a little recoil at the end

Animating with Deformers

Now's the time to animate the arm coiling back, using the winch's timing, as it is driving the arm. Since the catapult's arm is supported by a brace and the whole idea of a catapult is based on tension, you have to bend the arm back as the winch pulls it.

You'll use a deformer just as you did in the axe-modeling exercise in Chapter 6, but you'll be animating it. Follow these steps:

1. Switch to the Animation menu set. Select the Arm1 group, and choose **Deform → Create Nonlinear → Bend** to create a bend deformer perpendicular with your arm. Select the deformer and rotate it to line it up with the arm.

2. With the bend deformer selected, look in the Channel box for bend1 under the INPUTS section, and click it to expand its attributes. Try entering **0.5** for **Curvature**. The catapult arm bends sideways more than likely. Rotate the deformer so that the arm is bending back instead.

3. Now, you don't want the arm's base to bend back, just the basket side. And you want it to bend at the brace point, not in the middle where it is now. Move the deformer down the length of the arm until the middle lines up with the support brace of the arm.

4. To prevent the bottom of the arm from bending, change the **Low Bound** attribute to 0. To keep the basket from bending, set the **High Bound** attribute to 0.9.

> The **Low Bound** and **High Bound** attributes control how far up and down the deformer the object is affected. The **Envelope** attribute for a deformer governs how much *overall* the object is affected, with 0 not affecting the geometry at all.

5. Instead of trying to match the speed, ease in and out, and set the gross keyframes for the arm pulling back first. Reset **Curvature** to 0, and set a key for **Curvature** at frame 1. (Select bend1's **Curvature** in the Channel box, right-click, and choose Key Selected from the shortcut menu.)

6. Go to frame 60, and set **Curvature** to 0.8. If Auto Key is turned on, this sets a keyframe; otherwise, set a key manually. (See Figure 8.31.)

7. If you playback the animation, you'll notice that the way the winch winds back and the arm bends don't really match. In the Graph Editor, you can adjust the animation curve on the bend deformer to match the winch's curve.

8. Insert a key on the **Curvature** curve at frame 42, and move it up to match the curvature you created for the winch.

Figure 8.31

Bend the arm back at frame 60.

9. Insert a new key at frame 70, and make the arm bend back up a bit as the winch recoils. Set **Curvature** to about 0.79 from 0.8. (See Figure 8.32.)

10. Go to frame 90 and set a key again at **Curvature** of 0, set a key at 0.82 for frame 97 to create anticipation, and then keyframe at frame 103 to release the arm and fire its imaginary payload with a **Curvature** of –0.8.

11. Now you'll add some rotation to the arm for dramatic effect. At about frame 100, during the release, the arm is almost straight. Select the Arm1 group, and set a rotation key on the X axis. Go to frame 105, and rotate the arm to 45 to the left in the X axis. If the starting rotation of the arm is at 30 (as it is in the sample file), set an X-axis rotation key of 75 at frame 105.

12. Notice that the arm is bending strangely now that it's being rotated. It is moving off the deformer, so its influence is changing for the worse. To fix this, go back to frame 100, and group the deformer under the Arm1 group.

13. Work on setting keyframes on the deformer and the arm's rotation so that it falls back down onto the support brace and quivers a bit until it becomes straight again. The animation curve for the bend deformer should look like Figure 8.33. The rotation of the arm should look like Figure 8.34. Remember to make the tangents on the keys where the arm bounces off the brace linear and the peaks flat, like the ball's bounce from before.

Figure 8.32

Try to match the relative curvature of the winch's animation curve with the bend deformer's animation curve.

Figure 8.33

The animation curve for the arm's vibration back and forth as it comes to a rest

Figure 8.34

**The animation curve
for the arm's rotation
as it heaves up and
falls back down, com-
ing to an easy rest
on the brace**

The file `catapult_anim_v02.mb` will give you a good reference to check out timing of the arm bend and rotation.

Without getting into a lot more detail here, try your hand at animating the catapult on your own. Here are some items you'll want to animate to make this a complete animation:

- Spin the winch around as the arm releases, as if its rope is being yanked away from it.

- Animate the entire catapult rocking forward and backward as the arm releases, sort of like a car would rock when you jump onto the hood.

- Move the catapult forward on a road, spinning its wheels as best you can to match the distance it travels.

- Design and build your own catapult and animate it along the same lines.

Summary

Animating a complex system such as the catapult involves creating layers of animation based on facets of the mechanics of the system's movement. With the catapult, you tackled the individual parts separately and then worked to unify the animations.

The same is true of the bouncing ball and axe-throwing exercises. The different needs of the animation were addressed one by one, starting with the gross animation and ending with finishing touches to add weight. Finally, the art of timing brings the entire effort into a cohesive whole.

Even when animation is already applied, it is simple to change *how* the animation is accomplished as you did with path animation or even to replace the animated object entirely.

Animation is the art of observation, interpretation, and implementation. Learning to see how things move, deciphering why they move as they do, and then applying all that to your Maya scene is what animation is all about.

CHAPTER 9

Further Animation Topics

Now that you have a little more animation experience, you'll get into some deeper animation topics that introduce more involved toolsets. Make sure to take the principles covered in this book and its examples further for yourself. Animation is an ever-growing exploration, and you should use this text as a stepping-off point. For everything you're being exposed to here, there are many, many more techniques to discover. Topics include:

- **Skeletons and Kinematics**

- **Skeletons: The Hand**

- **Inverse Kinematics**

- **Basic Relationships: Constraints**

- **Basic Relationships: Set Driven Keys**

Skeletons and Kinematics

In your physical body, your muscles move your bones, and as your bones move, parts of your body move. Bones are your internal framework.

In CG animation, a skeleton is an armature built into a 3D model that drives the geometry. You insert a skeleton into a CG model and attach or bind it to the geometry. The skeleton's bones are animated (typically with rotations), which in turn move the parts of the geometry to which they are attached. Using a skeleton allows for bending and deformation of the attached geometry at *joints* of the skeleton. A skeleton is of course useful for character work, but skeletons have many more uses. Any time you need to drive the geometry of a model with an internal system, such as a whip or a tree bending in the wind, you can use skeletons.

Skeletons and Hierarchy

Skeletons rely on hierarchies. Bones are created in a hierarchical manner, resulting in a *root joint* that is the parent of all the joints beneath it in the hierarchy. For example a hip joint can be the root joint of a leg skeleton system in which the *knee joint* is the leg's child, the *ankle joint* belongs to the knee, and the five *toe joints* are the ankle's children. (See Figure 9.1.)

Using skeletons, you can easily create an immediate hierarchy system with which to animate. Furthermore, pieces of geometry need not deform to be attached to a bone system.

Figure 9.1

A leg skeleton and its hierarchy

Objects can be grouped with or under joints. They move under their parent joint and rotate around that joint's pivot as opposed to their own pivot point.

A skeleton is really just a collection of grouped and properly positioned pivot points called joints that you use to move your geometry, whether it deforms or not. A *bone* is defined as the length between each joint. Bones don't actually do anything more than show you the skeletal system.

Inverse Kinematics (IK) and *Forward Kinematics* (FK) are the methods you use to animate a skeletal system. FK rotates the bones directly at their top joint to assume poses. This method closely resembles stop-motion animation in which a puppet, along with its underlying armature, is posed frame by frame. With FK, the animator moves the character into position by rotating the joints that run the geometry.

Hip joint

Bone

Knee joint

Bone

Ankle joint

Joint at the
tip of the foot

The rotation of a joint affects the position of the bones and joints beneath it in the hierarchy (see Figure 9.2). If you rotate the hip up, the knee and ankle will swing up as if kicking.

Figure 9.2

In Forward Kinematics, the joints are rotated directly.

If you rotate the knee down, the ankle pivots down as if seated. The form of motion moves the way you would expect it in hierarchies and is therefore called *Forward Kinematics*.

IK uses a more complex, but often easier system of *IK handles* that are attached to the tip of a joint system. The corresponding base of the IK system is attached farther up the skeleton hierarchy to a joint determined to be the root of that IK segment. It need not be the root joint of the entire skeleton, though.

The bones and joints in the IK chain are affected only by movement of the IK handle. When the handle moves, an *IK solver* figures out how to rotate all the joints to accommodate the new position of the IK handle. Moving an IK handle will cause the bones to rotate around their joints to accommodate a new position.

The effect is as if someone grabbed your hand and moved it. The person holding your hand is similar to an IK handle. Moving your hand causes the bones in your arm to rotate around the shoulder, elbow, and wrist. As you can see in Figure 9.3, the animation flows up the hierarchy and is therefore called Inverse Kinematics.

Forward Kinematics: The Block Man

To really understand skeletal hierarchy, take a look at a simple biped (two-legged) character made of shaped primitive blocks called *block man*. In Figure 9.4, each block represents a part of the body with the gaps in between the blocks representing points where the body can pivot.

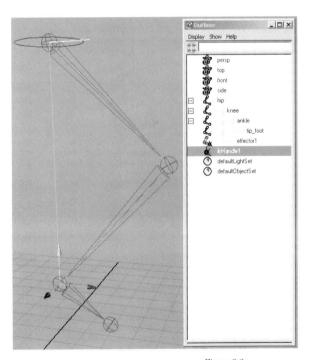

Figure 9.3

In Inverse Kinematics, the joints rotate in response to the IK handle's position.

The pivot of each body block is placed to represent the appropriate joint location. For example, the shin's pivot is located at the knee. Each block is then grouped up the chain so

Figure 9.4

The block man's cubes arranged

that the foot moves with the shin, which moves with the thigh, which moves with the pelvis.

The hands are grouped under the arms, which group under the shoulders and so forth, down the spine to the pelvis. The head groups under the first neck block, and so on, down the spine to the pelvis. The pelvis is the center of the body, which is known as the root of the figure.

The way this figure is grouped (see Figure 9.5) represents how the hierarchy of a character works. Each body part is attached and becomes the child of the part "above" it in the chain.

Load the file `block_man_v02.mb` from the CD for a good reference of the grouping structure. This file shows you what a skeleton hierarchy does.

Using the Hypergraph, you can position the nodes in any way you want. In the Hypergraph, choose **Options → Layout → Freeform Layout** to enable this feature. To make selections easier, you can arrange the nodes as if they were on a body (see Figure 9.6). You can toggle between freeform and automatic, and your freeform layout will be retained.

Creating the Skeleton

The basis of how the block man is laid out and grouped is what skeletons are all about. Skeletons make character animation easier by automating, at the very least, the hierarchy and pivot placement described earlier.

THE PELVIS AS ROOT

Traditionally, the pelvis is the basis of all biped setups. The root of any skeletal system (whether using bones or geometry as the example) is the character's pivot point, the center of balance. Since biped characters center themselves on two feet, their pelvis becomes the root of their skeletal system. In CGI, the pelvis becomes the parent node of the whole system and is the node used to move or orient the entire character. In a skeleton system, this would be the root joint.

The root is then the top parent of the system below it and runs the entire chain. Thus, selecting character parts straight from the Outliner or the Hypergraph is sometimes easier. You can, therefore, see that a good naming convention is always important with character setups.

You'll use the block man to create a skeleton. Load `block_man_v01.mb` from the Block_Man project. This is the same as `block_man_v02.mb`, but this version is not grouped.

Figure 9.5

Pivot placements and grouping

1. Maximize the front view window. Switch to the Animation menu set by using the drop-down menu or by pressing F2.

2. Activate the Joint tool by choosing **Skeleton → Joint Tool**. Your cursor will turn into a cross.

3. Click in the middle of the pelvis to place the first joint, the root joint of the skeleton.

4. Shift+LM click up to the space between the pelvis and the waist.

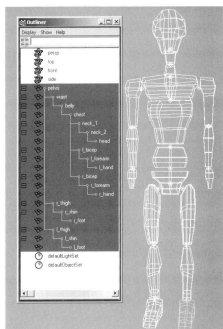

By pressing Shift as you click, you create a joint in a straight line from the last joint placement. A bone is created between the two joints, as a visual guide to the skeleton. The placement of the joints does depend on the active view; so placing a second joint in a different view may place the joint in an awkward location.

Figure 9.6

A freeform layout in the Hypergraph

5. Click more joints up the spine at the gaps between the body parts as shown.

6. You need to start a new branch of joints leading into the legs and arms. You'll begin with the arms. With the Joint tool still active, press the Up arrow key three times to move up the hierarchy of joints to the one between the neck and chest parts.

> Pressing the Up arrow key takes you up one node in a hierarchy; pressing the Down arrow key takes you down one node in a hierarchy. This approach also applies to skeletons, since they are hierarchies.

7. From this joint, click to place the right joint at the top of the right bicep. Click down to create joints at the elbow, at the wrist, and at the tip of the hand.

8. Press the Up arrow to *pick walk* up the chain to the neck/chest joint, and repeat the step 7 to create the joints for the left arm as shown.

9. To start another string of joints in the first leg, pick walk back up the skeleton until you're at the pelvis root joint.

10. Now from the root joint at the pelvis, click to create a joint at the tip of the right thigh and work down to the knee and ankle. (Place the ankle joint at the middle of the foot, as shown, as opposed to the gap between the shin and foot as shown. Press the spacebar to return to the four-way view, and maximize the side view. Click to create a joint at the tip of the foot. This allows you to place a joint in the proper axis.

11. Return to the front view, and press the Up arrow to get back to the pelvis joint. Repeat step 10 to create joints for the left leg. After you place your joints, press Enter.

Attaching to the Skeleton

You now have a full skeleton for your character. To attach the geometry, all you need do is parent the body parts under their appropriate joints. Before you get to that, take a few minutes and name all the joints in the Outliner to make the scene easier to manage. Figure 9.7 shows the names used in the project on the CD.

You can also load the `block_man_skeleton_v01.mb` file from the Block_Man project to get to this point.

To parent the block man's geometry to the skeleton, follow these steps:

1. Starting with the right foot, parent it under the right ankle joint (rt_ankle) by MM dragging it to rt_ankle in the Outliner or the Hypergraph. You don't want to parent it under the right foot joint (rt_foot) because you need the foot geometry to pivot with that foot bone and inherit the rotations from the ankle above it. Parent the left foot under the left ankle (lt_ankle).

2. Parent the rest of the body parts under their respective joints as shown in Figure 9.8.

   - Shins under the knees and thighs under the hips

   - Hands under the wrists and forearms under the elbows

   - Biceps under the shoulders

   - Head under the head joint (the joint between the head and the top neck geometry)

   - The top neck geometry under the joint between the two neck pieces

   - The bottom neck geometry under the joint between the chest and the neck

   - The chest under the joint between the chest and belly pieces

   - The belly under the joint between the belly and waist

   - The pelvis with the root joint

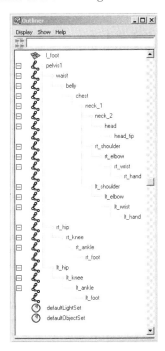

Figure 9.7

A consistent naming scheme for joints makes it easy to keep track of them.

Figure 9.8

Views of the skeleton and geometry hierarchy in the Outliner and the Hypergraph

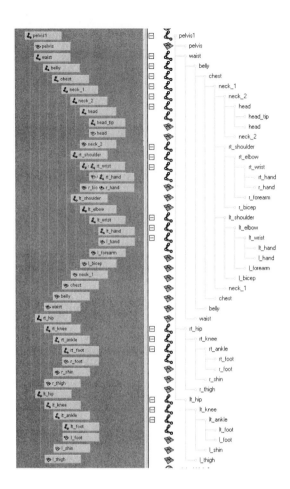

The Block Man: Walk Cycle

A walk cycle is an animation that takes the character through a few steps that can be repeated many times so that the character seems to be taking numerous steps. In a cycle, it is important to make sure the position of the first frame matches the position of the last frame so that when the animation sequence is cycled, there is no "pop" in the motion at that point.

Now try animating this character's walk cycle using FK on the skeleton. You'll find the workflow straightforward, as if you were adjusting positions on a doll.

Load the `block_man_skeleton_v02.mb` file from the Block_Man project on the CD for the properly grouped model and skeleton.

Use the key poses in the following figures to guide you in animating the body as it walks. You'll key at five-frame intervals to lay down the gross animation. You can go back and adjust the timing of the joint rotations in the Graph Editor to make the animation better. The white leg and arm are behind the body, farther from the camera.

This animation is also called *pose* animation because you are posing the character from keyframe to keyframe.

Starting Out: Frames 1 and 5

Figure 9.9 shows the character's starting position. Here you'll set a key for this position and then begin the walk cycle by moving the joints into their second position and keyframing that.

1. At frame 1, set a key for the rotation of all the joints. It's easiest to marquee select all the joints in the Outliner or the Hypergraph. Since you're using pose animation here, you'll need to make sure all the joints are keyframed at every step, even if Auto Keyframe is turned on. Also set a position keyframe for just the pelvis joint.

> A quick way to select all the joints and only the joints is to filter the Outliner view to show only joints. In the Outliner, choose **Show → Objects → Joints**. To reset the Outliner, choose **Show → Show All**.

2. Go to frame 5. Rotate the back leg (the block man's right, white leg) back, and rotate the foot to make it level again. Lower the body (select and move the pelvis joint) to line up the back heel with the ground. This will keep the man on the ground as he goes through the walk cycle, though he won't actually move forward yet.

3. Rotate the near leg (the man's left leg) forward, bend the knee, and pivot the foot up a bit.

4. Rotate the back arm forward, and rotate the near arm back (opposite from the legs). Bend the arms at the elbows.

5. Bend the man forward at the waist, bend neck_1 forward, and tilt the head back up to compensate a little. Figure 9.10 shows the pose at this point.

6. Select everything in the Outliner, and set a rotation key. You're setting a pose for all the joints, which will ensure that all body parts are in synch.

> If you don't key everything every step of the way, some parts of the body will not key with Auto Keyframe properly because the last time they moved may have been two steps previous.

Frame 10

Figure 9.11 shows the position you'll keyframe at frame 10; it's approximately mid-stride for the first leg.

1. Go to Frame 10. Rotate the back leg out farther, and level the foot. Lower the body to place the man on the ground.

2. Rotate the front leg out, straighten the knee, and flatten the foot to place it on the ground. This is mid-stride. Swing the arms in their current direction a touch more. Bend the torso forward some more. Make sure you set a key for all the joints.

Frame 15

Figure 9.12 shows the position you'll keyframe at frame 15. At this point, the character begins to shift his weight to the front leg as it plants on the ground, and the character also begins lifting the back leg.

1. Go to frame 15. Rotate the front leg back toward the body, and raise the body as the man steps to keep the front foot flat on the ground. Rotate the back knee up to lift the foot, and rotate the foot down to make him push off the toe.

2. Start swinging the arms in the opposite direction. Start straightening the torso back up, but bend the head forward a bit.

Frame 20

At frame 20, the man will shift all his weight on the front leg and move his body over that leg, lifting his rear leg to begin its swing out front to finish the stride. Figure 9.13 shows the pose.

1. Rotate the front leg almost straight under the man, and lift up the body to keep the front foot on the ground. Lift the rear leg and swing it forward.

2. Straighten the torso and keep the arms swinging in their new direction. Key all the joints.

Figure 9.9

The character's starting position

Figure 9.10

The second pose (frame 5)

Figure 9.11

The third pose (frame 10)

Frame 25

Now the man will swing his whole body forward, pivoting on the left leg (the dark one) to put himself off center and ready to fall forward into the next step. Figure 9.14 shows the pose.

1. Go to frame 25.
2. Rotate the front (dark) leg back behind the man, and swing the white leg up and ready to take the next step. Lower the body to keep the now rear foot (the dark one) on the ground.

Frame 30

Use Figure 9.15 as a guide for creating the next pose. Notice that it is similar to the pose at frame 10 (in Figure 9.11). As a matter of fact, the only major difference is really which leg and arm are out in front. Everything else should be about the same. You'll want some variety in the exact positions to make the animation more interesting, but the poses are much the same.

Figure 9.12

The fourth pose (frame 15)

Figure 9.13

The fifth pose (frame 20)

Figure 9.14

The sixth pose (frame 25)

Figure 9.15

The seventh pose (frame 30)

Completing the Cycle

You've finished a set of poses taking the character's first step. The next set of poses for your walk cycle will correspond to the first set, only now the other leg and arm correspond to these positions. For example, you animated the left leg taking a step forward in the first series of poses. The next series of poses will have to do with the right leg. The pose at frame 35 corresponds to the pose at frame 15. Frame 40 matches frame 20. You can start a new series of poses with the left leg.

Once a 30-frame section is complete, you will need to return to the animation through the Graph Editor. Adjust all the keyframes that you set at five-frame intervals to make the animation more realistic. Right now you have only the gross keyframes in place, so the timing is off. Your next step is to time the frames properly. This is ultimately a matter of how the animation looks to you.

Logistically speaking, some poses take a little less time to achieve than the evenly spaced five frames you used. For example, achieving the second pose from the start position should take four frames. The third pose (see Figure 9.10 earlier in the chapter) from frame 5 to frame 10 should take four frames. The next frame section originally from frame 10 to 15 (the fourth pose; see Figure 9.11 earlier in the chapter) should also take only three frames. To accomplish this easily, follow these steps:

1. Select the top node of the skeleton (the pelvis), and open the Graph Editor. On the pelvis node in the left side of the Graph Editor, Shift+click the plus sign to open the entire tree of nodes beneath the pelvis. All the animated channels will show their curves to the right.

2. Marquee select all the keyframes beyond frame 1, not including frame 1. Press the W key to active the Translate tool. Shift MM click in the Graph Editor, and drag the keys horizontally to move them all one unit (frame) to the left. The second pose now goes from frame 1 to frame 4.

3. Deselect the keys at frame 4 by holding down the Ctrl key and marquee selecting all the keys at frame 4. Shift drag the remaining selected keys 1 unit to the left. The third pose now goes from frame 4 to frame 8.

4. Deselect the keys at frame 8 and Shift drag the selected keys to the left two frames so that the fourth pose animates from frame 8 to frame 9. Deselect the frame 11 keys, and move the rest over two frames to the left so that the section runs from frame 11 to frame 14. The next section should go from frame 14 to frame 18. The final section should go from frame 18 to frame 22.

5. Continue to set and adjust keys for another cycle or two of the walk. The majority of time spent in animating something like this involves using the Graph Editor to time out the keyframes to make the animation look believable. Also try offsetting some of the arm rotations a frame to the left or right to break up the monotony that arises from having everything keyed on the same frame.

Load the file `block_walk_v01.mov` or `block_walk_v01.avi` of this walk cycle from the images folder of the Block_Man project on the CD to see the animation in motion. It's a rough cycle, and you have to keep adjusting the character's height to keep the feet on the ground. This is where IK comes in handy, as you'll see later in this chapter. Also, the file `block_man_skeleton_walk_v01.mb` in the Block_Man project has the keyframed cycle for you to play with and continue animating.

Walk Cycle Wrap-Up

This walk cycle animation is more about getting comfortable with keyframing and skeletons than it is with creating great walk cycles, so give yourself some time to practice and get better. Animating walk cycles is a good way to hone your animation skills. There are several great books devoted to character rigging and animation alone, and you can research the field for ways to become more proficient. But keep in mind you only need the bare technical essentials to make a good animation. Movement and timing is what makes animation good, not the setup or the model, so keep at this simple way of making a walk cycle to hone your timing skills.

Skeletons: The Hand

For another foray into a skeletal system, you can give yourself a hand—literally. You'll use a skeleton to deform the geometry to animate it as a hand would move.

Load the file `poly_hand_skeleton_v01.ma` from the Poly_Hand_Anim project on the CD. The hand initially looks like this:

You'll use it to create a bone structure to make the hand animate. This is called *rigging*.

Rigging the Hand

To create the first bones of the hand, follow these steps:

1. Maximize the top view window. Switch to the Animation menu set by using the drop-down menu or by pressing F2.

2. Activate the Joint tool by choosing **Skeleton → Joint Tool**. Your cursor will turn into a cross.

3. Click at the base of the wrist to place the first joint. This will be the root joint of the hand.

4. Shift + LM click the bottom part of the palm.

5. Place joints down through the thumb from this second joint according to the corresponding bones in Figure 9.16.

6. To start another string of joints into the palm, press the Up arrow key four times until you're at the second joint at the base of the palm.

Figure 9.16

The joints in the hand

7. The next joint you place will be a branch from this joint. Place that joint in the middle of the palm. Place another joint up farther along the palm, and then branch it out to the index finger. Press the Up arrow key to return to that upper palm joint, and start a new branch into the middle finger. Repeat to place joints for the remaining fingers as shown in Figure 9.16. With these joints placed, you have a simple skeleton rig for the hand. This rig allows you quite a bit of hand and finger movement.

Check the other views (see Figure 9.17), and you'll see you need to tweak your joint positions to fit the hand. Ideally you want the joints to be set inside your intended geometry in the same way that real bones are laid out.

To position the joints, you can use either of two Maya tools: Move or Move Pivot. First you'll try the Move tool. Select the tip joint for the pinkie. It needs to be lowered into the pinkie itself. Select the Move tool (press W), and move it down into the tip of the pinkie. Now move on to the top pinkie knuckle. Notice that if you move the knuckle, the tip will move as well.

It's best to move joints as pivots. Since joints are nothing more than pivots, go into the move pivot mode (press the Ins key) to move joints. Select the top pinkie knuckle joint, and move it with Move Pivot (press Ins) instead. Only the joint moves, and the bones adjust to the new positioning. Set the positions on the remaining joints as shown in Figures 9.18 and 9.19.

Figure 9.17

**Four views of the hand
with initial placement
of the joints**

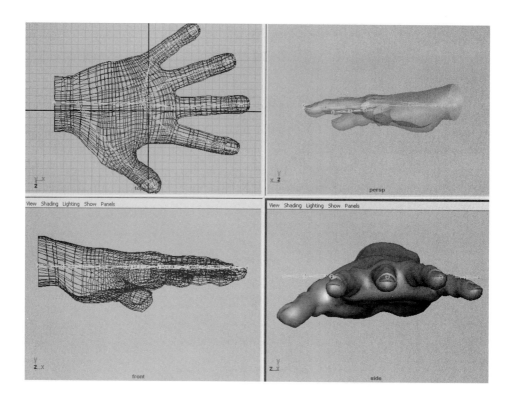

Figure 9.18

**The joints of the hand
placed properly in the
geometry**

Figure 9.19

Second view of the hand's skeleton

Binding to Geometry

An integral part of rigging a character or an object with a skeleton is *binding*, also known as *skinning*. Binding is another way to attach geometry to a skeletal system. Whereas with the block man you directly attached the whole pieces of geometry to the bones through parenting, binding involves attaching *clusters*, or groups of vertices or CVs, of the geometry to the skeleton to allow it to deform the model. This is typically how skeletons are used in character animation work. (For more on grouping and parenting, refer to Chapter 3's exercise on the nine planets.)

The basic technique of binding a character is easy. However, Maya gives you tremendous control over how your geometry deforms.

Binding Overview

Binding is in theory identical to the lattice deformer you saw in Chapter 6. A lattice is attached to an object and exerts influence only on parts of the model, according to the sections of the lattice. Each section affects a NURBS surface's CVs or a polygon surface's vertices within its borders, and as a section of the lattice moves, it takes with it those points of the model.

Skeletal binding does much the same thing. It attaches the model's points to the bones, and as the bones pivot around their joints, the section of the model that is attached follows.

By attaching vertices or CVs (depending on your geometry) to a skeleton, you can bend or distort the geometry. When a bone moves or rotates about its joint, it pulls with it the points that are attached to it. The geometry then deforms to fit the new configuration of the bones bound to it.

You can directly bind geometry to a skeleton in two ways: using Smooth Bind and using Rigid Bind. You can indirectly deform geometry using deformers and lattices attached to skeletons, but here you'll use the direct methods. Figures 9.20 shows a Rigid Bind, and Figure 9.21 shows a Smooth Bind.

Create a tall cylinder, with a span of 16 or more. The more spans you have in the deformable model, the better it will bend. Duplicate the cylinder, and move it over in your window. Now in the front view, create a four-bone (five-joint) skeleton that starts at the bottom of the first cylinder and goes straight up the middle, ending at the tip. Duplicate the skeleton, and move it to the center of the second cylinder.

CREATING A RIGID BIND

A Rigid Bind is the simpler of the two, because only one surface point (vertex or CV) is affected by a joint at a time. A Rigid Bind groups the CVs of a NURBS or the vertices of a polygon into *joint clusters* that are then attached to the bones. No one surface point is influenced by more than one joint.

Thus, bending a model about a joint with a Rigid Bind yields a more articulate crease than a Smooth Bind, which allows more than one joint to affect the CV or vertex, resulting in a more rounded and smooth bend.

To create a rigid bind, select the first skeleton and shift select its cylinder. In the Animation Menu Set, click on **Skin → Bind Skin → Rigid Bind** ❏.

Figure 9.20

Rigid Bind of a cylinder. The crease is pronounced.

Figure 9.21

Smooth Bind of the cylinder shown in Figure 9.20. The crease is smoother, yet less defined.

In the option box, you'll find almost everything you need is already the default. The Bind To parameter lets you Rigid Bind the entire skeleton to the geometry or just the joints selected. Using Selected Joints gives you the option of using just part of a skeleton system to Rigid Bind, giving you flexibility in how your rig affects the model. You'll leave that option on Complete Skeleton to attach the whole thing.

Click the Color Joints check box to set a different color for each joint in the bind, which can make for an easier workflow. The Bind Method parameter deals with how the points in the model will be attached. The default, Closest Point, will organize the points into skin point sets according to which joint they are closest. They are then assigned to be influenced by that joint only.

The Partition Set option lets you define your own points before you bind and select which points are set to which joints. If you define a partition set for each joint you have, Maya then assigns each set to the nearest joint. For example, you can define some points at the top of the surface to be a part of a set controlled by a joint in the bottom part. Closest Point is the best option for most work.

Using the defaults and turning on Color Joints, click the Bind Skin button in the option box. The root of the skeleton is now selected, and the cylinder turns magenta, signifying it has input connections (such as history).

CREATING A SMOOTH BIND

A Smooth Bind allows a joint to influence more than one skin point on the model. This allows for areas of the model farther from the joint to bend when that joint rotates. Joints influence points to varying degrees between 0 and 1 across the surface, decreasing in influence the farther the point is from the joint. The multiple influences on a point all need to add up to 1 across all the joints that influence it. Maya automatically generates the proper influence amounts upon binding, although the animator can change these values later.

To create a Smooth Bind, select the second skeleton and its cylinder, and choose **Skin → Bind Skin → Smooth Bind □**.

In the option box, you'll find the familiar Bind To parameter. You will also find, under the Bind Methods pull down menu, the options Closest Joint and Closest Distance. Choosing Closest Joint assigns the skin points to the nearest joint in the hierarchy. This is most commonly used for character work, because it pays attention to the way the skeleton is laid out.

For example, a surface point on the right leg would not be affected by the thigh joint on the left leg simply because it is near it on the model. Closest Distance on the other hand disregards a joint's position in the hierarchy of the skeleton and simply assigns influences according to how far the point is from the joint.

Max Influences sets a limit on how many joints can affect a single point. Dropoff Rate determines how a joint's influence diminishes on points farther from it. For example, with a Smooth Bind one shoulder joint can influence, to varying degrees, points stretching down the arm and into the chest and belly. By limiting these two parameters, you can control how much of your model is pulled along by a particular joint.

Using all the defaults is typically best. So click Bind Skin in the option box, and your second cylinder will be smooth bound to the bones.

Bend both cylinders to get a feel for how each creases at the bending joints. Figure 9.22 shows the difference.

DETACHING A SKELETON

If you make a mistake or you simply want to do away with your binding, select the skeleton and its geometry and choose **Skin → Detach Skin**. The model will snap to its original shape before the bind was applied and the joints rotated.

You'll find that it's quite common to bind and detach skeletons several times on the same model as you try to figure out exactly the configuration that will work best for you and your animation.

If you find yourself needing to go back to the initial position of the skeleton at the point of binding it to the model, you can automatically set the skeleton back to the bind pose after any rotations have been applied to any of its joints. Simply select the skeleton and choose **Skin → Go to Bind Pose,** and the skeleton and model will snap back into the position they were when you bound them together. It is also best to set your skeleton to bind the pose whenever you edit your binding weights.

Figure 9.22

Rigid and smooth bound cylinders. The smaller cylinder is rigid bound, and the larger is smooth bound.

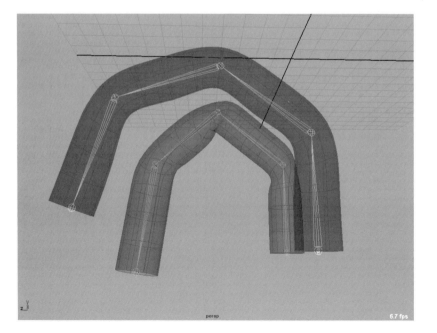

A MODELING TRICK USING A SKELETON

An easy way to create bends and creases in a model is to create the surface without the bend and use a skeleton to deform it the way you want. You can then detach the skin and *bake* the history so that the surface retains its deformation, but loses its connection to the skeleton.

    Bind your geometry to the skeleton chain using Smooth Bind or Rigid Bind. Bend the skeleton to deform the geometry, and then choose **Skin → Detach Skin ☐**. In the option box, set the History parameter to Bake History and click Detach. The model will retain its deformed state, but will lose all connections to the skeleton. This is just like using a nonlinear or lattice deformer on an object and then deleting the object's history to rid it of the deformer. With a detached skin, however, you won't lose any other history already applied to that object, as you would if you deleted history through he Edit menu.

Binding the Hand: Rigid

Since you'll want definitive creases at the finger joints, you'll use a Rigid Bind for the hand.

    Load your hand and positioned skeleton, or use the file `poly_hand_skeleton_v02.ma` from the Poly_Hand_Anim project on the CD. Now follow these steps to Rigid Bind the hand:

1. Select the skeleton's root at the wrist, and Shift+select the top node of the hand. Select the hand's top node, especially in the CD file, to make sure you select the fingernails as well.

2. Choose **Skin → Bind Skin → Rigid Bind ☐**. Turn on Color Joints, and click the Bind Skin button in the option box. You're bound and ready to animate the hand.

3. Select some of the finger joints and rotate them. Notice how the model creases at the knuckles. If you rotate far enough, the model will fold in over itself, especially since this model is polygonal.

Editing a Rigid Bind

Having a Rigid Bind doesn't mean your creases always have to be this hard. With *flexors* (basically a lattice, as seen in Chapter 6), you can smooth out specific areas of a joint for a better look. This becomes useful at shoulder joints or hip joints where a crease like an elbow is not desired. In this case, it will help smooth out the knuckles so the geometry doesn't fold over itself as in the previous graphic.

1. Choose **Skin → Go to Bind Pose** to reset your skeleton.

2. Select the middle knuckle of the index finger, and choose **Skin → Edit Rigid Skin → Create Flexor** to open the option box for Create Flexor.

3. You'll notice that these options are similar to the lattice you created in Chapter 6 to edit the model. You can adjust the number of divisions later through the Attribute Editor, so you don't need to know exactly what you require before you create the flexor. Click Create to display a lattice at the joint position, as shown in Figure 9.23.

4. In the Outliner, drill down to the jointFfdLatticeGroup node now attached under that knuckle joint in the hierarchy. Select the lattice as well as its base so you can adjust the size and, if need be, position of the flexor, just as you did on the lattice work earlier. Resize the flexor so that it better conforms to the knuckle, and elongate it so that it covers more of the finger, as shown in Figure 9.24.

Figure 9.23

Creating a flexor at the middle knuckle

Figure 9.24

Scaling the flexor to fit better on the knuckle

5. Scaling and positioning the flexor (when both lattice and base nodes are selected) will make the joint bend smoother, without affecting more than is necessary. By elongating the flexor here, you smooth out the knuckle's bend and prevent the polygons from bending over each other and still maintain a crisp crease, as shown in Figure 9.25.

6. Create flexors for the other knuckles that will need them. Be sure to scale the flexors to make the most efficient use of them and fit them only where they need to be. Figure 9.26 shows how the finger reacts when bending with flexors at each joint.

Figure 9.25

The knuckle's crease is now sharp, but the geometry does not fold over itself as before.

The scene `poly_hand_skeleton_v03.ma` from the Poly_Hand_Anim project on the CD has the hand rigid bound with flexors on one finger for your reference. Start with it to create flexors for the rest of the fingers, and animate the hand making some sign language positions, grabbing a pencil, or pressing a button.

Figure 9.26

Flexors along the index finger

Binding the Hand: Smooth

Now try skinning the hand with a Smooth Bind.

Load your pre-bound hand or `poly_hand_skeleton_v02.ma` from the Poly_Hand_Anim project on the CD. Now follow these steps to Smooth Bind the hand:

1. Select the root at the wrist and the top node of the hand. Choose Skin → Bind Skin → Smooth Bind.

2. Try rotating some of the knuckle joints to see how the fingers respond. Go back to bind pose when you're done.

3. Rotate the middle knuckle of the index finger down. Notice how the knuckle gets thinner the more you bend the finger there. Go to the top knuckle of the index finger and rotate that joint. Notice that part of the hand moves with the finger. This is again exaggerated because the hand is polygonal, so its deformations seem more severe than a NURBS model of the same hand. Figure 9.27 shows the result of bending at the index finger.

Editing a Smooth Bind

You usually edit a Smooth Bind by *painting skin weights*. Since points on the model are influenced by multiple joints in a Smooth Bind, you will need to adjust just how much influence is exerted by these joints on the same points.

1. Make sure you are in shaded mode (press 5). Select the hand, and then choose Skin → Edit Smooth Skin → Paint Skin Weights Tool ❐.

> You paint skin weights on the affected geometry and not on the joints themselves, so you need to select the model and not the skeleton before invoking this tool.

Figure 9.27

Bending at the index finger causes some unwanted deformation.

2. Your hand should now turn black, with a bit of light gray at the wrist. The option box will appear, listing the joints that are connected to the hand.

3. The color value (between white and black) determines how much the selected joint in the option box is exerting on that part of the geometry. It's best to name your joints properly so that selecting from this window is easier and more intuitive. If you loaded the file from the CD, you'll need to do this to make the scene organized and easier to work with.

You could, however, select the joints in the viewport by RM clicking them.

a. Switch into wireframe mode (press 4). RM click and hold on the top index finger joint to display a marking menu. Drag up to highlight Paint Weights, and that joint will turn cyan and be selected in your Paint Weights tool.

b. Switch back to shaded mode (press 5) to see the influence of that joint on the model.

4. In the option box, make sure the Paint Operation button under the Paint Weights section is set to Replace. Change the Value slider to 0. In the Brush section, the Radius(U) and Radius(L) govern the size of your brush. Make sure the Opacity slider is set to 1.

5. Using the LM, paint the black value around parts of the hand and palm that should not be affected by the index finger bending at its top knuckle, as shown in Figure 9.28.

Skin weights must always be *normalized* in a Smooth Bind, meaning the values have to add up to 1. When you reduce the influence of a joint on an area of the surface, it is automatically shifted to other joints in the hierarchy that have influence over that area, so those joints are now more responsible for its movement.

6. Smooth out the area where it goes from white to black. In the Tool Options window, set Paint Operations to Smooth. Use the RM to smooth the area around the knuckle for a cleaner deformation. Your index knuckle should now bend beautifully.

You can exit the Paint Skin Weights tool by selecting another tool (press W for Translate, for example), and your view will return to regular shaded mode. Try bending the rest of the fingers and painting their influences, and then animate the hand making gestures or grabbing an object using FK animation to set keys on the rotations.

Keep in mind, when you paint weights on polygons, that you will be painting using the UVs. So a polygonal mesh may need you to re-create its UVs with a UV projection map for the Paint Weights tool to function properly, especially when importing and exporting the weight maps from one mesh to another, a procedure you won't encounter till later in your Maya experience.

The scene `poly_hand_skeleton_v04.ma` from the Poly_Hand_Anim project on the CD has the hand smooth bound with painted weights on the index finger for your reference. Try painting the other knuckles as needed for your animation.

THE JOB OF RIGGING

Rigging work is essential to getting a good animation from your model. In a professional shop, it usually falls under the domain of a technical director, who oversees the setup of characters and may also model their geometry. In general, time spent on rigging pays off in easier animation. (It's possible to over-rig a model, creating automation in ways that constrain your flexibility and creativity in animating the model; but if you're just beginning to work with Maya, the risk of that is slight.)

Inverse Kinematics

With IK, you have tools that let you plant a foot where it needs to be, so you're not always moving the skeleton or model to compensate and keep the heel in place.

For legs, IK is nothing short of a blessing. There is no clearly preferable workflow to suggest when dealing with rigging arms and hands, however. Many people use IK on hands as well, but it can be better to animate the legs with IK and animate every other part of the body with FK. IK is best used when parts of the body (such as the feet) need to be planted at times. Planting the hands is not necessary for a walk cycle, and having IK handles on the arms may create additional work while animating them.

Rigging the IK legs

Now it's back to the block man. Switch to that project and load your version or the `block_man_skeleton_v02.mb` file from the Block_Man project on the CD.

You will create an IK chain from the hip to the ankle on each foot. Creating the IK from the hip to the toe will not work as well.

Since IK automatically bends the joints in its chain according to where its end-effector, or IK handle is located, it has to choose which way to bend at a particular joint. To prevent IK from choosing the wrong way, you will first nudge the knees slightly to let the IK solver know which way that joint is supposed to go. Follow these steps:

Figure 9.29

IK handles on both ankles with the roots at the hip joints

1. Select the two knee joints. In pivot mode (press Ins), move the knees a little bit forward to create a slight crook in the leg.

2. Open the IK Handle tool by choosing **Skeleton → IK Handle Tool**. You cursor will change to a cross.

3. Select the start joint for the IK chain. This will be the root of this chain. Click the left thigh joint, and then pick your end effector at the heel joint. Repeat for the other leg. Figure 9.29 shows handles on both ankles.

   If for some reason you can't manage to pick a joint for the IK tool, make sure in your viewport that **Show → Pivots** is turned on. Also, if you have difficulty seeing the handles, you can increase their size by choosing **Display → IK Handle Size**.

4. Move the IK handles around, and see how the legs react. When you're done, reset the IK handle positions.

5. Grab the top joint of the skeleton, the pelvis joint. Move the joint, and the entire body moves with it. Now select both ankle IK handles and set a translation key for them (press Shift+W). Now grab the pelvis joint again and move it. The feet now stick

to their positions on the ground. Move the pelvis down, and the legs bend at the knees. Notice how the feet bend into the ground, though (below left).

6. Move the pelvis back to the origin. You'll now create an IK handle for the foot so that the foot stays flat on the ground. Open the IK Handle tool. For the start joint select the ankle; and for the end-effector, select the joint at the tip of the foot. Repeat for the other foot.

> You can invoke the last tool you used by pressing Y.

7. Set a translate key for the foot IK handles. Move the pelvis down, and the legs bend at the knees and the ankle, keeping the feet flush on the ground (below right).

Creating an IK Walk Cycle

Because the feet will stick to the ground, creating a walk cycle with IK animation will be far easier than using FK. Making the animation look good is still a tough job that requires a lot of practice.

Load `block_man_IK_v01.mb` from the Block_Man project on the CD, or use your own IK-rigged block man with handles at the ankles and feet. The white leg and arm are again on the far side of the character. You'll set keys at every five frames again for the gross animation. To keep this short, you'll just go over setting poses with the feet. You can always return to the scene to add animation to the upper body with FK as you did earlier in this chapter.

1. On frame 1, set translate keys on the pelvis joint and all four IK handles for their start position.

2. Go to frame 5, and move the pelvis forward about 1 unit. The legs and feet will lift up off the ground a bit and strain to keep their position. Lower the pelvis to get the feet flat on the ground again. Set a key for the pelvis. Because Auto Keyframe is turned on, all keys are set for this animation. (With the FK animation, you set keys for everything at every pose.)

3. Grab the near ankle's and foot's IK handles, and move them forward and up to match the following pose (below left).

4. Go to frame 10. Move the front foot forward and plant it on the ground. Move the pelvis another ¾ unit. Set translation keys for the rear ankle and foot handles where they are. Make sure to place the pelvis so that the rear foot is almost flat on the ground. Match the following pose(below middle).

5. Go to frame 15. Move the pelvis another 2 units to center the body over the front foot. Lift the rear ankle and foot IK handles up to bend the knee, and bring the knee up a bit. Match the following pose (below right).

6. Go to frame 20. Move the pelvis forward 1 unit, and swing the white leg forward as in the following pose (below left).

7. Move the pelvis ¾ of a unit forward, and plant the front leg down. Set keys for the rear leg and foot where they stand. Match the following pose (below right).

The next pose should match the pose in frame 10, though with the other leg. Continue the cycle, with each successive pose matching the one 15 frames before it on the opposite side. And don't forget to add FK animation to the top of the body to give your character some weight.

Further Uses for IK Chains

Many animators use IK chains more often in effects animation than in character work. IK chains can drive whips and ropes, flutter flags, bounce pony tails, pump pistons, as well as move legs and arms.

For example, you can use a different type of IK chain, the *spline IK chain,* to control the shape of your bone chain with a NURBS spline. This is great for snakes and other long deforming objects.

To create a spline IK chain, choose **Skeleton → IK Spline Handle Tool**, and then select your top joint and end-effector. Maya will create a spline running the length of the bone chain. Adjusting the curvature of the spline will in turn drive the bones, which in turn drive the geometry bound to them. Figure 9.30 shows a spline curve affecting the curvature of the bones in its spline IK chain.

Basic Relationships: Constraints

As you know, Maya is all about relationships between object nodes. You can create animation on one object based on the animation of another object by setting up a relationship between the objects. The simplest way to do that (outside of grouping) is to create a *constraint*. For example, you can "glue" one object to another's position or rotation through a constraint.

A constraint creates a direct relationship between the source and target object's **Translate** or **Rotate** attributes. This section explores six types of constraints: point, orient, scale, aim, geometry, and normal.

The Point Constraint

To attach a source object to a target object but only have the source follow the position of the target, use a point constraint. This will connect only the **Translate** attributes of the source to the target. To use this method, select the target object(s), and then Shift+select the source object. In the Animation menu set, choose **Constrain → Point □**.

The options allow you to set an offset that will create a gap between the source and the target. Constraints are based on the pivots of the objects, so a point constraint will snap the source at its pivot point to the pivot point of the target. Offset would dictate the distance between their pivots in any of the axes.

You can constrain the same source to more than one target object. The source will then take up the average position between the multiple targets. By setting the Weight slider in the option box, you can create more of an influence on the source by any of the targets.

In Figure 9.31, a cone has been point constrained to a sphere. Wherever the sphere goes, the cone follows. This is different from parenting the cone to the sphere in that only its translations are affected by the sphere. If you rotate or scale the sphere, the cone will not rotate or scale with it.

Although you can now blend keyframe animation with constraint animation in Maya 5.0, as a beginner to Maya animation, consider that once you set a point constraint you should be

Figure 9.30

A spline IK chain is driven by the curvature of a NURBS spline. Adjusting the curve's CVs moves the joints.

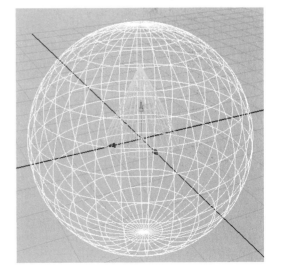

Figure 9.31

A cone point constrained to a sphere follows the sphere's position.

unable to control the cone's **Translate** attributes since they are being driven by the sphere's translations.

Point constraints are perfect to animate a character carrying a cane or a sword, for example. The rotations on the sword are still free to animate, but the sword is attached to the character's belt and will follow the character throughout the scene.

The Orient Constraint

An orient constraint will attach the source's **Rotation** attributes to the target's **Rotation** attributes. Select the target object(s) first, and then Shift+select the source object. In the Animation menu set, choose **Constrain → Orient □**.

The Offset parameter allows you to set an offset in any axis. Otherwise, the source will assume the exact orientation of the target. In the case of multiple targets, the source will use the average of their orientations. Figure 9.32 shows the cone's orientation following an elongated sphere (the target).

A rotation constraint saves a lot of hassle when you have to animate an object to keep rotating in the same direction as another object. For example, if two speedboats are cruising along neck and neck and one turns, the other could turn to match, keeping them both on course. You could also set offsets and animate them to make the second boat look as if it's reacting to the other so that the animation doesn't look too perfect.

The Scale Constraint

A scale constraint will attach the source's **Scale** attributes to the target's **Scale** attributes. Select the target object(s) first, and then Shift+select the source object. In the Animation menu set, choose **Constrain → Scale □**.

Figure 9.32

The cone's rotations will match the sphere's rotations.

The Offset parameter allows you set a scale offset in any axis. Otherwise, the source will assume the exact scale of the target. The source will use the average of the scales of multiple targets. Figure 9.33 shows the cone's scale matching the target sphere.

The scale constraint is good for matching the sizes of objects. For example, if an air hose is inflating a string of balloons, constraining the balloons to one target saves you the hassle of animating all their **Scale** attributes in unison. Or if a cartoon character's eyes are bugging out at something, you can scale constrain one to the other so that both bug out in the same time and proportion.

The Aim Constraint

The aim constraint adjusts the source's rotations so that the source always points to the target object. Select the target object(s) first, and then Shift+select the source object. In the Animation menu set, choose **Constrain → Aim ☐**.

The aim constraint has more options than the other constraints because you need to specify which axis of the source is to point to the target. You do so using the Aim Vector and Up Vector settings.

The Aim Vector setting specifies which axis of the source is the "front" and will point to the target. In the cone and sphere examples, you would set the Aim Vector of the cone to 0,1,0 to make the Y axis the "front" so that the cone's point aims at the sphere. If Aim Vector is set to 1,0,0, for example, the cone's side points to the sphere. Figure 9.34 shows the cone pointing to the sphere with an Aim Vector setting of 0,1,0.

The Offset values will create an offset on the source's **Rotation** attributes, tilting it one way or another. The Up Vector setting specifies which way the cone will face when it's pointing to the sphere.

Aim constraints are perfect for animating cameras to follow a subject, such as a car at a racetrack.

Geometry and Normal Constraints

The geometry and normal constraints will constrain the source object to the surface of the target object (as long as it's a NURBS or poly mesh).

With a geometry constraint, the source object attaches at its pivot point to the surface of the target. It will try to keep its own position as best it can, shifting as its target surface changes beneath it. Again, select the target, select the source object, and choose **Constrain → Geometry**.

Figure 9.33

The cone will now match the sphere's scale.

Figure 9.34

The cone aiming at the sphere

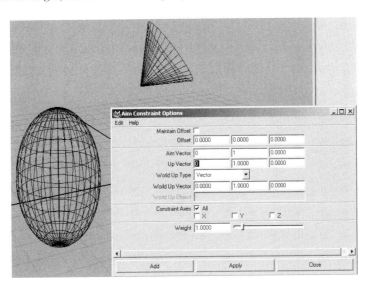

Using a geometry constraint is useful when you want to keep an object on a deforming surface, such as a floating boat on a lake. Figure 9.35 shows the cone after it's been geometry constrained to a NURBS plane that is being deformed by a wave deformer (choose **Deform →** **Create NonLinear → Wave**). The cone will sit on the surface as the waves ripple through, but it will not rock back and forth to stay oriented with the surface.

To get the cone to orient itself so that it truly floats on the surface, you need to use a normal constraint. Using a normal constraint rotates the cone to follow the surface's normals, keeping it perpendicular to the surface.

> A surface normal is an imaginary perpendicular tangent line that emanates from all surfaces to give the surface direction.

The normal constraint is similar to the aim constraint, and its options are similar. Using the Aim Vector setting, you specify which way "is up" for the object to define the orientation that the source should maintain. This setting will not, however, constrain the location of the source to the target. If you want a floating effect, use a geometry and a normal constraint to get the cone to bob up and down and roll back and forth as the waves ripple along (see Figure 9.36).

Figure 9.35

With a geometry constraint, the cone sits on the deforming surface.

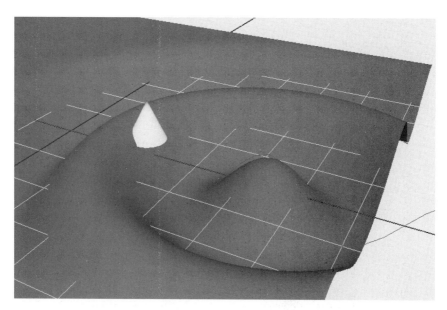

Parent, Tangent, and Pole Vector Constraints

There are three more constraints possible in Maya, and these are the Parent, Tangent, and Pole Constraints. Here is a brief explanation of these three constraints.

Parent Constraint A Parent Constraint constrains an object's translation and rotation to that of another object by mimicking a parent-child relationship, without actually needing to parent the former object under the latter. This constraint is useful in keeping objects aligned together, but without having to actually group them together, and not having to worry about such grouping issues as needing to scale the parent and not the child.

Tangent Constraint A Tangent Constraint keeps an object's orientation so that the object always points along a curve's direction. This constraint is usually used along with a geometry constraint or path animation, to keep the object traveling along a curve pointed in the right direction no matter the direction of the curve.

Pole Vector Constraint When animating with IK, IK handles generate a *Pole Vector* that can be used to keep any joints in the IK chain from flipping around should the joint be rotated beyond 180 degrees of motion. These constraints are used extensively in character animation rigs.

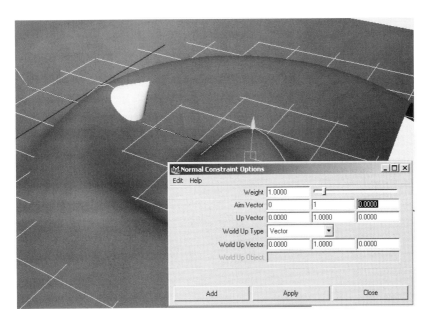

Figure 9.36

The cone now animates to float on the water surface, using both geometry and normal constraints.

Basic Relationships: Set Driven Keys

A favorite feature for character riggers is the set driven key (SDK). A set drive key establishes a relationship for objects that lets you create controls that drive certain features of a character or an object in a scene.

Before you can use an SDK, you must create extra attributes and attach them to the top node of a character. These new attributes drive part of the character's animation. The term *character* is used broadly here. For example, you can set up a vehicle so that an SDK turns its wheels.

Let's start with a simple SDK relationship between two objects. You will create a relationship between a ball and a cone. As the ball moves up in the Y axis, the cone spins in the X axis. As the ball descends, the cone spins back. You will then revisit the hand and setup SDK on the skeleton that animates the model.

Creating a Set Driven Key

To create a simple SDK to make a sphere control the animation of a cone's rotation, follow these steps:

1. Create a NURBS sphere and a cone in a new scene. Move the cone to the side of thee sphere, and lay it on its side.

2. Select the sphere, and in the Animation menu set, choose **Animate → Set Key ❏**. The Set Driven Key window opens with the nurbsSphere1 object selected in the lower half of the window in the Driven section. Its attributes are listed on the right, as you can see in Figure 9.37.

3. You want the sphere to drive the animation of the cone, so you need to switch the sphere to be the driver and not what's driven. Click the Load Driver button to list the sphere in the top half of the window.

4. Select the cone, and click the Load Driven button to display the cone's attributes in the bottom half of the window.

5. In the Driver section, select the sphere's **translateY** attribute. In the Driven section, select the cone's **rotateX** attribute. Click the Key button to set an SDK that essentially

says that when the sphere is on the ground (Y=0), the cone's X rotation is 0 since both attributes are currently 0. The cone's **rotateX** attribute turns orange in the Channel box, meaning a driven key has been set.

6. Select the sphere and raise it up in Y to a height of 5. Select the cone and rotate it in X to 1800 to make it spin properly. Click the Key button in the Set Drive Key window to specify that when the sphere is at a height of 5, the cone's **rotateX** attribute will be 1800°. As the sphere's height increases from 0 to 5, the cone spins from 0 to 1800 in X.

Figure 9.37

The Set Driven Key window

An Advanced Set Driven Key: The Hand

Automating some animations on a character is indispensable to an animator. This can't be truer than setting up an SDK for hand control. After you model and bind a hand to a skeleton, you're ready for an SDK.

Open the scene `poly_hand_skeleton_v05.ma` from the Poly_Hand_Anim project on the CD, or use your own file that has the hand and its skeleton and is bound (either smooth or rigid) to the skin. Your file should not have animation, though. Set your hand to the bind pose before you begin.

Creating a New Attribute

First, you'll create a new attribute called **index_pull** to control a contracting finger.

1. Select the hand. (It's best to select the top node instead of just the poly mesh of the hand.) In the polySurface2 tab of the Attribute Editor, click the Extra Attributes section. For now, at least, this section is empty.

2. In the Attribute Editor menu, choose **Attributes → Add Attribute** to open the Add Attribute window, which is shown in Figure 9.38. In the Attribute Name field, enter **index_pull**. Be sure that the Make Attribute Keyable check box is checked and that the Float option is selected in the Data Type section. In the Numeric Attribute Properties section, set Minimum to 0, set Maximum to 10, and set Default to 0. Click OK.

Figure 9.38

The Add Attribute window

After you click OK, the Index_pull slider appears in the Attribute Editor and the Channel box. This attribute alone will control the entire index finger.

Assigning the Set Driven Key

To set up the relationships with the SDK, follow these steps:

Figure 9.39

The Set Drive Key window for the hand

1. With the top hand node selected, open the Set Driven Key window (choose **Animate →** **Set Key ❏**). Click Load Driver to specify that the hand drive the animation.

2. Since you're animating the index finger pulling back, you'll want to drive the rotations of the top three knuckles. Shift+select all three knuckles on the index finger. Click the Load Driven button. All three knuckles will appear on the bottom.

3. Select the hand's **index_pull** attribute and the three knuckles' **rotateY** attributes, as shown in Figure 9.39.

4. With the rotations of the knuckles at 0 and the **index_pull** attribute at 0 as well, click the Key button to set the first relationship. When **index_pull** is at 0, the finger will be extended.

5. Select the top hand node, and set the **index_pull** attribute to 5.

6. Select the fingertip's knuckle (joint11 in the CD file), and rotate it in Y to 20. Select the next joint up the chain (the middle knuckle, joint10), and rotate it to 35 in the Y axis. Select the final index knuckle (joint9), and rotate it in the Y axis to 5. Click the Key button. When the **index_pull** attribute is at 5, the finger will assume this bent position.

7. Select the top hand node, and set **index_pull** to 10.

8. Select each of the three knuckles. Set the tip to rotate to 65 in Y. Set the middle knuckle to 60. Set the last knuckle to 50. Click the Key button to see the result shown in Figure 9.40.

Select the top hand node, and change the value of the **index_pull** attribute to animate your finger. All you need do to pull the finger is to set keys on that attribute, without having to constantly rotate the knuckles. Furthermore, you can setup a single SDK to control the bending of all the fingers at once, or one SDK for each finger for more control.

Open the scene `poly_hand_skeleton_v06.ma` from the Poly_Hand_Anim project on the CD, to see the hand with the SDK setup on the index finger.

Summary

The true work in animation comes from recognizing what to do in the face of certain tasks, and how to approach their solutions. Maya offers a large animation toolset, and the more you become familiar with the tools, the better you'll be able to judge which tools to use in your work. Don't stop where this chapter does; experiment with the rest of the features not covered here and see what happens.

Animation is about observation and interpretation. The animator's duty is to understand how and why something moves and to translate that into their medium without losing the movement's fidelity, tenacity, or honesty.

Only through observant and patient eyes will you be able to see the essence of motion. Learning to remember and represent that motion is the art of animation. And you, as the artist, drive that art, not the medium and not the tool.

Figure 9.40

The bent index finger

Beginners' Gallery

On the following pages, you will find a combination of images by new Maya artists, as well as some images from the book to inspire your own creativity as you become more familiar with 3D in general and Maya specifically.

Some of these artists have been using Maya for only a short period of time, and already they've been able to use the tools and techniques they've learned to channel their artistic eye and creativity into some beautiful and interesting imagery.

This **Still Life** was modeled and textured by Maya students Juan Guitierrez and Robert Jauregui. The fruit still life was modeled by Guitierrez using mostly polygons. The textures were created by Jauregui, who took this opportunity to learn all about UV texture space and mapping polygons, since this was his first texturing experience inside Maya. Dariush Derakhshani laid out the scene, lit it, and rendered it to show off Maya's rendering and lighting capabilities.

ABOVE: The **Pool Table** was modeled by Victor Garza to demonstrate modeling techniques to an introductory Maya class and to show the students how to be creative in putting surfaces together to form a complex object. Once Garza modeled the table, he and Dariush Derakhshani textured and lit the scene for photorealism. **BELOW:** Dariush Derakhshani created this box full of **Marbles** to test out mental ray for Maya and its capabilities. The scene is made of very simple geometry, with the majority of the work going into lighting and rendering using mental ray for Maya.

Mahyar Abousaeedi and Ed Chen had two years of experience with Maya when they created the animation **Free Radicals**. All objects are NURBS models and the textures were created using a combination of UV and projection maps. Texturing, shading, lighting, and rendering were done with Renderman 11, and the compositing and focus-blur effects were created in Shake.

ABOVE: This is from artist Alexander Hupperich's short film **Dragon**. Using polygons in Maya, he modeled half of it at a relatively low poly count, mirrored the geometry, then edited one side to add a more lifelike asymmetry. **BELOW:** This robot was created as part of a short film called **Dronez**. First, Hupperich drew some concept sketches and Manuel Macha did the modeling. Because this was a hard surface model with no deformations or organic feeling, they used a mixture of polys, NURBS, and subdivision surfaces. Hupperich, graduated from The German Film School in February, 2003. You can see his work at www.huppi.de.

Megan E. Orosz modeled **Grieg** using a NURBS patch and stitch technique (which allowed for an even distribution of Maya Fur over the surface of the character). Rigging was based on anatomical pictures of the Devon Rex and the eyes are three separate pieces: a glossy outer globe, a ramp-shaded inner globe, and a black half circle for the iris. Orosz had been using Maya for a year and a half at the time she created the animation. Orosz created Grieg for the animated short **Eddie**, which can be seen at www.motoons.net.

ABOVE: Maya's Paint Effects allow you to create effects like plants and **Flowers** quickly and easily to be used in your environments. Dariush Derakhshani created this image as an example in **Chapter 12** to illustrate how you can create grass and flowers using a few strokes of Maya's different preset grass and flower brushes. **BELOW:** Ed Anderson created this **Golden Spider** with simple geometric shapes in Maya . The spider web consists of lofted circles with soft bodies applied. Anderson rendered out each light separately and composited in Photoshop. The body has a hair texture map and Maya's Fur applied to it.

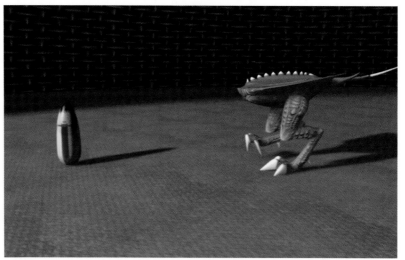

ABOVE: The head, **Me**, by Victor J. Garza, was modeled 9 months after Garza first opened the Maya software package. He used NURBS to model the head because NURBS gives a great organic feel. For the hair and facial hair he used Maya's poly tools to get a sharp edge on the geometry. **BELOW:** This image is from an animated short by Kamal Katami called **The Alpha Beast**. Katami modeled in polygons, and then converted to subdivisions, using the original polys for texturing. He used three texture maps for his main character: a color map, a bump map, and a diffuse map. The environment and lights were a separate file that was imported into each scene.

CHAPTER 10

Maya Lighting

Light shapes the world by showing us what we see. It helps create a sense of depth, it initiates the perception of color, and it allows us to distinguish shape and form. And this reality of light needs to be as faithfully reproduced in CG as possible for a successful scene. The trick is learning to see light and its astonishing effects on the world around us. Topics include:

- **Basic Lighting Concepts**
- **Maya Lights**
- **Adding Shadows**
- **Lighting Effects**
- **Tips for Using and Animating Lights**

Basic Lighting Concepts

It is no surprise that Maya's lighting resembles actual direct lighting techniques used in photography and filmmaking. Lights of various kinds are placed around the scene to illuminate the subjects of the scene as they would for a still life or a portrait. Your scene and what's in it dictate, to some degree at least, what lights you put where. And choosing the *type* of lights to be used depends on the desired effect.

At the most basic level, you want your lights to illuminate the scene. Without lights, your cameras have nothing to capture. Although it seems rather easy to throw your lights in, turn them all on, and render the scene, that couldn't be further from the truth.

Lighting is the backbone of CG. Although it is technically easy to insert and configure lights, it is *how* you light that will make or break your scene. And that really only comes with a good deal of experience and experimentation, as well as a good eye and some patience.

This chapter will familiarize you with the basic techniques of lighting a scene in Maya and start you on the road to finding more.

Learning to See

There are so many nuances to the real-world lighting around us that we take them for granted. We intuitively understand what we see and how it's lit and infer a tremendous amount of visual information without much consideration. With CG lighting, you must re-create these nuances for your scene. That amounts to all the *work* of lighting.

The most valuable thing you can do to improve your lighting technique is to re-learn how you see your environment. Simply put, refuse to take for granted what you see. Question why things look the way they do, and you'll find the answers almost always come around to lighting.

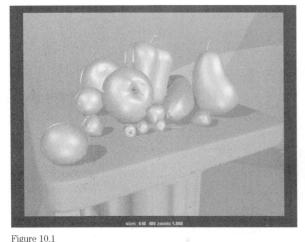

Figure 10.1

An over-lit still life

Figure 10.2

An under-lit still life

Take note of the distinction between light and dark in the room you're in now. Notice the difference in the brightness of highlights and how they dissipate into diffused light and then into shadow.

When you start understanding how real light affects objects, you'll be much better equipped to generate your own light. After all, the key to good lighting starts with the desire to simply create an interesting image.

What Your Scene Needs

Ideally, your scene will need areas of highlight and shadow. Over-lighting a scene will flatten everything and diminish details. This is perhaps the number one mistake of beginners. Figure 10.1 shows a still life with too many bright lights, which only serve to flatten the image and remove any sense of color and depth.

Similarly, under-lighting your scene will make it *muddy*, gray and rather lifeless, as well as cover your details in darkness and flatten the entire frame. Figure 10.2 shows the still-life under-lit. The bumps and curves of the mesh are hardly noticeable.

Finding a good middle ground to lighting your scene is key. Like a photographer, you want your image to have the full range of exposure. You want the richest blacks to the brightest whites in your frame to create a deep sense of detail. Even though you may not have an absolute black to white in the rendered image, the concept is appealing. As in Figure 10.3, light and shadow complement each other and work to show the features of your surface.

Three-Point Lighting

Since your scene needs to be rendered, and lighting can be a fairly heavy computational process when it comes to rendering, there is the added task of keeping your lighting efficient. That means not using dozens of lights for every part of the scene.

The traditional approach to efficiently lighting an object, culled from filmmaking and television, starts with *three-point lighting*. In this setup, three distinct roles are used to light the subject of a shot. More than one light may be used for each of the three roles, but the scene should in effect seem to have only one primary, or key, light, a softer light to fill the scene, and a back light to pop the subject out from the background.

Three-point lighting ensures that the primary subject's features are not just illuminated, but featured with highlights and shadow. Using three different directions and qualities of light creates the best level of depth. Figure 10.4 shows a schematic of a basic three-point setup.

Figure 10.3

Balanced lighting creates a more interesting picture.

Figure 10.4

A three-point lighting schematic

Key Light

A *key* light is placed in front of the subject and off to the side to provide the principal light on the subject. Since it is usually off center, the key light creates one side of brighter light, increasing the depth of the shot. This light also provides the primary shadows and gives the important sense of lighting direction in the shot.

Although it is possible for several lights to fulfill the role of key light in a scene, for example, three ceiling lights overhead, one light should dominate, creating a definitive direction. Figure 10.5 shows the subject being lit by only a key light, although it is physically composed of two lights.

The direction of the two lights remains the same, and one takes intensity precedence over the other and casts shadows. The effect creates a single key light, which produces a moody still life.

Fill Light

A more diffused light than the key light, the fill light seems directionless and evenly spread across the subject's dark side. This serves to fill the rest of the subject with light and decrease the dark area caused by the key light.

The fill light is not meant to cast any shadows onto the subject or background itself and is actually used to help soften the shadows created by the key light. Figure 10.6 shows the still life with an added fill light. Notice how it softens the shadows and illuminates the dark areas the key light misses.

Figure 10.5

Key light only

Figure 10.6

A fill light is now included.

Typically, you place the fill light in front of the subject and aim it so that it comes from the opposite side of the key light to target the dark side of the subject. Even though the still life in Figure 10.6 is still a fairly moody composition, there is much more visible than with only the key light in Figure 10.5.

Back Light

The back, or rim, light is placed behind the subject to create a bit of a halo, which helps to pop the subject out in the shot. Thus, the subject has more presence against its background. Figure 10.7 shows how helpful a back light can be.

Figure 10.7

A back light pops the subject right out.

The back light serves to bring the fruit in this still life out from the background and add some highlights to the edges, giving the composition more focus on the fruit.

Don't confuse the back light with the background light, which lights the environment behind the subject.

Using Three-Point Lighting

The three-point lighting system is used for the primary subject of the scene. Since it is based on position and angle of the subject to the camera, a new setup is needed when the camera is moved for a different shot in the same scene. Three-point lighting is therefore not scene specific, but shot specific.

Once the lighting is set up for the subject of a shot, the background must be lit. Use a directed primary light source that matches the direction of the key light for the main light, and use a softer fill light to illuminate the rest of the scene and soften the primary shadows.

Practical Lighting

Practical lighting is a theatrical term describing any lights in a scene that are cast from lighting objects within the scene. For example, a desk lamp on a table in the background of a scene would need practical lighting when it's on. You never want the practical lighting to interfere with the main lighting of the scene, unless the scene's lighting is explicitly coming from such a source.

Each light-emitting object in your CG scene doesn't necessarily need its own Maya light. Rendering tricks such as *glow* (for glow effects; see the "Lighting Effects" section later in this chapter) can simulate the effect that a light is turned on, without actually having to use a Maya light. Of course, if you need the practical light to illuminate something in the scene, you need to create a light for it.

Maya Lights

Six types of light are available in Maya: Ambient, Directional, Point, Spot, Area, and Volume. How you use each dictates whether they become key, fill, or rim lights. Each light can fill any of those roles, although some are better for some jobs than others. The most commonly used light types for most scenes are Spot, Directional, and Ambient.

To create each light, choose **Create → Lights** and click the light type.

Figure 10.8

A typical light's Attribute Editor

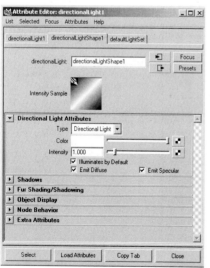

Common Light Attributes

Lights in Maya are treated as any other object nodes. They can be transformed, rotated, scaled, duplicated, deleted, and so forth and are visible as nodes in the Hypergraph and Outliner alongside other objects in the scene. Like any other node, lights have attributes that govern how they function. Figure 10.8 shows the Attribute Editor for a typical light.

When you select any light type and then open the Attribute Editor, you'll see the following attributes and options.

Type This drop-down menu sets the type of light. You can change from one light type to another (for instance, from Spot to Point)at any time.

Color This attribute controls the color cast by the light. The darker the color, the dimmer the light. You can use **Color** in conjunction with **Intensity** to govern brightness, although it's best to leave that to Intensity only.

Figure 10.9

Lighting renders can be separated for greater control later.

Full render   Diffuse only render   Specular only render

Intensity This attribute specifies how much light is cast. The higher the intensity, the brighter the illumination.

Illuminates by Default This check box deals with light linking, or the ability to illuminate specific objects with specific lights. Clearing this check box causes the light to not illuminate all objects by default. Keep this check box checked unless you are linking lights to specific objects. This book will not cover light-linking workflow.

Emit Diffuse and Emit Specular These two check boxes are not available with the Ambient light type. For all other light types, they toggle on or off the ability to cast diffuse lighting or specular highlights on an object. This is useful for creating specific render passes to give you precise control of your final image. For example, turning off Emit Diffuse will cast only specular highlights in your scene. This, once rendered, would be a highlight pass that can be separately adjusted and then composited on to your final image. You'll find more on this later this chapter. Figure 10.9 shows how you can separate renders to better control lighting details when the image is composited back together.

Figure 10.10

Ambient light

Light Types

Beyond the common light attributes, each light type carries its own attributes that govern its particular settings.

Ambient Lights

Ambient lights cast an even light across the entire scene. These lights are great for creating a quick, even illumination in a scene, but as you can see in Figure 10.10, they run the risk of flattening the composition. They are perhaps best used sparingly and at low intensities as fill lights or background lights.

Figure 10.11

A low Ambient Shade setting flattens the image.

Ambient Shade = 0.1   Ambient Shade = 1.0

The *Ambient Shade* slider in the Attribute Editor governs how flat the lighting will be. The lower the value, the flatter the lighting. Figure 10.11 shows the effect of two contrasting Ambient Shade settings.

Directional Lights

Directional lights cast a light in a general direction evenly across the scene (see Figure 10.12). These lights are perhaps second to Spot lights as the most commonly used light type. They are perfect for sunlight or general indoor lighting, for key lights, and for fill and back lights. They give a perfect sense of direction without having to come from a specific source.

Point Lights

A Point light casts light from a single specific point in space, similar to a bare lightbulb. Its light is spread evenly from the emission point (see Figure 10.13).

Figure 10.12

Directional light

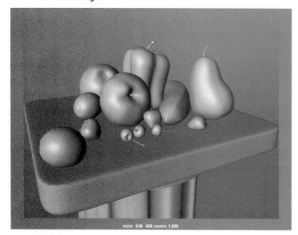

Using the **Decay Rate** drop-down menu in the Attribute Editor, you can set how a Point light's intensity diminishes over distance. With No Decay, the Point light will illuminate an object far away as evenly as it does up close. This is the most common setting for most applications.

Setting the Decay Rate to **Linear**, **Quadratic**, or **Cubic** will require you to exponentially increase the intensity level to compensate for the decay. You can use decay rates settings to illuminate nearby objects and to leave distant ones unaffected. In reality, lights have decay rates. But in CG, they don't really need to unless the falloff effect is called for (as in Figure 10.14). Clever lighting can easily avoid this cumbersome calculation.

Figure 10.13

A Point light placed in the front right of frame

Figure 10.14

A Point light with a decay rate set

Point lights are good for effects such as candlelight or mood setting.

Spot Lights

Spot lights are arguably the most often used lights in Maya because they can be used for keys, fills, or rims; and they are highly efficient,, casting light in specific areas, just like a real spotlight.

Similar to a Directional light, Spot lights emphasize direction. But these lights, unlike directionals, emit from a specific point and radiate out in a cone shape, whereas a directional emits from an infinite source from a certain direction. As such, Spot lights can create a circular focus of light on the geometry much like a flashlight on a wall, whereas directionals spread the light evenly. Figure 10.15 shows a Spot light on the still life.

The following attributes govern the behavior of Spot lights.

Decay Rate Specifies that the light's intensity falls off with distance, as with the Point light. Again, the intensity needs to increase exponentially to account for any decay.

Cone Angle Sets the width of the cone of light emitted by the spotlight. The wider a cone, the more calculation intensive it becomes.

Penumbra Angle Specifies how much the intensity at the edges of the cone and hence the circular focus dissipate. (See Figure 10.16.) A negative value softens the light into the width of the cone, decreasing the size of the focus; a positive value softens away from the cone.

Figure 10.15

Using a Spot light

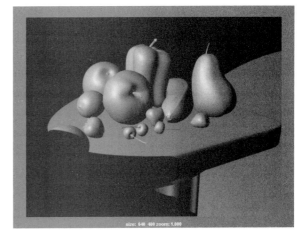

Figure 10.16

The Penumbra Angle attribute controls the softness of the edge of a spotlight.

Penumbra = 0   Penumbra = -10   Penumbra = 10

Dropoff Specifies how much light is decayed along the distance of the cone. The higher the dropoff, the dimmer the light gets farther along the length of the cone. This effect is much better to use than a decay rate and gives similar results.

Most practical lights are created with Spot lights. For example, a desk lamp's light is best simulated with a Spot light. Spot lights are also the lights of choice to cast shadows. You'll find more on shadows later in the chapter.

Area Lights

Area lights emit light from a flat rectangular shape only (see Figure 10.17). They behave similarly to Point lights except that they emit from an area and not from a single point. You can still set a decay rate, just as you can with Point lights. Area lights are the only lights whose scale affects their intensity. The larger an area light, the brighter the light.

Since you can control the size of the area of light being emitted, these lights are good for creating effects such as a sliver of light falling onto an object from a crack in a door, as in Figure 10.18, overhead skylights, or the simulation of large diffused lighting fixtures such as some overhead office lights. Use Area lights when you need to light a specific area of an object.

Figure 10.17

An Area light and its placement

Volume Lights

Volume lights (see Figure 10.19) emit light from a specific 3D volumetric area as opposed to an area light's flat rectangle. Proximity is important for a volume light, as is its scale.

A Volume light can have the following attributes,

Light Shape A Volume light can be in the shape of a sphere, a box, a cylinder, or a cone. You select a shape from the Light Shape drop-down menu.

Color Range This section of attributes sets the color of the light using a built-in ramp. The ramp (from right to left) specifies the color from inside to outside. For instance, a white to black ramp from right to left creates a white light at the center of the Volume light that grades down to black toward the outer edge.

Volume Light Dir This attribute sets the direction for the light's color range. Outward lights from inside out, Inward lights from the volume's edge in to the center, and Down Axis lights as a gradient in an axis of the light.

Figure 10.18

An Area light as a sliver and its placement

Figure 10.19

A Volume light and placement

Arc and Cone End Radius This attribute defines the shape for the volume.

Penumbra For cylinder and cone shapes, this attribute adjusts how much the light dims along the edge of its length.

Use Volume lights when you need to control the specific area in which light is cast or when you need an object to move into and out of a particular area of light. Volume lights are also great for creating volumetric lighting effects such as areas of lit fog. For volumetric effects, see the "Volumetric Lighting" section later in this chapter.

Lighting a Scene

It's best to start with just a couple of light types such as Directional and Spot, before turning to the more sophisticated types such as Area and Volume.

Getting the essence of lighting is far more important in the beginning than understanding the nuances of all the attributes of a light. At first, limit yourself to spots and directionals with the occasional ambient use.

Adding Shadows

Don't be too quick to create an abundance of light in your scene, eager to show off your models and textures. Shrouding objects in darkness and shadow is just as important as revealing them in light. You can say a lot visually by not showing parts of a whole, leaving some interpretation to the audience.

A careful balance of light and dark is important for a composition. As Figure 10.20 shows, the reality of a scene is greatly increased with the simple addition of well placed shadows. Don't be afraid of the dark. Use it liberally, but in balance.

Figure 10.20

Darkness and shadow help create a sense of reality, depth, and mood to an otherwise simple still life

Figure 10.21

Directional light with Depth Map shadows render faster and usually are detailed enough.

Creating Shadows in Maya

Maya lights do not cast shadows by default; you need to enable this feature in the light's Attribute Editor. When you do that however, lights can cast shadows in one of two ways, depending on how the scene will be rendered.

The more common way of the two methods to create shadows is by using Depth Map Shadows. Once you enable shadow maps (by clicking the Use Depth Map Shadows checkbox in the Shadows area of a light's Attribute Editor), Maya generates shadow maps that locate where shadows fall by following the path of the light backward from the lighted object to the light itself. Shadow maps create fast accurate shadows through Maya's renderer. See the next section on how to create Shadow Map shadows.

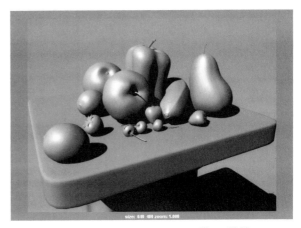

Figure 10.22

Directional light with Raytraced shadows produce more detailed shadows, but slower renders.

The second method to cast shadows is achieved by *raytracing* with Maya's software renderer. With raytracing enabled in the Render Globals window and raytracing shadows enabled for each light, you can create *raytraced shadows*. See Chapter 11 for more on rendering.

Raytracing involves tracing a ray of light from every light source in all directions and tracing their reflection to the camera lens. Thus, you can create more accurate shadows with raytracing. However, this render takes significantly longer to calculate. See later this chapter on how to create raytraced shadows.

Only in cases where you want a soft and diffused shadow or a very sharp and crisp-edged shadow is needed will you need to turn on raytraced shadows. See Figures 10.21 and 10.22.

Figure 10.23

Turning on shadow maps in the Attribute Editor for a Directional light

Shadow Map Shadows

You can turn on shadow maps for every light type except Ambient through the light type's Attribute Editor, as shown in Figure 10.23.

The **Dmap Resolution** defaults at 512. The higher this resolution, the better defined the shadows. Figure 10.21 was rendered with a **Dmap Resolution** of 4096, a relatively high value. Figure 10.24 is the same render with a **Dmap Resolution** of 768. Most shadows will be detailed enough with a **Dmap Resolution** of 1024.

Now, directional lights are not the best lights to use for detailed shadow map shadows because they require a high resolution; however, their raytraced shadows are extremely well done, as shown in Figure 10.22, earlier in this chapter.

Figure 10.24

The Dmap Resolution setting affects shadow quality for shadow maps.

Figure 10.25

Spot lights cast faster and more detailed shadow map shadows.

Spot lights create shadow maps with greater accuracy at lower **Dmap Resolution** settings and faster render times. As such, spots are preferred to directionals for shadow-casting lights. Figure 10.25 shows the same render with a Spot light and a **Dmap Resolution** setting of only 1024, ¼ the size of the Directional light's **Dmap Resolution**.

Trying to squeeze a detailed shadow map from a Directional light with an absurdly high **Dmap Resolution** setting may crash your system. In these cases, it is wiser to use a Spot light. If a Spot light cannot be used (for example, when an even Directional light is needed instead), use raytraced shadows.

Raytraced Shadows

Figure 10.26

The Spot light shown in Figure 10.25 but now with raytraced shadows

To enable raytraced shadows, turn on the light's **Use Ray Trace Shadows** setting in the Attribute Editor (see Figure 10.23) and enable raytracing in the Render Globals window. Choose **Window → Rendering Editors → Render Globals** or click the Render Globals icon ( ) in the Status line.

Figure 10.26 shows the Spot light from Figure 10.25, this time rendered with a raytraced shadow in Figure 10.26. Notice that there is not much difference in the renders. This shows how well you can detail spot shadow maps; and again, the rendering time is less than with raytraced shadows.

For an object that has a transparency map applied to its shader, however, only raytraced shadows can cast proper shadows. On the left in Figure 10.27 is a plane with a mapped checkerboard transparency casting a raytraced shadow over the still life. On the right is the same light using shadow maps instead of raytraced shadows.

Figure 10.27

Only raytraced shadows work with transparencies.

Raytraced Shadow   Shadow Map Shadow

Controlling Shadows per Object

You can specify whether an object can cast and receive shadows in Maya to better control your lighting. For example, if you have geometry in front of a shadow casting light, but you do not want it to cast a shadow, you can manually turn that feature off for that object only.

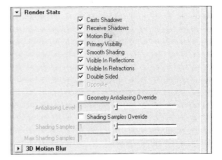

To turn off shadow casting for an object, select the object and open its Attribute Editor. In the Render Stats section is a group of check boxes that control the render properties of the object. Clear the **Casts Shadows** check box. If you do not want the object to receive shadows, clear the **Receive Shadows** check box.

Lighting Effects

In CG, you must fake certain traits of light in the real world. Using certain methods, you can create smoky light beams, glowing lights, and lens flares. Although some of these effects fall under the domain of rendering and shader tricks, they are best explored in the context of lighting; they are indeed created by light in the real world.

Volumetric Lighting

How do you create an effect such as a flashlight beam shining through fog? This lighting effect is called *volumetric lighting,* and you can use it to create some stunning results, which can sometimes be time-consuming to render.

You cannot apply volumetric effects to Ambient and Directional light types. To add a volumetric effect, select the light, and in the Attribute Editor under the Light Effects section, click the checkered map button to the right of the **Light Fog** attribute. This will create a new render node that will appear in the Hypershade and Multilister windows. Once you click the Map button, the Attribute Editor will take you to the lightFog node.

Fog Spread = 0.5   Fog Spread = 2.0

The way Maya handles volumetric lights is to attach a lightFog node to the light. The **Color** and **Density** attributes under this node control the brightness, thickness, and color of the fog attached to that light. Furthermore, in the light's Attribute Editor, you can control the fog with the **Fog Spread** and **Fog Intensity** settings. **Fog Intensity** will increase the brightness of the fog, and **Fog Spread** controls how well the fog is defined within its confines. For example, a spotlight with a fog will show the fog in its cone. Figure 10.28 shows how spread affects the conical fog shape.

> To remove a fog effect, right-click the Light Fog label in the light's Attribute Editor and choose Break Connections from the context menu.

If you want the light fog-cast shadows to make rays of light within the fog, simply turn on Shadow Maps for the light. You will have to increase the **Dmap Resolution** for a higher-quality image.

Lens Flare

Lens flare and *light glow,* illustrated in Figure 10.29, mimic the real-world effect created when light strikes a lens or when the light source is visible in the frame. The flare is created when the light hits the lens at a particular angle and causes a reflection of itself in the optics of the lens.

To enable a light glow, under the Light Effects section in the light's Attribute Editor, click the checkered map button next to the **Light Glow** attribute to create an OpticalFX node that will appear in the Hypershade and Multilister. The Attribute Editor will shift focus to that new node, which will control the behavior of the light glow and lens flare. The OpticalFX node will contain the following attributes and settings:

Glow Type Setting this attribute specifies the kind of glow: Linear, Exponential, Ball, Lens Flare, and Rim Halo. These define the size and shape of the glow from the light.

Halo Type Specifying a halo will create a foggy halo around the light in addition to the glow. Controls for the halo can be found under the Halo section in the Attribute Editor.

Star Points Setting this attribute specifies the number of star points the glow generates.

Rotation Setting this attribute rotates the orientation of the star points.

Radial Frequency Used in conjunction with the **Glow Radial Noise** attribute (see the next item) in the Glow section, this attribute defines the smoothness of any added glow noise.

Glow Radial Noise Setting this attribute adds noise to the glow effect, creating light and dark patches within the glow for a more random look.

Figure 10.29

Light glow and lens flare turned on for the back light

Glow Radial Noise = 0   Glow Radial Noise = 0.5

Glow Color Setting this attribute specifies the color of the glow.

Glow Intensity and Spread Setting these attributes specifies the brightness and thickness of the glow and how well it fades away.

To turn on a lens flare along with the light glow, simply click the **Lens Flare** check box at the top right in the Attribute Editor for opticalFX. The attributes under the Lens Flare section will control the look of the flare.

Light glows and flares can be highly effective in scenes, adding credibility to the lighting, but they are often misused or, worse, overused in CG. Used sparingly and with subtlety, lens flares can go a long way toward adding a nice touch to your scene.

Shader Glow Effects

To create a glowing effect, it is sometimes better to place a glow on a geometry's shader instead of the light itself. Since a light must be seen in the shot and pointed at the camera to see any light glow and flare, a shader glow is sometimes more desirable. This process will composite a glow on the object assigned the glow shader to simulate a volumetric light such as a street lamp on a foggy night. Shader glows have far less render cost than true volumetric lights.

Try This: To light a still-life scene, follow these steps:

1. Open the `still_life_v03.mb` file in the Lighting project on the CD. Create a spotlight, place it over the still life, and aim it directly down onto the fruit. Turn on **Shadow Maps** for the light, and set Dmap Resolution to 1024. Set **Penumbra Angle** to 10 and **Intensity** to 1.5. Press 7 for lighted mode in the *Camera1* view panel to see how the light is being cast.

2. The spotlight will provide the practical light in the scene. You will place a bare bulb on a wire directly above the fruit. Create a NURBS sphere and position it right over the fruit, but in the frame for *Camera1* to see. In the Render Stats section of the Attribute Editor for the sphere, turn off **Casts Shadows**.

3. Create a long, thin cylinder for the lightbulb's wire, and position it as if the bulb were hanging from it. Turn off **Casts Shadows** for it as well.

4. Create a black PhongE shader to assign to the cylinder.

5. Create a Phong shader for the bulb and assign it to the NURBS sphere. Set its **Color** to a pale, light yellow, and make it about 50% transparent.

6. Select the spotlight and set its **Color** to the same yellow. You can do this easily through the Color Chooser. With the shader for the bulb selected, open the Color Chooser by clicking the pale yellow color you just made. Click the right arrow to place the yellow color in the swatches to the right of the main color swatch, or RMB click any of the swatches.

7. Now pick the spot light, and click its **Color** attribute to set the Color Chooser to that color. Simply LMB click the yellow swatch you created to get the same color on the light. For detail's sake, make the light's color less saturated. Click Accept to close the Color Chooser window.

8. To make the shader glow for the bulb, open the Hypershade and select the bulb's Phong material. In the Attribute Editor, in the Special Effects section, drag the **Glow Intensity** slider from 0 to 1.0. If you render the frame, you'll see the glow not quite enough to

make it a convincing lightbulb yet. In the Hypershade, select the shaderGlow1 node. This node controls all the glows in the scene.

9. Set the **Quality** to 0.1. In the Glow section, set **Glow Intensity** to 6.0, set **Glow Spread** to 0.5, and set **Glow Radial Noise** to 0.2.

The scene file `still_life_v04.mb` contains the full scene for your reference. See Figure 10.30 for the final result.

Further Practice

The best way to learn about lighting is to light some scenes.

The file `still_life_v01.mb` in the Lighting project on the CD contains the scene of the still life with no lights for you to play with lighting and shadow methods. The file `still_life_v02.mb` contains the same scene, but with three-point lighting already set up.

Notice in the `still_life_v02.mb` file that two lights make up the key light (spotLight1 and spotLight2). One light makes up the fill light (directionalLight1), and two lights (spotLight3 and spotLight4) make up the back light.

Tips for Using and Animating Lights

When lighting a scene, invoking a lighting mode in your perspective or camera view panel will give you great feedback on the relative brightness and direction of your lights. Most computer system's graphics cards can handle a maximum of eight lights in lighted mode, with some professional cards increasing this capability.

You invoke lighted mode by pressing the number 7 on your keyboard (not through the number pad on the side). You must first be in shaded mode (press 5) or texture mode (press 6) for lighted mode.

Figure 10.30

The bare lightbulb over the still life is created with a shader glow.

Maya's IPR render is also useful when lighting a scene. This almost real-time updating renderer will give you a high-quality render of your scene as you adjust your lights. Chapter 11 will explore the IPR renderer.

Animating a Light

Any attributes of a light can be animated in the same way that you animate any other object attribute. You cannot, however, animate a light's type. To edit a light's animation, you need only select the light and open the Graph Editor to access its keyframes. You can set keyframes on **Intensity**, **Penumbra Angle**, **Color**, and so on within the Channel box or the Attribute Editor. Right-click the name of the attribute, and choose Key Selected from the context menu.

> By animating a light's intensity, you can simulate the real-world appearance of a light turning on or off. To turn on a light, create a quickly increasing curve so that its brightness arcs up slowly at first before climbing to full brightness. This animation better mimics the way real lights turn on and off than simply enabling or disabling them in your scene.

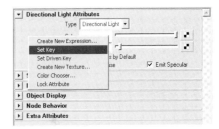

Animating the color of a light, as well as the color for a shader, will set keyframes for the color's RGB values as three separate keyframes. The Graph Editor will show a separate curve for the red, green, and blue channels of color when you animate a light's color. You can set all three keys at once by right-clicking the color attribute in the Attribute Editor and choosing Set Key from the context menu.

In addition, lights can be animated to be moved, scaled, and rotated like any other object.

Using the Show Manipulator Tool for Lights

An easy way to manipulate lights is to use their special manipulator (invoked by pressing T). For example, pressing T (or clicking the Show Manipulator icon [ ] in the toolbox) to select the Show Manipulator tool with a spotlight selected will give you two translate manipulators in the view panel.

This will allow you to move the source or target of the light to better aim it. By clicking the cyan circle that appears below the source's translate manipulator, you can toggle through a number of manipulators to adjust the spotlight's settings such as cone angle (two clicks clockwise) and penumbra angle (three clicks clockwise). The manipulator for cone angle is shown here.

A source and target translate manipulator is available for all the light types through the Show Manipulator tool as well.

Summary

Lighting is truly the linchpin of CG. It can make or break a scene with the flick of a switch. Lighting goes hand in hand with rendering and shading, and the more you understand about all three functions, the better your scenes will look.

As mentioned before, the trick to lighting is understanding how light works in reality and how to approximate its effects in Maya. That comes with practice, so don't be afraid to experiment with lighting and shading schemes on all your projects.

CHAPTER 11

Maya Rendering

Rendering is the last step in creating your CG work. It is the process by which the computer calculates the surface properties, the lighting and shadows, and the movement and shape of objects and saves a sequence of images. Although the computer does all the thinking at this point, you still need to set up your cameras and the render to get exactly what you want.

This chapter will show you how to render out your scene using Maya's software renderer and how to create reflections and refractions and will introduce you to Maya's other rendering methods. In this chapter, you will use the wine bottle and still life from previous chapters and animate a camera to render out a sequence.

- **The Rendering Setup**
- **Previewing Your Render**
- **Reflections and Refractions**
- **Using Cameras**
- **Motion Blur**
- **Batch Rendering**
- **Rendering the Wine Bottle**

The Rendering Setup

When your scene is complete and you're ready to start a render, you'll need to set up how you want it rendered. Although this is the last part of the CG process, in some way it should have been in your thinking all along. If you create models and textures with the final image in mind and gear the lighting toward showing off the scene with elegance, the final touches are relatively easy to set up.

First, you need to decide which render engine you will use: Maya Software (the most common), Maya Hardware, mental ray for Maya, or Maya Vector. Each engine renders differently and yields different results entirely. The choice of rendering methods depends on your final look.

Some steps in the creation of your scene, from modeling to lighting, will depend on which render engine you plan to use. It is therefore best to choose your render engine as you begin creating your scene.

> You will render most scenes using the Maya Software renderer. All illustrations and examples in the previous chapters were rendered using Maya Software.

The Render Global Settings

Regardless of the type of render, you need to specify a set of common attributes in the Render Global Settings window. As shown in Figure 11.1, you use the options in this window to set up all your rendering preferences, including the resolution, file type, frame range and so forth. Choose **Window → Rendering Editors → Render Globals** to open the Render Global Settings window.

The Render Global Settings window has two tabs: the Common tab and a tab for the rendering method being used (Maya Software, Maya Hardware, mental ray, or Maya Vector). The Common tab contains the settings common to all the rendering methods.

Choosing a Filename

Rendered images are typically identified by a filename, a frame number, and an extension, in the form `filename.####.ext`, for example, `stillife.0234.tif`.

In the File Name Prefix text box, enter the image sequence name. If you don't enter anything in this text box, Maya automatically names your rendered images after your scene file (`stillife` in the example). When dealing with numerous scene files, this is the preferred naming convention; using it, you can immediately identify the scene file from which a particular image file was rendered.

The frame number portion of an image sequence name (`0234` in the example) identifies which frame in the sequence the image represents. In the Frame/Animation Ext drop-down list box, select name.#.ext to render out a sequence of files. If you leave this setting at the default of `name.ext`, only a single frame will render, no matter the animation range in the Time Slider.

> Name.#.ext is perhaps the most commonly used convention as opposed to name.ext.# or name.# because it allows you to identify the file type easily in Windows. While Macintosh OS X is not as picky about the order of number and extension, most Mac compositing software (like AfterEffects and Shake) wants file names that end in the three-letter extension. Therefore it is best for both Mac and Windows to use the name.#.ext format.

The extension portion of the image name is a three-letter abbreviation for the type of file you are writing to disk. By specifying in the Frame/Animation Ext drop-down list box that you want an extension appended to each image filename, you ensure that you can identify the file type.

Image Format

In the Image Format drop-down list box, select the type of image file you want to render. Maya then adds the appropriate extension to the filename.

You can save your images in a wide range of formats. The format you choose depends on your own preference and your final output needs. For example, JPEG (Joint Photographic Experts Group) files may be great for the small file sizes preferred on the Internet, but their color compression and lack of alpha channel (a feature discussed later in this chapter) make them undesirable for professional film or television production work.

It's best to render a sequence of images rather than a movie file for a couple of reasons. First, you would want your renders to be their best quality with little to no image compression. Second, if a render fails during a movie render, you must re-render the entire sequence. With an image sequence, however, you can pick up where the last frame left off. The best file type format to render to is TIFF (Tagged Image File Format). This format enjoys universal support, has little to no compression, and supports an alpha channel. Almost all image-editing and compositing packages can read Targa and TIFF formatted files, so either is a safe choice most of the time. Also, the SGI (Silicon Graphics Image) and Maya IFF (Maya Image File Format) formats are good, though some image editors may not be able to load them without a plug-in. For more on image formats, see Chapter 1.

Figure 11.1

The Render Global Settings window

Frame Range

Choosing the frame range ensures that your entire animation is rendered out. Maya defaults to the range 1–10, which you may often need to change to render your entire sequence. If you still have the **Frame/Animation Ext** attribute set to name (Single Frame), the frame range text boxes will be grayed out. You must choose a naming convention other than name (Single Frame) first.

Once you have selected a naming convention other than `name (Single Frame)`, enter the **Start Frame** and **End Frame** attributes for part of the sequence or the entire sequence. These attributes are also helpful if you need to render parts of the sequence at different times. By specifying new start and end frames, you can render different portions of a sequence or pick up where a previous render left off.

The **By Frame** attribute specifies the intervals at which the sequence will render. For example, if you want to render only all the odd-numbered frames, set the **Start Frame** attribute to 1, and set the **By Frame** attribute to 2. If you want to render only even-numbered frames, set the **Start Frame** attribute to 2 and set the **By Frame** attribute to 2. And so on. Typically you leave the **By Frame** attribute set to 1 so that Maya renders each frame. In certain cases, such as in previsualization work, it may be necessary to render only every second or third frame instead.

The **Frame Padding** attribute has to do with the way an operating system, such as Windows or Mac OS X, orders its files by inserting leading zeros in the frame number. If the **Frame Padding** attribute is set to 2, for example, a single zero precedes every single-digit frame number in the filename. In this case, frame 8 is `name.08.tif` as opposed to `name.8.tif` (which is set to a padding of 1). If the **Frame Padding** attribute is set to 4, the filename contains three leading zeros, and thus frame 8 is `name.0008.tif`.

Figure 11.2

Images rendered without frame padding (left). Frame padding makes file sequences easier to organize (right).

Large sequences of files are much easier to organize if they all have a frame padding of at least 3. They will be much easier to see in a file browser such as Windows Explorer and will be ordered properly. The upper part of Figure 11.2 shows an image sequence without padding, and the lower part shows the same sequence with padding. Notice that the files without padding are not in numeric order. Because rendering can generate a large number of files, it's important to be able to manage them efficiently.

Image Channels

Image files are composed of red, green, and blue channels. Each channel specifies the amount of that primary additive color in the image. (See Chapter 2 for more on how computers define color.) In addition, some file formats can also save a fourth channel, called the alpha channel. This channel defines the transparency level of the image. Just as the red channel defines how much red is in an area of the image, the alpha channel defines how transparent the image is

when layered or composited on another image. If the alpha channel is black, the image is perfectly see-through. If the alpha channel is white, the image is opaque. The alpha channel is also known as the matte. An object with a transparency will render with a gray alpha channel, as shown in Figure 11.3.

The alpha channel is displayed in the Render View window. As discussed later in this chapter, your test-renders also display in this window.

Figure 11.3

This wine bottle's transparency renders with a gray alpha channel.

> To view an image's alpha channel in the Render View window, click the Display Alpha Channel icon. To reset the view to RGB (full-color view), click the Display RGB Channels icon.

Select the channels you want to render by clicking the check boxes shown here.

Most renders will have RGB as well as alpha channels selected, so leave the RGB Channel

(Color) and the Alpha Channel (Mask) check boxes checked at all times. Note, however, that JPEG, GIF (Graphics Interchange Format), and Windows bitmap files do not support alpha channels regardless of whether the Alpha Channel (Mask) check box is checked.

> Only a few file formats, such as Maya IFF, support the depth channel. This grayscale channel resembles the alpha channel, but conveys depth information, that is, the distance of an object from the camera. The Depth Channel (Z Depth) setting is typically used when compositing images.

Setting Resolution

The **Resolution** attribute sets the pixel size of the image to be rendered. In the Resolution section of the Render Global Settings window, you can select a resolution from the Presets drop-down list box. The commonly used resolution for professional broadcast is 720 × 486 NTSC (National Television System Committee), which appears as CCIR 601/Quantel NTSC in the Presets list. To composite Maya CG into a home shot DV (digital video) movie, you use the standard DV resolution of 720 × 480 to render your scene, but you must enter that resolution manually in the Width and Height fields. (For more on resolutions, see Chapter 1.)

The **Device Aspect Ratio** and **Pixel Aspect Ratio** attributes adjust the width of the image to accommodate certain professional output needs; you need not adjust them here.

> Make sure your **Pixel Aspect Ratio** attribute is set to 1 before you render unless you need to render CCIR 601/Quantel NTSC for broadcast needs; otherwise, your image may look squeezed or widened in comparison with any live-action footage you composite into.

The higher your resolution, the longer the scene will take to render. Doubling the resolution may quadruple the render time. With large frame sequences, it's advisable to render tests at half the resolution of the final output or less to save time.

Besides the image resolution, the image quality of a render also dictates how long a render will take. In addition to turning down the resolution of for a test, you can also use a lower-quality render. Each rendering method has its own set of quality settings, which are explained in the following section.

Selecting a Render Engine

New with Maya 5 is the ability to select a render engine in the Render Global Settings window. Although Maya Software is commonly used for most applications, the other rendering methods give you flexibility in choosing a final look for your project.

Maya Software

Maya Software, the default software rendering method, can capture just about everything you would want in your scene, from reflections to motion blur and transparencies. You will find that almost all your Maya projects will render through the software rendering method, although you can use it in a couple of ways.

USING RAYTRACING

Raytracing, a topic introduced in Chapter 10, is used to incorporate two optical effects into a rendering that the default software rendering method cannot handle. Raytracing literally traces rays of light from each light source to every object in the shot and then traces the light's reflection from the object to the camera's lens. This allows true *reflections* and *refractions* to appear in the render, as well as highly defined shadows. (For more on shadows, see Chapter 10.)

Since the default software renderer renders the same image without true reflections or refractions and can generate detailed shadows with shadow maps, the only reason to use raytracing is for reflective and refractive surfaces as well as raytraced shadows.

True Reflections   True reflections occur when every object (other than those with reflections explicitly turned off through the Render Stats setting in the Attribute Editor) in the scene reflects in the reflective surface. Although it is possible to simulate reflections in Maya Software using *reflection maps*, true reflections can only be generated through raytracing. (In Chapter 9, the axe project shows how to apply reflection maps.)

As with raytraced shadows, raytraced reflections need to be enabled. To do so, click Raytracing in the Raytracing Quality section of the Maya Software tab in the Render Global Settings window. Unlike raytraced shadows, however, raytraced reflections need not be explicitly turned on through the lights.

As soon as raytracing is enabled, any reflective surface will receive a true reflection of the objects and environment in the scene. Even objects with reflection maps will reflect in other objects. For more on reflection maps, see the "Reflections and Refractions" section later in this chapter.

Refractions   Refractions occur when light bends as it passes through one medium into another medium of different density. For example, a pencil in a glass of water will appear to be broken. The light bouncing off the pencil refracts as it travels from the water into the air, bending a bit during the transition. That displaces the view of the pencil under the water, making it seem broken.

RENDER QUALITY

With software rendering, the render quality depends most noticeably on *anti-aliasing*. Anti-aliasing is the effect when pixels appear to blur together to soften a jagged edge on an angled line. Increasing the anti-aliasing level of a render produces an image that has smoother angles and curves. The Render Global Settings window contains presets that specifies this level and a few others to set the quality of your render.

1. In the Render Global Settings window, make sure Maya Software is selected in the Render Using drop-down list box, and click the Maya Software tab.

2. In the Anti-Aliasing section, select either Preview Quality or Production Quality from the Quality Preset drop-down list box.

The upper image in Figure 11.4 shows the fruit still life from Chapter 10 rendered with the Preview Quality preset; the lower image shows the same image with the Production Quality preset.

Figure 11.4

With Preview Quality (left) the edges of the fruit are jagged. With Production Quality (right) the jaggedness is gone.

Of course, the higher the quality, the longer the render time. As you become more experienced, you will be better able to balance uncompromised quality with efficient render times.

Maya Hardware

The hardware rendering method uses your graphic card's processor to render the scene. Hardware renders are similar to what you see when you play a 3D video game. The data output by the game is fed directly into the graphics pipeline of your hardware setup and is rendered on-the-fly as you play.

This results in much faster render times, but does lack some of the features and quality you get from a software render. In Figure 11.5, the top image shows the wine bottle from Chapter 10 as rendered through hardware. The render time is blazingly fast, but the quality suffers. The lower image shows the software render of the same frame.

Using Maya Hardware is a good way to test-render a scene before a final render and still see near-final results. However, since only a few professional video cards fully support Maya's hardware rendering method, this book relies on software rendering.

To specify hardware quality, select a level from the Samples drop-down list box in the Render Global Settings window.

Figure 11.5

The hardware-rendered wine bottle (left) lacks some subtleties. The software-rendered wine bottle shows better specularity and surface detail (right).

mental ray for Maya

The mental ray for Maya rendering method lets you emulate the behavior of light even more realistically than the other rendering methods. Based on raytracing, mental ray takes the concept further by adding photon maps to the light traces. That is, it projects photons from lights and records their behavior. The end result allows the phenomena of light *caustics* and *bounce,* also known as *radiosity* and *global illumination.*

Caustics is the scattering of light reflections off and through semitransparent objects, such as the light that shines on the ceiling of an indoor pool or the sunshine at the bottom of an outdoor pool. Global illumination is the effect of light reflected from one object to another. For example, if you place a red ball inside a gray box and shine a light into the box, the walls and floor of that box appear slightly red. The light from the ball reflects onto the walls and tints them with its color. Also, the light from the floor of the box bounces and helps illuminate the underside of the ball.

For example, the Figures 11.6 and 11.7 show a scene file that has a dozen or so glass spheres inside an enclosed box. The box has four holes in the top, and two spotlights with shadows turned on are positioned outside the box, shining in through the holes. Figure 11.6 shows a typical software render. The spheres under the holes are visible, and the rest of the box is in shadow.

However, rendering through mental ray for Maya (see Figure 11.7), the light that enters the box bounces around the scene and illuminates the other spheres. The color of the spheres also colors the area immediately around them due to global illumination. Additionally, the light shines through the semitransparent spheres and casts caustic highlights on the floor. (You'll see the full effect in the color section of this book.)

Figure 11.6

The Maya Software render of the box of spheres scene

Figure 11.7

The mental ray for Maya render of the scene in Figure 11.6

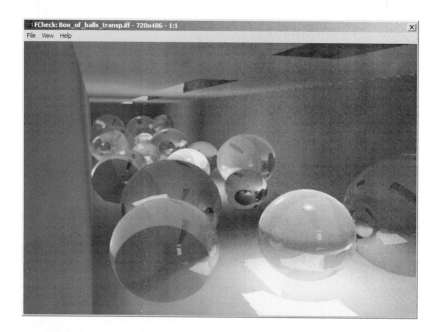

Figure 11.8

The fruit still life as a vector render

The mental ray for Maya renderer is a truly advanced and intricate rendering language and will not be covered aside from this overview. It is primarily used for renders that require a highly sophisticated lighting look, and to use it you need to be experienced with lighting and rendering.

Maya Vector

Vector rendering, new to Maya 5, lets you render your objects with an illustrated or cartoon look. You can render "ink" outlines of your characters to composite over flat-color passes. Figure 11.8 shows the fruit still-life scene rendered with Maya Vector.

Maya Vector can output animated files in Macromedia Flash format for direct use in web pages and animations, as well as Adobe Illustrator files and the usual list of image formats. To specify the attribute settings for Maya Vector, you use the Maya Vector tab in the Render Global Settings window (see Figure 11.9).

In the Fill Options section, click the Fill Objects check box and select the number of colors for each object to set the look of the render. If you want the renderer to include an outline of the edges of your geometry, in the Edge Options section click the Include Edges check box and set the line weights.

Previewing Your Render: The Render View Window

The Render View window automatically opens when you test-render a frame. To open it manually, choose **Window → Rendering Editors → Render View**. Your current scene renders in the Render View window. Figure 11.10 shows the important icons in this window.

Redo Previous Render Renders the last-rendered view panel.

Render Region Renders only the selected portion of an image. To select a portion of an image, click within the image in the Render View window and drag a red box around a region.

Open Render Globals Window Opens the Render Global Settings window.

Display RGB Channels Displays the full color of the image.

Display Alpha Channel Displays only the alpha matte of the render as a black-and-white image.

Display Real Size Resets the image size to 100% to make sure the image displays properly. When the Render View window is resized or you select a new render resolution, the image renders to fit the window, the image is resized if need be. If your render looks blocky, make sure the Render View window is displaying at real size before adjusting the options in the Render Global Settings window.

Select a Renderer Lets you select the rendering method. This is the same as selecting it in the Render Global Settings window.

Figure 11.9

The Maya Vector rendering settings

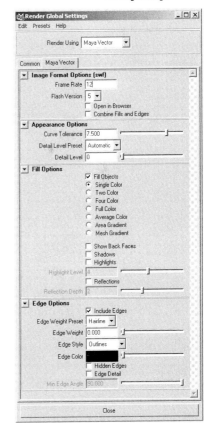

Figure 11.10

The Render View window

Saving/Loading an Image

Although you typically use the Render View window to test a scene, you can also use it to save single frames by choosing **File → Save Image** to save in all Maya's supported image formats. Likewise, choose **File → Open Image** to display any previously rendered image file in this window. If your task in Maya is to create a single frame, this is the best way to render and save it.

Keep/Remove Image

The Render View window is a prime place to see adjustments to various parts of your scene. You can store images in its buffer by clicking the Keep Image icon. When you do, a scroll bar appears at the bottom of the window, and you can scroll through any saved images. This is handy for making a change, rendering it, and scrolling back and forth between the old saved image and the new render to make sure the change is to your liking. You can store a number of images in the buffer. For a faster way to preview changes, use IPR rendering.

IPR Rendering

A fast way to preview changes to your scene is to use Maya's IPR (Interactive Photoreal Rendering). After you IPR render a view panel, specify the region you want to tune by dragging a box around that area of the image in the Render View window. Maya updates that region every time you make a shader or lighting change to the scene. Figure 11.11 shows the fruit still life as an IPR render as the color and specular levels are being fine-tuned.

IPR is perfect for finding just the right lighting and specular levels. It will not, however, register any raytracing elements such as refractions or true reflections. But overall, IPR quality is close to that of a full software render while still allowing you to watch your tuning in real time. As it's used to fine-tune textures and lighting, IPR will not register shifts in the Timeline or changes to the geometry.

Reflections and Refractions

You can either map or raytrace reflections. As you saw in Chapter 9, it is rather simple to create a reflection map for an object. Simply assign a Phong, PhongE, Blinn, or Anisotropic material to your object and make sure the **Reflectivity** attribute is greater than zero. Then click the the Reflected Color map button to add a texture or a file as a map to create the reflection. (See the axe project in Chapter 7 for more on reflection maps and shaders.)

Figure 11.11

IPR rendering lets you fine-tune your textures and lighting with near real-time feedback.

To generate true reflections, however, you will need to enable raytracing. Mapping textures to the reflected color is not necessary when raytracing is enabled, as Maya will simply reflect any objects in the scene that fall in the proper line of sight.

Raytraced Reflections

To enable raytraced reflections, simply use a material with a **Reflectivity** attribute such as a Phong, and open the Render Global Settings window. Choose Maya Software, and in the Maya Software tab, click the Raytracing check box in the Raytracing Quality section.

The sliders control the quality of the render by specifying how many times to reflect or refract for any given object. Setting Reflections to 2, for example, enables an object's reflection in a second object to appear as part of its reflection in a third object.

The top image in Figure 11.12 shows the still life reflecting onto the surface of its table. In this case, Reflections is set to 1. If you increase Reflections to 2, however, you'll see the reflections of the pieces of fruit in each other also reflecting in the surface of the table. Notice the difference in the reflections of the fruit in the table between the two renders.

Each shader also has a setting to limit the number of reflections for the objects assigned to it. This allows you to increase the number of reflections on a per shader basis, as needed. Raytraced reflections can consume valuable render resources and time, so it's a good idea to make your scene efficient. You don't want to reflect more than necessary.

To access a shader's reflection limits, select the shader in the Hypershade and open the Attribute Editor. In the Raytrace Options section, drag the Reflection Limit slider to set the maximum number of reflections for that shader. The lower of this value or the Reflections value in the Render Global Settings window will dictate how many reflections are rendered for every object attached to that shader. The default shader reflection limit is 1, so make sure you change the Reflections value as well as each shader's value if you want more than one level of reflection.

Figure 11.12

(Left) Reflections set to 1. (Right) Reflections set to 2.

Furthermore, you might want some objects not to cast reflections in a scene with ray-traced reflections. To specify that an object does not cast reflections, select the object in a Maya panel and open the Attribute Editor. In the Render Stats section, clear the Visible In Reflections check box.

Rendering Refractions

Refractions are also a raytraced-only ability. Refractions require than an object be semitransparent so that you can see through it to the object(s) behind it that are being refracted. To control refractions, you use the shader.

To enable refractions, select the appropriate shader in the Hypershade, and open the Attribute Editor. In the Raytrace Options section, click the Refractions check box. Now you need to set a refractive index for the shader and a refraction limit, similar to the reflection limit.

The refractive index must be greater or less than 1 to cause a refraction. Typically, a number within 0.2 of 1 is perfect for most refraction effects. The top image in Figure 11.13 is raytraced with a refractive index of 1.2 on the wine bottle and glasses; the lower image has a refractive index of 0.8 on both bottle and glasses.

You can specify whether an object is visible in a refracting object by clicking or clearing the Visible In Refractions check box in the Render Stats section of the object's Attribute Editor.

Using Cameras

Cameras capture all the animation fun in the scene. In theory, Maya's cameras work in the same way as real cameras. The more you know about photography, the easier these concepts are to understand.

The term *cameras*, in essence, refers to the perspective views. You can have as many cameras in the scene as you want, but it's wise to have a camera you're planning to render with that is placed to frame the shot and not moved and another camera to act as the perspective work view that you can move around your scene as you work. The original persp panel fits that role well, though it can be used as a render camera just as easily.

Figure 11.13

(Left) Refractive index of 1.2. (Right) Refractive index of 0.8.

You can also render any of your work windows to test-render orthogonal views of your model the same way you render a perspective view.

Creating a Camera

The simplest way to create a new camera is to choose **Panels → Perspective → New**. This creates a new camera node in Maya and sets that active panel to its view.

You can select a camera and transform it (move it, rotate it, scale it) just as you would select and transform any other object in Maya to be animated or just positioned. Furthermore, you can move a camera and rotate it using the Alt key and mouse button combinations.

For example, click inside a new Maya scene perspective window to make it active. Select that view's camera by choosing **View → Select Camera**. The camera's attributes appear in the Channel box. Try moving the view around using the Alt key and mouse button combinations. Notice how the attributes change to reflect the new position and rotation of the camera. You can animate the camera—for example, zoom in or out or pan across the scene—by setting keyframes on any of these attributes.

Camera Types

You can create three types of cameras for your scene: single-node, two-node, and three-node.

Single-node cameras are the most common. This camera consists of a single camera node that you move and rotate as you would any other object for proper positioning.

Two-node cameras are made up of the camera node and an aim node. You use the aim node to point the camera as opposed to rotating it to orient it properly. This is useful for animating a camera following an object. You animate the movement of the aim node to follow your object like a car around a race track. The camera pivots to follow its aim point and, hence, the object.

The three-node camera has a camera node, an aim node, and an up node. The additional up node is to orient the camera's up direction. This gives you the ability to animate the side-to-side rotation of the camera as well as its aim direction.

The persp panel's camera is a single-node camera. To create any of these cameras, choose **Create → Cameras** and then choose the type of camera. You can also change the type of a camera at any time through the Attribute Editor.

Camera Attributes

As an example, load the `still_life_render_v02.mb` scene from the Lighting project on the CD. You'll see a green box in the persp panel that displays the resolution (set to 640 × 480) and the name of the camera (camera1).

Special attributes control the function of camera nodes. To set these attributes, follow these steps:

1. With your camera1 camera selected, open the Attribute Editor (press Ctrl+A or choose View → Camera Attribute Editor).

2. At the top of the window, select the type of camera controls you want. The **Controls** attribute sets the type of camera from single- to two- to three-control nodes. Figure 11.14 shows Attribute Editor for the camera.

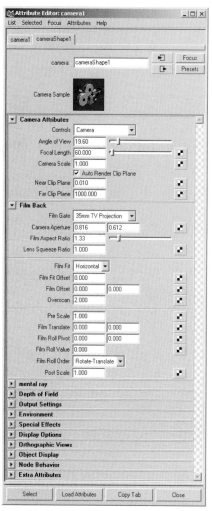

Figure 11.14

The Attribute Editor for the camera

Focal Length

The **Focal Length** attribute specifies the length of the lens. The lower the focal length (a.k.a. short lens), the wider the view. At very low numbers, however, the image will be distorted, as you can see in the comparison in Figure 11.15. The higher the focal length, the closer the subject seems to the camera.

Although adjusting the **Focal Length** attribute of a camera zooms in and out, it is not the same as moving the camera closer to your subject using the Alt+RM and MM procedure to zoom in view panels. Focal length zooming can create optical distortions such as can be created with a fish-eye lens. It is best to animate the camera to truck in and out to zoom in a scene rather than animate the focal length.

When you want to animate your camera getting closer to the subject of your shot, it's best to animate the camera and not the focal length. However, if you need to match some CG element in Maya to a photograph or video you've imported as an image plane, set your camera's focal length to match that of the real camera used for the background.

Clipping Planes

All cameras in Maya have clipping planes that restrict the amount of information that can be seen through that camera. The clipping plane is defined by the **Near Clip Plane** and **Far Clip Plane** attributes. These set the minimum and maximum distance, respectively, of the clipping plane. Any object or portion of an object that passes beyond these distances will not show in the window and should not render.

Focal Length = 35   Focal Length = 8   Focal Length = 60

Figure 11.15

Different focal lengths

If you notice objects disappearing as you move your camera and create a scene, it may be because of the clipping plane. Increase the **Far Clip Plane** attribute, and the objects should reappear in the view.

Film Back

The **Film Back** attributes concern the type of output you'll be dealing with once your renders are finished and you're ready to put your animation on tape, DVD, film, or what have you.

Film Gate Defines the aspect ratio of your camera's view. Most images that are output to television have an aspect ratio of 1:1.33, exemplified by the 35mm TV Projection selection in the Film Gate drop-down list box. (For more on aspect ratios, see Chapter 1.)

Film Fit When set to Overscan, lets you resize the view without changing the film gate that will render. For example, the scene on the left is set up with an Overscan setting of 1.3, allowing you to see more than what will render, which is defined by the outline box. The scene on the right is set up with an Overscan setting of 2, which increases how much you see in the camera1 panel but does not change the view when rendered.

You can turn the green box in the panel on and off through the Attribute Editor for the camera. In the Display Options section are Display Film Gate and Display Resolution check boxes. Ideally, these two green boxes should align perfectly in the view pane. If the resolution box (the solid green line) does not line up with the film gate box (the dashed green

line), change your film gate selection to match the resolution's aspect ratio in the Render Global Settings window. A resolution of 640 × 480, for example, has an aspect ratio of 1.33, the same as the 35mm TV Projection film gate currently selected for this scene.

Environment

In the Environment section you will find attributes to adjust the background color that renders and to create an image plane. As you saw in the axe-modeling project in Chapter 4, importing image planes can help improve your scene.

In Chapter 4, you imported a drawing of an axe by choosing View → Image Plane → Import **Image** in the persp panel. You can also import an image plane by clicking the Create button in the Environment section of the Attribute Editor.

Click the color swatch next to Background Color to change the background color in your renders using the Color Chooser. The slider will allow you control the value, or brightness of

the current color. Neither will change the background color of your view panels however.

Motion Blur

Motion blur is an optical illusion that occurs when an object moves fast in front of a camera: it looks blurred as it crosses the frame. Maya renders out motion blur in two ways: 2D blur or 3D blur.

- In the 2D blur process, Maya calculates after the frame is rendered. Any objects moving in the frame are blurred with a 2D filter effect. The 2D blur is quite effective for most applications.

- The 3D blur process is calculated while a frame of the sequence is rendering. Every motion-blur–enabled object is blurred with typically better results than 2D blur, but at a cost of a much longer render time.

> Neither blur method will render in a reflection or a refraction, and to use motion blurred shadows, you need to use the mental ray rendering method, which is an advanced topic.

To enable motion blur, open the Render Global Settings window, and in the Motion Blur section, click the Motion Blur check box . Then choose 2D or 3D blur.

Typically, you control the amount of blur rendered for 2D and 3D by setting the **Blur By Frame** attribute. The higher the number, the greater the blur. Using additional controls, however, you can increase or decrease the 2Dblur effect in the render. The **Blur Length** attribute affects the streakiness of the blur to further increase or decrease the amount of motion blur set with the **Blur By Frame** attribute.

Use motion blur sparingly in most scenes. It takes a careful eye to choose the right blur amount for an object.

> Setting a camera's **Shutter Angle** attribute (in the camera's Attribute Editor in the Special Effects section) also affects the amount of blur rendered. The higher the number, the greater the blur.

Batch Rendering

You've used single-frame rendering numerous times to see a scene in the Render View window. But how do you start a render of an animation sequence? That is called batch rendering in Maya. To batch render an entire scene, follow these steps:

1. Open the Render Global Settings window.

2. Choose Maya Software to render with, enter the start and end frame of your animation, and select your image format. Select your quality and resolution settings and the camera you want to render.

> Be sure to select name.#.ext in the Frame/Animation Ext drop-down list box to render out a sequence of files. Remember, if you leave the default setting, which is name.ext, only a single frame renders.

3. In the main Maya window, choose **Render → Batch Render** ❒ to open the Batch Render Frame dialog box, as shown in Figure 11.16.

4. If you have a multiprocessor machine, select how many CPUs you would like to use to render your scene.

5. Click Batch Render to render the frame range you specified in the Render Global Setting window. The render occurs in the background, and you will see progress updates in the Command line at the bottom of your Maya screen and in the Script Editor window if you open it.

To see a frame as the batch render is in progress, choose **Render → Show Batch Render**. To cancel a batch render, choose **Render → Cancel Batch Render**.

Figure 11.16

The Batch Render Frame dialog box

When you batch render, your image files are written to the images folder of the current project. Make sure your project is properly set; otherwise, your files will end up in an unexpected folder. You can always see the render path and the image name at the top of the Render Global Settings window.

Rendering the Wine Bottle

In this section, you'll set up and render an animated camera to move over 25 frames of the wine bottle exercise begun in Chapter 9.

Load `still_life_render_v01.mb` from the Lighting project on the CD. You will adjust your render settings and some shader properties to make the wine bottle look more like glass, picking up where Chapter 9 left off.

Selecting Render Globals Options

Begin by setting your resolution and quality settings in the Render Global Setting window.

1. Open the Render Global Settings window, and select Maya Software. Click the Maya Software tab.

2. From the Quality drop-down list box, select Production Quality. This will preset the appropriate settings to produce a high-quality render.

3. Click the Common tab.

4. Set Frame/Animation Ext to name.#.ext, set Start Frame to 1, set End Frame to 25, and set Frame Padding to 2.

5. From the Image Format drop-down list box, select Tiff.

6. Make sure that Renderable Objects is set to Render All and that Camera is set to camera1.

7. In the Resolution section, set Preset to 640 × 480.

Setting up the Scene

Now set up some of the objects in the scene itself. The wine bottle has been imported into the still life scene, and three wine glasses have been added. All the lights are in place, as is the camera.

Start by setting this scene up to raytrace to get true reflections and refractions.

1. Turn on refractions for the glass shaders. In the H_S, select the Glasses material and open the Attribute Editor. In the Raytrace Options section, click the Refractions check box and set Refractive Index to 1.2. Set Reflection Limit to 2. Now select the Wine_Bottle material, and repeat the previous steps.

2. Since your lights' shadows are set to shadow maps, you need to change them to raytraced shadows. Remember that semitransparent objects cast solid shadows unless

shadows are raytraced, so the glasses and wine bottle will cast shadows as if they were solid and not glass. In the Outliner, select spotLight1. In the Attribute Editor, in the Shadows section, enable Use Ray Trace Shadows. Notice that the shadow map options turn off. Repeat these steps for the remaining two shadow-casting lights: spotLight4 and spotLight3. Figure 11.17 shows the three shadow-casting lights in the scene.

> You cannot select all three lights at once to turn on raytraced shadows in the Attribute Editor. Any adjustments you make in the Attribute Editor affect only the most recently selected object, not multiple selections.

3. Open the Render Global Settings window, and turn on raytracing in the Raytracing Quality section. Set Reflections to 2.

Setting up the Camera

Next you'll set up the camera to render the scene.

1. Open the camera's Attribute Editor through the camera1 panel (choose **Views → Camera Attribute Editor**).

2. Select the Display Film Gate option in the Display Options section to turn on a dashed green box in the camera1 panel. Enable the Display Resolution option. Notice that the two boxes are not aligned.

3. Since the resolution is 640 × 480, you will use a 1.33 aspect ratio. Select 35mm TV Projection from the Film Gate drop-down list box. The two green boxes now align. Although it's not absolutely necessary to match the resolution with the film gate, it's definitely good practice to do so, especially if you will later insert CG in live-action videos.

4. As soon as you change the film gate, the framing of the scene changes. You'll have to move the camera out to frame the entire still life. If you try moving the camera with the Alt key and mouse button combinations to zoom out, you'll notice that you cannot move the camera in this scene. The movement attributes for the camera have been locked to prevent accidental movement that would disrupt the shot.

5. To unlock the camera, choose **View → Select Camera**. The camera's attributes will appear in the Channel box. Notice that some are grayed out, signifying that they are locked and cannot be changed. Highlight the locked attributes and RM choose Unlock Selection in the Channel box.

Figure 11.17

Shadow lights

6. Create an animated camera move to slowly pull out to reveal the still life over 25 frames. Set your Range Slider to 1 to 25 frames. Go to frame 1. The camera1 view should be similar to that shown here. Select all three Translate and Rotate channels in the Channel box, and RM choose Key Selected to set keyframes for the first camera position.

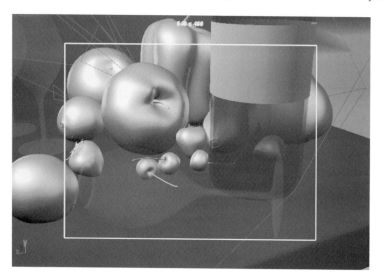

7. Zoom (actually truck) the camera out by pressing Alt+LM+MM to a wider framing to reveal the entire still life seen here. Highlight the Translate and Rotate channels again in the Channel box, and set keyframes for them.

You can choose to lock the camera again to prevent accidentally moving the view once you set your keyframes, especially if Auto Keyframe is on. Just select the **Transform** and **Rotate** attributes in the Channel box and RM choose Lock Selected.

Scrub your animation, and you'll see a pullout revealing the full scene. Now all that remains is to render the sequence.

Batch Rendering and Playing Back the Sequence

Now you're ready to render out the 25-frame sequence. Choose **Render** → **Batch Render**.

Since you are raytracing this scene at full resolution, this render should take anywhere from 20 minutes to an hour. To chart the progress of the render, open the Script Editor by clicking its icon on the Help line or by choosing **Window** → **General Editors** → **Script Editor**.

To see the frames playback, you will need a program that can load the images in sequence and play them back for you. You can also import the image sequence into a compositing or editing program such as Adobe After Effects or Premiere to playback as a clip and edit as you wish.

For a quick view, however, you can use FCheck, a frame viewer that is included with Maya. This small and surprisingly powerful program plays back your images in real time so that you can judge your finished animation. To use FCheck, follow these steps:

1. In Windows, choose **Start** → **Programs** → **Alias Wavefront** → **Maya 5.0** → **FCheck** to open the FCheck window, as shown in Figure 11.18.

2. Choose **File** → **Open Animation**.

3. In the file browser, find your images folder in your project and click the first frame of the sequence you want to playback. FCheck loads the images frame by frame into RAM and then plays them back in real time. Some computers with low RAM may not get real-time playback, however.

Figure 11.18

FCheck, shown here with a sample image, plays back your rendered sequence.

Summary

Getting to this point of a scene can take some work, but once you see the results playing back on your screen, the work all seems more than worth it. Nothing is more fulfilling than seeing your creation come to life, and that's what rendering is all about.

But don't consider the rendering process a mere pushbutton solution when planning your animations. Always allow enough time to ensure that your animations render properly and at their best quality. Most beginners seriously underestimate the time needed to properly complete this step in CG production.

After you create numerous scenes and render them out, you'll begin to understand how to construct your next scenes so that they render better and faster. Just be sure to keep on top of your file management; rendering can produce a bevy of files all over the place!

CHAPTER 12

Maya Dynamics

Maya is renowned for creating special effects animation that simulates not only physical phenomena such as smoke and fire, but also natural movement of colliding bodies. Behind that latter type of animation is the Maya dynamics engine; sophisticated software that creates realistic-looking motion based on the principles of physics.

Another powerful Maya animation tool, Paint Effects, can create dynamic fields of grass and flowers, a head full of hair, and other such systems in a matter of minutes.

Topics include:

- **An Overview of Dynamics**
- **Rigid and Soft Dynamic Bodies**
- **Animating with Dynamics: the Pool Table**
- **Particle Dynamics**
- **Creating Particles**
- **Animating a Particle Effect: Steam**
- **Introduction to Paint Effects**

An Overview of Dynamics

Dynamics is the simulation of motion through the application of the principles of physics. Rather than assigning keyframes to objects to animate them, with Maya dynamics you assign physical characteristics that define how that object behaves in a real world simulation. You create the objects as usual in Maya and then convert them to *dynamic bodies*. These objects are now defined through dynamic attributes you've added to them, which affect how the objects behave in a dynamic simulation.

Dynamic bodies are affected by external forces called fields, which exert a force on them to create motion. Fields can range from wind forces to gravity, and can have their own specific effects on dynamic bodies. You'll learn how to use fields later this chapter.

In Maya, dynamic objects are categorized as bodies, particles, and fluids. Dynamic bodies are created from geometric surfaces and are used for physical objects like bouncing balls. Particles are merely points in space with renderable properties that behave dynamically. Particles are used for natural effects like fire and smoke. Particles will be covered in the latter half of this chapter. Fluids, available in Maya Unlimited only, are in essence volumetric particles that can exhibit surface properties. Fluid dynamics can be used for natural effects such as billowing clouds or plumes of smoke. Fluid dynamics is an advanced topic and will not be covered in this book.

Rigid and Soft Dynamic Bodies

There are two types of dynamic bodies, rigid and soft. Rigid bodies are solid objects such as a pair of dice or a baseball that move and rotate according to the dynamics applied to them. Fields and collisions affect the entire object and move it accordingly. Soft bodies are malleable surfaces that deform dynamically, such as drapes in the wind or a bouncing rubber ball. In brief, this is accomplished by making the surface points (NURBS, CVs, or Polygon vertices) of the soft body object dynamic instead of making the whole object dynamic, so that the forces and collisions of the scene affect these surface points, making them move to deform their surface.

In this section, you'll learn about rigid body dynamics. Soft bodies are an advanced topic and will not be covered in this book.

Creating Active and Passive Rigid Body Objects

Any surface geometry in Maya can be converted to a rigid body. Once converted, that surface can respond to the effects of fields and take part in collisions. When one Maya object hits another in a dynamic simulation, Maya automatically calculates the animation of the colliding objects according to their velocity and other dynamic properties such as mass.

There are two types of rigid bodies: active and passive. An active rigid body is affected by collisions and fields. A passive rigid body is not affected by fields and remains still when it collides with another object. A passive rigid body is used solely to be a surface with which to collide active rigid bodies.

The best way to see how the two types of rigid bodies behave is to create some and animate them. In this section, you'll do that in the classic animation exercise of a bouncing ball.

To create a bouncing ball using Maya rigid bodies, follow these steps:

1. Create a polygonal plane and scale it out to be a ground surface.

2. Create a poly sphere and position it above the ground a number of units, as shown in Figure 12.1.

3. Switch to the Dynamics menu set (by choosing Dynamics from the main menu pull down bar). Select the poly sphere, and choose **Soft/ Rigid Bodies → Create Active Rigid Body**. Notice that the sphere's **Translate** and **Rotate** attributes have now turned yellow. This signifies that there is a dynamic input for those attributes, and, as such, you cannot set keyframes on any of them. The dynamics engine drives the movement and rotation of the active rigid body sphere.

Figure 12.1

Place a poly sphere a few units above a poly plane ground surface.

4. Select the ground plane, and choose **Soft/Rigid Bodies → Create Passive Rigid Body**. This will set the poly plane as a passive rigid body to serve as the floor on which to bounce your active rigid ball. For this exercise, ignore the various creation options and **Rigid Body** attributes; you'll explore the most important of those later in this chapter.

5. To put the ball into motion, you need to create a field to affect it. Select the sphere, and choose **Fields → Gravity**. By selecting the active rigid object(s) while you create the field, you connect that field to the objects automatically. Fields affect only the active rigid bodies to which they are connected. If you hadn't established this connection initially, you could still do so later, through the Dynamic Relationships Editor. You'll find more on this process later in this chapter.

If you try to scrub the Timeline, you will notice that the animation does not run properly. Since dynamics is a simulation of physics, no keyframes are set. You must play the scene from start to finish for the calculations to execute properly. You must also play the scene using the Play Every Frame option. Click the Animation Options button to the right of the Range Slider, or choose **Window → Settings/Preferences → Preferences**. In the Preferences window, choose **Settings → Timeline**. Choose Play Every Frame from the Playback Speed menu.

To playback the simulation, set your frame range from 1 to at least 500. Go to frame 1, and click Play. Make sure you have the proper Playback Speed settings in your Preferences window; otherwise, the simulation will not play properly.

When the simulation plays, you'll notice the sphere begins to fall after a few frames and collides with the ground plane, bouncing back up.

As an experiment, try turning the passive body plane into an active body, using the following steps.

1. Select the plane and open the Attribute Editor.

2. In the rigidBody2 tab in the Attribute Editor, click the Active check box to turn it on. This will switch the plane from a passive body to an active body.

3. Play the simulation, and you'll see the ball fall to hit the plane and knock it away. Because the plane is now an active body, it will be moved by collisions. Since it was not connected to the gravity field, however, it does not fall with the ball.

To connect the now active body plane to the gravity field, open the Dynamic Relationships window, which is shown in Figure 12.2 (choose **Window → Relationship Editors → Dynamic Relationships**).

> You can also connect a dynamic object to a field by selecting the dynamic objects and then the desired field and choosing **Fields → Affect Selected Object(s)**. This method is more useful for connecting multiple dynamic objects to a field.

On the left is an Outliner list of the objects in your scene. On the right is a listing of Fields (default), Collisions, Emitters, or All. Simply select the geometry (pPlane1) on the left side, and then connect it to the gravity field by selecting the gravityField1 node on the right.

Once you connect the gravity field to the plane and run the simulation, you will see the plane fall away with the ball. Since the two fall at the same rate set by the single gravity field, they will never collide. To disconnect the plane from the gravity, unselect the gravity field in the right panel.

RELATIONSHIP EDITORS

The relationship editors, such as the Dynamics Relationship window are a means to connect two nodes together to create a special relationship between them. The Dynamics Relationship window specializes in connecting dynamic attributes so that fields and particles and rigid bodies can interact in a simulation. Another example of a relationship editor is the Light Linking window, which allows you to connect lights to geometry so that only that one object is lit by them. These are fairly advanced topics, however as you learn more about Maya, their use will become integral in your workflow.

Turning the active body plane back to a passive floor is as simple as returning to frame 1, the beginning of the simulation, and clearing the **Active** attribute in the Attribute Editor. By turning the active body back to a passive body you regain an unmovable floor with which the ball can collide and bounce on.

Moving a Rigid Body

Since Maya's dynamics engine controls the movement of any active rigid bodies, you cannot set keyframes on their translation or rotation. With a passive object, however, you can set keyframes on translation and rotation as you can with any other Maya object. Since the object is not active, the dynamics engine does not regulate its movement with fields or collisions.

Rather, any movement the passive body has through regular keyframe animation is translated into momentum that is passed on to any active rigid bodies with which the passive body collides. Think of a baseball bat that strikes a baseball. The baseball bat is a passive rigid body that you have animated to swing with keyframes. The baseball is an active rigid body that is hit by (collides with) the bat as it swings. The momentum of the bat is transferred to the ball, and the ball is sent flying into the stadium stands.

You'll see an example of this in action in the next tutorial.

Rigid Body Attributes

What makes an object a rigid body is the addition of several attributes that help govern how it behaves in a dynamic simulation. Here is a rundown of the more important attributes for both passive and active rigid bodies as they pertain to collisions.

Mass　Sets the relative mass of the rigid body. Set on active or passive rigid bodies, mass is a factor in how much momentum is transferred from one object to another. A more massive object will push a less massive one with less effort and will itself be less prone to movement when hit. Mass is relative from one object to another. If all rigid bodies have the same mass value, there is no difference in the simulation.

Static and Dynamic Friction sliders　Set how much friction the rigid body has while at rest (static) and while in motion (dynamic). Friction specifies how much the object resists moving or being moved while at rest. A friction setting of 0 makes the rigid body move freely, allowing it to slide effortlessly as if on ice.

Bounciness　Specifies how resilient the body is upon collision. The higher the bounciness value, the more bounce the object will have upon collision.

Damping　Creates a drag on the object in dynamic motion so that it will slow down over time. The higher the damping, the more the body's motion diminishes.

Figure 12.2

The Dynamic Relationships window

Animating with Dynamics: The Pool Table

This exercise will take you through the creation of a simple pool table scene in which you will use dynamics to animate a cue ball striking two balls on a pool table.

Creating the Pool Table and the Balls

You will create a simple pool table as a collision surface for the pool balls. To create the table, follow these steps:

1. Create a polygonal plane for the surface of the table. Scale it to 10 along its height and length.

2. To create the pocket holes, you'll make two simple holes in opposite corners. The easiest way is to duplicate the tabletop plane and offset slightly in both directions as shown here. This will create a pair of square holes in the corners for the ball to drop through. For this simple exercise, it will do perfectly well.

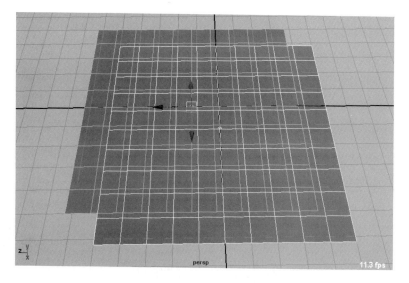

3. Create a polygonal cube, and scale it to fit one edge of the plane to create a rail. Duplicate the cube three times, and then move and rotate the pieces to create the rails around the table as shown in Figure 12.3.

4. Create three poly spheres, and then scale and place them as shown. It is important to place them slightly above the pool table surface. Although it's not imperative to have the same exact location as shown, it's a good idea to get rather close to the layout shown.

Figure 12.3

A simple pool table

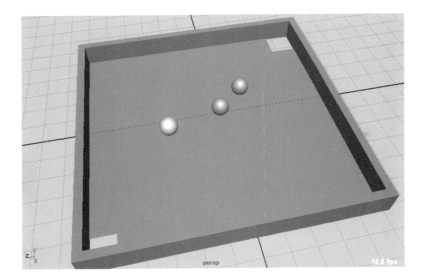

The spheres are placed a bit over the table surface so that the geometries' surfaces are not accidentally crossing each other; surfaces that cross each other are said to be interpenetrating. When surfaces interpenetrate, the dynamics results will be unwelcome. Starting all colliding rigid bodies a little bit away from each other should guarantee their surfaces do not interpenetrate.

5. Create shaders for the pool balls as follows:

   - In the Hypershade, create three new Blinn shaders. Make the first Blinn's color white and assign it to the ball the farthest from the corner. This is the cue ball.

   - Press 6 to enter texture mode in the persp panel. The second ball, in between the cue and the third ball, will be a striped yellow ball, the 9 ball. On the **Color** attribute of the second Blinn shader, create a ramp. Set Interpolation to None to create a hard edge between the colors. Create three positions on the ramp to make a yellow stripe on white, as shown in Figure 12.4.

   - The third ball will be the black 8 ball, a solid color except for two circles of white on the top and bottom sides where the number 8 is printed on a real 8 ball. Create a similar ramp for the third Blinn shader, except using black instead of yellow and the ramp positions shown in Figure 12.5. Rotate the 8 ball to see the shaders better. Figure 12.6 shows all three balls with their textures applied.

Figure 12.4

Create a yellow stripe in the middle of a white ramp to make a striped pool ball.

Figure 12.5

The ramp for the 8 ball's color

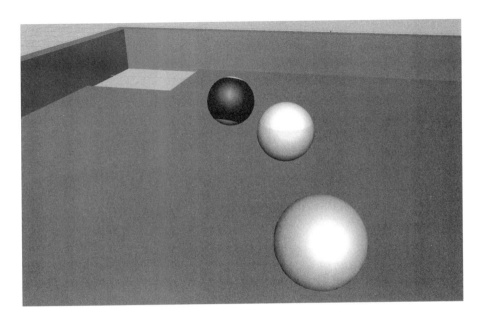

Figure 12.6

The pool balls in texture view

Use the file `Table_v1.mb` in the scenes folder of the Pool_Table project on the CD as a reference or to catch up to this point.

Creating Rigid Bodies

You need to define the pool table as a passive rigid body and define the pool balls as active rigid bodies. Follow these steps:

1. Select the two planes that make up the tabletop and the four cubes that are the side rails. Choose **Soft/Rigid Bodies → Create Passive Rigid Body**.

2. Select the three balls and choose **Soft/Rigid Bodies → Create Active Rigid Body** to make them active rigid bodies.

3. With all three pool balls selected, create a gravity field by choosing **Fields → Gravity**. The gravity field will automatically connect to all three balls.

4. Run the simulation to make sure the balls fall slightly to the tabletop and that none of them interpenetrate the table surface. If any of them do, Maya will select the offending geometry and display an error message in the command feedback line, turning it red.

ADVANCED TIP: ADDING NUMBERS

For a further challenge, see Chapter 7's instructions for importing an image file to use as a texture, and try to create the 8 and 9 printed numbers as image files to import and map into the white areas of the black and yellow cue balls using layered shaders.

Animating Rigid Bodies

The next step is to put the cue ball (the white sphere) into motion so that it hits the 9 ball (yellow) into the 8 ball (black) to sink it into the corner pocket. The easiest way to do this is to keyframe the cue ball's translation from its starting point to hit into the 9 ball. But since active rigid bodies cannot be keyframed, you will have to turn the cue ball into a passive rigid body. To do that, follow these steps:

1. Select the cue ball (the white ball). Notice the **Active** attribute in the Channel box. (You may have to scroll down; it's at the bottom.) It is set to On.

2. Rewind your animation to the first frame. Choose **Soft/Rigid Bodies → Set Passive Key**. Notice that the **Active** attribute has turned yellow. You have set a keyframe for the active state of the cue ball, and it now reads Off. You can toggle rigid bodies between passive and active. Maya has also set translation and rotation keyframes for the cue ball.

3. Go to frame 10. Move the cue ball with the Translate tool so that its outer surface passes through the 9 ball (the yellow-striped ball) slightly as shown. Choose **Soft/Rigid Bodies → Set Passive Key**.

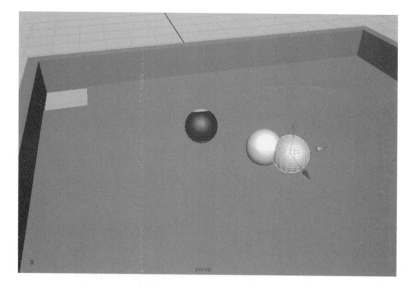

4. Go to frame 11, and choose **Soft/Rigid Bodies → Set Active Key**. This will turn the cue ball back into an active rigid body in the frame after it strikes the yellow 9 ball.

By animating the ball as a passive rigid body, keyframing its translation, and then turning it back to active, you easily set the dynamic simulation in motion. The cue ball animates from its start position and hits the yellow 9 ball. Maya's dynamics engine calculates the collisions on the 9 ball and sets it into motion; it then strikes the black 8 ball, which should roll into the corner pocket. The dynamics engine, at frame 11, also calculates the movement of the cue ball after it strikes the 9 ball, so you do not have to animate it ricocheting.

Go to the start frame and playback the simulation. The cue ball knocks the 9 ball into the 8 ball. The 8 ball rolls into the corner, and the 9 ball bounces off to the right. If the 8 ball is not hit into the corner, you will have to edit your cue ball's keyframes to hit the 9 ball at the correct angle to hit it into the 8 ball into the corner pocket.

At the current settings however, the 8 ball bounces out of the corner without falling through the hole. You need to control the bounciness of the collisions:

1. Go back to the first frame. Select all three balls. In the Channel box, change the **Bounciness** attribute from 0.6 to 0.2. Once you set the attribute value in the Channel box, Maya will set the value for all three spheres concurrently.

> Changing the **Bounciness** attribute through the Attribute Editor changes the value for only one sphere. You will have to change the value for each sphere individually in the Attribute Editor. This is true for all values changed on multiple objects through the Attribute Editor.

2. Playback the animation, and you'll see that the balls do not ricochet off each other and the sides of the pool table with as much spring. The 8 ball should now fall through the hole.

You can load the scene file `Table_2.mb` from the Pool_Table project on the CD to compare your work.

Additional Rigid Body Attributes

In addition, using the pool table setup without any animation, try playing with the rigid body attributes to see how they affect the rigid body in question. Some of these attributes are defined here:

Initial Velocity Gives the rigid body an initial "push" to move it in the corresponding axis.

Initial Spin Gives the rigid body object an initial twist to start the rotation of the object in that axis.

Impulse Position Gives the object a constant push in that axis. The effect is cumulative; the object will accelerate if the impulse is not turned off.

Spin Impulse Rotates the object constantly in the desired axis. The spin will accelerate if the impulse is not turned off.

Center of Mass (0,0,0) Places the center of the object's mass at its pivot point, typically at its geometric center. This value offsets the center of mass, so the rigid body object behaves as if its center of balance is offset, like trick dice or a top-weighted ball.

Creating animation with rigid bodies is straightforward and can go a long way toward creating natural-looking motion for your scene. Integrating such an animation into a final project can get fairly complicated, so it's prudent to become familiar with the workings of rigid body dynamics before relying on that sort of workflow for an animated project. You'll find most professionals use rigid body dynamics as a springboard to create realistic motion for their projects. The dynamics are often converted to keyframes and further tweaked by the animator to fit into a larger scene. Understanding the basics is easy; the rest comes with practice.

Here are a few suggestions for scenes using rigid body dynamics:

Bowling lane The bowling ball is keyframed as a passive object until it hits the active rigid pins at the end of the lane. This scene is simple to create and with which to practice tweaking all the dynamic attributes.

Dice Active rigid dice are thrown into a passive rigid craps table. This exercise challenges your dynamics abilities as well as your modeling skills if you create an accurate craps table.

Game of marbles This scene challenges your texturing and rendering abilities as well as your dynamics abilities.

Particle Dynamics

Like rigid body objects, particles are moved dynamically using collisions and fields. In short, a *particle* is a point in space that is given renderable properties; that is, it can render out. When particles are used en masse, they can create effects such as smoke, a swarm of insects, fireworks, and so on. Although particles can be an advanced and involved aspect of Maya, it is important to have some exposure to them as you begin to learn Maya.

Much of what you learned about rigid body dynamics transfers to particles verbatim. However, it is important to think of particle animation as a manipulation of a larger system rather than as controlling every single particle in the simulation. You control fields and dynamic attributes to govern the motion of the system as a whole.

For example, with the pool table you control the motion of the cue ball and let Maya dynamics calculate the motion of the other balls after they collide. Each ball is a distinct part of the scene and renders out as a distinct object in the frame. Particles are most often used together in large numbers so that the entirety is rendered out to create an effect. To control a particle system, you'll create an emitter and define fields and attributes that control the particles' movement.

Creating Particles

Typical workflow for creating a particle effect in Maya breaks into two parts: motion and rendering. First, you create and define the behavior of particles through *emission*. An *emitter* is a Maya object that creates the particles themselves. After creating fields and adjusting particle behavior within a dynamic simulation, much like you would do with rigid body motion, you give the particles renderable qualities to define how they look. This second aspect of the workflow defines how the particles "come together" to create the desired effect, such as steam. You will make a steaming teakettle later in this chapter.

To create a particle system, follow these steps:

1. Make sure you are in the Dynamics menu set, and then choose **Particles → Create Emitter** ❑. The option box gives you various creation options for the particles' emitter shown in Figure 12.7.

   The default settings will create an Omni emitter with a rate of 100 particles per second and a speed of 1.0. Click Create. A small round object (the emitter) will appear at the origin.

2. Click the Play button to play the scene. As with rigid body dynamics, you must also play the scene back using the Play Every Frame option. You cannot scrub or reverse play particles, unless you create a cache file. You will learn how to create a particle disk cache later in this chapter. But for the most part, particles need to be played back to run properly.

   You will notice a mass of small dots stream out of the emitter in all directions (see Figure 12.8). These are the particles themselves.

Figure 12.7

Creation options for a particle emitter

Emitter Attributes

You can control how particles are created and behave by changing the type of emitter and adjusting its attributes:

Omni Emits particles in all directions.

Directional Emits a spray of particles in a specific direction, as shown in Figure 12.9.

Volume Emits particles from within a specified volume, as in Figure 12.10. The volume can be a cube, a sphere, a cylinder, a cone, or a torus. By default, the particles may leave the perimeter of the volume.

Figure 12.8

An Omni emitter emits a swarm of little particles in all directions.

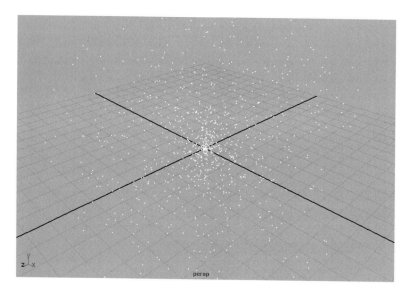

Figure 12.9

Particles sprayed in a specific direction

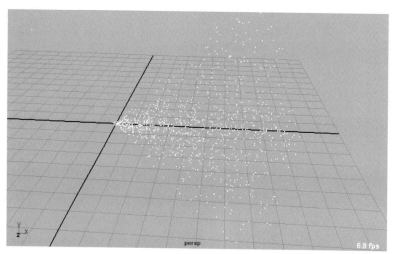

After you create an emitter, its attributes govern how the particles are released into the scene. Every emitter has the following attributes to control the emission:

Rate Governs how many particles are emitted per second.

Speed Specifies how fast the particles move out from the emitter.

Speed Random Randomizes the speed of the particles as they are emitted for a more natural look.

Min/Max Distance Emits particles within an offset distance from the emitter itself. You enter values for the Min and Max Distance setting. Figure 12.11 shows a directional emitter with a Min and Max Distance setting of 3.

Figure 12.10

Particles emit from anywhere inside the emitter's volume.

Figure 12.11

An emitter with a Min and Max Distance setting of 3 emits particles 3 units from itself.

Particle Attributes

Once created (or born) and set into motion by an emitter, particles rely on their own attributes and any fields or collisions in the scene to govern their motion, just like rigid body objects.

In Figure 12.12, you'll notice the Attribute Editor shows a number of tabs for the selected particle object. Particle1 is the particle object node. This has the familiar **Translate**, **Rotate**, and **Scale** attributes as most other object nodes. The shape node, particleShape1 is where all the important attributes are for a particle, and it is displayed by default. The third tab in the Attribute Editor is the emitter1 node that belongs to the particle's emitter. This makes it easier to toggle back and forth to adjust emitter and particle settings.

The Lifespan Attributes

When a particle is created, or born, you can give it a lifespan, which allows the particle to die when it reaches a certain point in time. Giving particles a lifespan is a good idea for a variety of reasons. As you'll see with the steaming teakettle later in the chapter, a particle that has a lifespan can change over its lifespan. For example, a particle might start out as white and fade away at the end of its life. A lifespan also helps keep the total number of particles in a scene to a minimum, which helps the scene run more efficiently.

You use the lifespan mode to select the type of lifespan for a particle:

Live Forever The particles in the scene can exist indefinitely.

Constant All particles die when their Lifespan value is reached. Lifespan is measured in seconds, so upon emission, a particle will exist for 30 frames in a scene setup at 30fps before it disappears.

Random Range This type sets a lifespan as in constant mode, but assigns a range value via the **Lifespan Random** attribute to allow some particles to live longer than others for a more natural effect.

LifespanPP Only This mode is used in conjunction with expressions that are programmed into the particle with MEL. Expressions are an advanced Maya concept and are not used in this book.

The Render Attributes

The Render attributes determine how your particles look and how they will render. Two types of particle rendering are used in Maya: software and hardware. Hardware particles are typically rendered out separate from anything else in the scene and are then composited with the rest of the scene. Because of this compound workflow for hardware particles,

Figure 12.12

Particle attributes

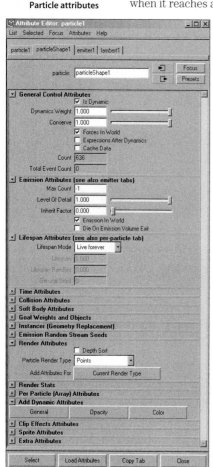

this book will introduce you to a software particle called Cloud. Cloud, like other software particles, can be rendered with the rest of a scene through the software renderer.

With your particles selected, open the Attribute Editor. In the Render Attributes section, you will find the Particle Render Type drop-down menu.

The three render types listed with the (s/w) suffix are software-rendered particles. All the other types can be rendered only through the hardware renderer. Select your render type, and then click the Add Attributes For Current Render Type button to create and add the proper attributes for the render type you selected.

For example, if you select the Cloud (s/w) render type from the menu, your particles change from dots on the screen to large circles.

Click the Add Attributes For button to display several new attributes that will control the look of the particles. Each particle render type has its own set of render attributes. The cloud particle type attributes added will be **Radius**, **Surface Shading**, and **Threshold**.

In the Per Particle (Array) Attributes section of the Attribute Editor are attributes that affect individual particles, as opposed to affecting the entire particle object as one unit.

For example, the **radius** attribute, which appeared when you clicked to create a Cloud render type, governs the radius, the size, of every particle in the system evenly. That is, with a radius setting of 1.5, each particle in that particle system (particle object) will have a radius of 1.5.

By allowing you to control certain attributes at an individual particle scale, Maya gives you immense power to create realistic-looking effects. In the case of your Cloud particle's radius, you can create an attribute called **radiusPP** (for radius Per Particle) so that each particle can have a different radius.

Rather than manually enter radius values for every single particle, you control **Per Particle** attributes by connecting textures or expressions to them in the Per Particle (Array) Attributes section of the Attribute Editor. Notice that there is already a **lifespanPP** attribute that allows you to control the lifespan for particles on an individual basis.

Caching Particles

You can cache the motion of your particles to memory or to disk to make editing your particle animation easier. To cache particles to your system's fast RAM memory, select the particle object you wish to cache and choose **Solvers → Memory Caching → Enable**. Playback your scene and the particles will cache into your memory for faster playback. You can also scrub your timeline to see your particle animation. If you make changes to your animation, the scene will not reflect the changes until you delete the cache from memory by selecting the particle object and choosing **Solvers → Memory Caching → Delete**. The amount of information the memory cache will be able to hold depends on the system RAM of your machine. While memory caching is much faster than disk caching, creating a disk cache will allow you to cache all the particles as they exist throughout their duration in your scene and ensures that the particles will be rendered correctly. You should create a particle disk cache before rendering.

Creating a Particle Cache File

Once you have created a particle scene, and you want to be able to scrub the timeline back and forth to see your particle motion and how it acts in the scene, you may create a particle disk cache. This will allow you to playback the scene as you wish, without running the simulation from the start and by every frame.

To create a particle disk cache, switch to the Dynamics menu set and choose **Solvers → Create Particle Disk Cache**. Maya will run the simulation according to the timeline and save the position of all the particle systems in the scene to cache files in your current project's *particle* folder. You will then be able to play your animation back and forth and the particles will run properly.

If you make any dynamics changes like emission rate or speed to the particles, you will need to detach the cache file from the scene for the changes to take effect. Choose **Solvers → Edit Oversampling or Cache Settings**, and uncheck the **Use Particle Disk Cache** check box.

Now that you understand the basics of particle dynamics, it's time to see for yourself how they work.

Animating a Particle Effect: Steam

You will create a spray of steam coming out of the spout of the teakettle you created in Chapter 6.

Emitting the Particles

The first step is to create an emitter to spray from the kettle's spout and to set up the motion and behavior of the particles:

1. Create a directional emitter and place it at the end of the spout as shown.

2. To set up the spray in the proper direction, adjust the attributes of the emitter. In the Distance/Direction Attributes section, change **Direction Y** from 0 to 1.5, and leave **Direction X** at 1 and **Direction Z** at 0. This will emit the particles at about a 70° angle up and away from the spout.

> The **Direction** attributes are relative. Entering a value of 1 for **Direction X** and a value of 2 for **Direction Y** will make the particles spray at twice the height (Y) of their lateral distance (X).

3. Playback your scene. You'll see particles emit in a straight line from the spout, as shown in Figure 12.13.

4. To change the particle emission to a spray, adjust the **Spread** attribute for the emitter. Click the emitter1 tab in the particle's Attribute Editor (or select the emitter to focus the Attribute Editor on it instead), and change the **Spread** attribute from 0 to 0.25. Figure 12.14 shows the new spray.

> The **Spread** attribute sets the cone angle for a directional emission. A value of 0 results in a thin line of particles. A value of 1 emits particles in a 180° arc.

5. The emission is rather slow for hot steam, so change the Speed setting for the emitter from 1 to 2, and change Speed Random from 0 to 1. This will create a random speed range between 1 and 3 for each particle. These two **Speed** attributes are found in the emitter's Attribute Editor in the Basic Emission Speed Attributes section.

Figure 12.13

Particles emit in a straight line from the spout.

Figure 12.14

**The emitter's Spread
attribute widens the
spray of particles.**

6. So that all the steam does not emit from the same exact point, set the emitter's Min Distance to 0.5 and its Max Distance to 1. This will create a range of offset between 0.5 and 1 for the particle to emit from, as shown.

Setting Particle Attributes

Now that you have the particles emitting properly from the spout, you'll adjust the particle attributes. Start by setting a lifespan for them and then add rendering attributes:

1. Select the particle object and open the Attribute Editor. For Lifespan Mode, select Random Range. Set Lifespan to 3 and Lifespan Random to 1. This will create a range of 2 to 4 for each particle's lifespan. (That's based on a lifespan of 3 plus or minus a random value from 0 to 1.)

You just added an attribute to the particle object, just as you added a new attribute for the set driven keys for the hand in Chapter 9.

2. Change Particle Render Type from Points to Clouds. The particles will be displayed as large circles that overlap each other. They are too large; however it is often desirable to have these particles overlap each other to make the steam look seamless.

3. You will control the radius of the particles individually, on a Per Particle basis, as opposed to changing the **Radius** attribute. In the particleShape1's Attribute Editor, in the Add Dynamic Attributes section, click the General button to open the Add Attribute:particleShape1 window. Click the Particle tab, and select **radiusPP**, as shown in Figure 12.15. This will add a **radiusPP** attribute to the Per Particle (Array) Attributes section of the Attribute Editor.

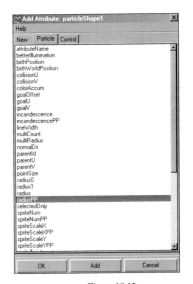

Figure 12.15

The Add Attribute window

For this attribute, you will assign a texture to the **radiusPP** to control the size of the particles. A particle's attribute, such as radiusPP, in Maya can read the color values from a texture and use the texture to control the particle's behavior, in this case its radius, or size.

The texture you will create for the **radiusPP** will be a ramp. Using a texture that has only one color will assign a static radius value to each particle. For example, if you use a white texture for the **radiusPP**, each particle will have a radius of 1.0. White, in this case, is read to be a value of 1; black is a value of 0.

Using a gradient such as a ramp texture that grades from black to white will change the radius of the particle along its lifespan. The radius for each particle will begin at 0 (black) at its birth and increase along its lifespan to a value of 1 (white) at its death. This is one reason that assigning an active lifespan mode to your particles is a good idea.

To assign a ramp texture to the **radiusPP** attribute, follow these steps:

1. RM click and hold in the gray text box of the **radiusPP** attribute. A marking menu will appear. Choose Create Ramp and release the mouse button. The **radiusPP** attribute will now read **arrayMapper1.outValuePP**. Simply put, a ramp is now assigned to this attribute that will control the radius of your particles as they grow older.

2. To edit the ramp, RM click **arrayMapper1.outValuePP** and choose **arrayMapper1.outValuePP → Edit Ramp** from the marking menu. The Attribute Editor will now display the ramp. For organization's sake, name the ramp radiusPP_ramp. The ramp also appears in the Hypershade and Multilister windows for editing.

3. Adjust the ramp settings so that the bottom is a dark gray and the top is a medium gray. Set the bottom gray to an HSV of 0,0,0.15 and the top color to an HSV of 0,0,0.5. This will make the steam particles small at birth (a radius of 0.15).

The ramp will make the particles grow to a maximum radius of 0.5 over their lifespan. The values are read from the bottom of the ramp at the beginning of a particle's life to the top of the ramp as the particle ages and dies. Playback the scene from the first frame, and you should have something similar to Figure 12.16.

Load the file `Kettle_Steam_v2.ma` from the Tea_Kettle project on the CD to check your work.

Setting Rendering Attributes

After you define the particle movement to your liking, you can create the proper look for them, and that means setting and adjusting rendering parameters for the particles. Since Maya has several types of particles, different particles are set up differently; this workflow applies only to the Cloud particle type.

Cloud particles render out when they are assigned a particle cloud shader. This shader is similar to the shaders you've used previously in this book. To create a steam shader for these particles, follow these steps:

1. Open the Hypershade window, and choose **Create → Volumetric Materials → Particle Cloud**. This will create a shader for use with Cloud particles. You will notice a particle-Cloud1 material already in the scene. Maya creates one by default in every new scene, but you will not use that one.

Figure 12.16

The particles grow as they spray out from the spout.

2. Double-click particleCloud2 to open the Attribute Editor. Rename the material to steam. Figure 12.17 shows the Attribute Editor for the steam shader material.

3. Change the color of the material from cyan to white. Now select the particles and assign the steam material to them by right-clicking the steam material in the Hypershade and choosing Assign Material to Selection from the marking menu.

Figure 12.17

The new steam shader material

4. In the Render Globals tab, set the resolution to 640 × 480, and in the Maya Software tab, set the Quality to Intermediate Quality. Run the animation and stop it when some steam has been emitted. Render a frame. It should look like Figure 12.18.

Render a 200-frame sequence of the scene at a lower resolution such as 320 × 240 to see how the particles look as they animate. (Check the frames with Fcheck. Refer to Chapter 11 for more on Fcheck.) First, the steam is far too thick and too opaque. Also in the animation you will notice that the particles "turn off" at the end of their lifespan.

Steam, however, dissipates. The particles here pop off when they die. You will need to make the particles gradually disappear as they grow older so that they are fully transparent at the end of their lifespan. This will make them fade instead of popping off. You will adjust the transparency of the steam material in the following steps:

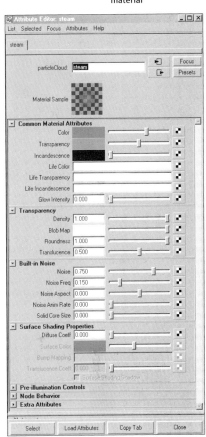

1. Select the steam material in the Hypershade, and open the Attribute Editor. Instead of merely setting a higher value for the **Transparency** attribute (by making the gray color brighter), you will need to make a new ramp texture for the steam material's **Life Transparency**. As a ramp texture assigned to the **radiusPP** created growing particles, this new ramp will make the particles fade (become more transparent) as they get older and become fully transparent at their death. To create a ramp on the **Life Transparency**, click the Texture button to the right of the text box in the Attribute Editor to open the Create Render Node window.

2. Click to create a ramp texture. Maya will create and display a particleSamplerInfo1 node in the Attribute Editor. You will not need to adjust this node, so select the new ramp node in the Hypershade to display its attributes in the Attribute Editor instead.

3. Rename the ramp from ramp2 to steam_transparency. Since the particles will read the ramp from bottom to top, set the bottom color to white. This will make the particles transparent at first. Set a medium gray color not too far above the black so that the particles fade in. Toward the top, set a white color. This will create a full transparency at the end of a particle's life. The ramp should look as shown to the left.

4. Render a frame to see the results. The steam will look more real and will animate better by just adding the transparency ramp to the lifespan of the particles. Compare the results (see Figure 12.19) to the previous render.

5. If you prefer not to have a gap between the spout and the steam, as this scene creates, try moving the emitter into the kettle's spout.

Load the file `Kettle_Steam_v3.ma` from the Steam_Kettle project on the CD to check your work.

Experiment with animating the **Rate** attribute of the emitter to make the steam animation more lifelike. Also, try animating the Speed values and playing with different **radiusPP** sizes. The steam you'll get from this tutorial, while looking good, will not be as lifelike as it could be. You can do a lot more the more you learn of Maya, but those techniques are beyond the scope of this book.

Once you feel comfortable with the steam exercise, try using the Cloud particle type to create steam for a mug of coffee. That steam moves much slower and is less defined than the blowing steam of the kettle and should pose a new challenge. Also try your hand at creating a smoke trail for a rocket ship or a wafting stream of cigarette smoke.

Figure 12.18

A single frame render of the steam

Figure 12.19

The steam dissipating more realistically

Cloud particles are the perfect particle type to begin with. As you feel more comfortable animating with Clouds, experiment with the other render types. The more you experiment with all particles, the easier they will be to harness. You'll quickly find Maya particles can create a wild array of realistic and stylized effects for your animations.

Introduction to Paint Effects

In Maya's effects arsenal is a tool called Paint Effects. Using Paint Effects, you can create a field of grass rippling in the wind, a head of hair or feathers, or even a colorful aurora in the sky. Paint Effects is a rendering effect found under the Rendering menu set that has incredible dynamic properties that can make leaves rustling in the wind, or trees swaying in a storm. Though it does not use the same dynamics engine as particles or rigid bodies do, Paint Effects uses its own dynamics calculations to create natural motion. It is one of Maya's most powerful tools, with features that go far beyond the scope of this introductory book. Here you will learn how to create a Paint Effects scene and how to access all the preset brushes to create your own effects.

Paint Effects use brushes to paint effects into your 3D scene. The brushes create strokes on a surface or in the Maya modeling views that produce tubes, which render out through Maya's software renderer. These Paint Effects tubes have dynamic properties, which means they can move according to their own forces. That means you can easily create a field of blowing grass.

Try This You will create a field of blowing grass and flowers, and it will take you all of five minutes.

1. Start with a new scene file. Maximize the perspective view. (Press the spacebar with the persp window active.)

2. Switch to the Rendering menu set. Choose **Select Paint Effects → Get Brush** to open the Visor window. The Visor window displays all the preset Paint Effects brushes that automatically create certain effects. Select the grasses folder in the to display the grass brushes available (see Figure 12.20). You can navigate the Visor window as you would navigate any other Maya window using the Alt key and the mouse buttons.

3. Click the grassWindWide.mel brush to activate the Paint Effects tool and set it to this grass brush. You cursor will change to a pencil icon.

4. In the persp window, click and drag two lines across the grid as shown to the right to create two Paint Effects strokes of blowing grass.

5. To change your brush to add some flowers in between the grass, choose **Select Paint Effects → Get Brush** and select the flowers folder. Select the dandelion_Yellow.mel brush. Your Paint Effects tool is now set to paint yellow flowers.

6. Click and drag a new stroke between the strokes of grass as shown.

7. Position your camera and render a frame. Make sure to use a large enough resolution such as 640×480 so that you can see the details. Render out a 120-frame sequence to see how the grass animates in the wind. Figure 12.21 shows a scene filled with grass strokes as well as a number of different flowers.

Once you create a Paint Effects stroke, you can edit the look and movement of the effect through the Attribute Editor. You'll notice, however, that there are a large number of attributes to edit with Paint Effects. The next section introduces the attributes that are most useful to the beginning Maya user.

Figure 12.20

The preset grasses brushes in the Visor window

Paint Effects Attributes

It is best to create a single stroke of Paint Effects in a blank scene and experiment with adjusting the various attributes to see how they affect the strokes. Select the stroke, and open the Attribute Editor. Switch to the stroke's tab to access the attributes. For example, for an African Lily Paint Effects stroke, the Attribute Editor tab is called africanlily1.

Each Paint Effects stroke produces tubes that render to create the desired effect. Each tube (you can think of a tube as a stalk) can grow to have branches, twigs, leaves, flowers, and buds. Each section of a tube has its own controls to give you the greatest flexibility in creating your effect. As you experiment with Paint Effects, you will begin to understand how each attribute contributes to the final look of the effect.

Here is a summary of some Paint Effects attributes:

Brush Profile Gives you control over how the tubes are generated from the stroke, namely with the **Brush Width** attribute. This will make tubes emit from a wider breadth from the stroke to cover more of an area.

Shading and Tube Shading Give you access to the color controls for the tubes on a stroke.

> **Color1 and Color2** From bottom to top, graduates from Color1 to Color 2 along the stalk only. The leaves and branches have their own color attributes, which you can display by choosing **Tubes → Creation → Growth**.
>
> **Incandescence1 and 2** Adds a gradient self-illumination to the tubes.
>
> **Transparency1 and 2** Adds a gradient transparency to each tube.
>
> **Hue/Sat/Value Rand** Add some randomness to the color of the tubes.

In the Tubes section, you will find all the attributes to control the growth of the Paint Effects effect. In the Creation subsection, you can access the following:

Tubes per Step Controls the number of tubes along the stroke. For example, this setting will increase or decrease the number of flowers for the africanlily1 stroke.

Length Min/Max Controls how tall the tubes are grown to make taller flowers or grass (or other effects).

Tube Width1 and Width2 Controls the width of the tubes, that is, the stalks of the flowers.

Figure 12.21

Paint Effects can add realistic-looking flowers and grass to any scene.

size: 640 480 zoom: 1.000 (Maya Software)

In the Growth subsection, you can access controls for branches, twigs, leaves, flowers, and buds for the Paint Effects strokes. Each attribute in these sections controls the number, size, and shape of those elements. Although not all Paint Effects strokes create flowers, all strokes contain these headings; some may or may not be active. Each stroke has its own settings.

The Behavior sub-section contains the controls for the dynamic forces affecting the tubes in a Paint Effects stroke. Adjust these attributes if you want your flowers blow more in the wind.

Paint Effects are rendered as a post process, which means they will not render in reflections or refractions as is. They are indeed processed and rendered after every other object in the scene is rendered out. They will, however, playback in the work panels to give you feedback on your dynamic settings.

New to Maya 5.0 however, is the ability to convert paint effects to polygonal surfaces that will render in the scene along with any other objects, so that they may indeed take part in reflections and refractions. To convert a paint effects stroke to polygons, select the stroke and choose **Modify → Convert → Paint Effects to Polygons**. The polygon paint effects tubes may still be edited by most of the paint effects attributes mentioned so far, though some, like color, will not affect the poly tubes. Instead the color information was converted into a shader that was assigned to the polygons. It's best to finalize your paint effects strokes before converting to polygons to avoid any confusion.

Paint Effects is indeed a strong Maya tool, with which complex effects such as a field of blowing flowers can be easily created. With that complexity comes a large number of controls to create a variety of effects. Fortunately, Maya comes with a generous sampling of preset brushes. Experiment with a few brushes and their attributes to see what kind of effects and strange plants you can create.

Summary

With power comes complexity of use. Maya dynamics has a rich feature set and compound controls. The best way to be exposed to Maya dynamics is to simply experiment. You will find that the workflow in dynamics is much more iterative than other Maya workflows, as you are required to experiment with different values frequently to see how they affect the final simulation. And with time, you will develop a strong sense of intuition, and you will accomplish more complex simulations faster and with greater effect.

Where Do You Go from Here?

You should feel encouraged to explore other resources of information and tutorials to expand your working knowledge of Maya. Several web sites on the Internet contain numerous tips, tricks, and tutorials for all aspects of Maya, including the author's new Maya education web site, The Maya FAQ (Frequently Asked Questions) at www.mayaFAQ.com. Also a great resource is Alias's own website: www.alias.com, which has a wide range of learning tools. Other texts such as *Maya 5 Savvy* will be valuable for more tutorials to expand your skill set as well. Check Chapter 1's bibliography for some suggestions. But you will surely find a wealth of information out there; and now that you have gained the all-important first exposure, you will be better equipped to forge ahead confidently.

The most important thing you should have learned from this book is that proficiency and competence with Maya comes with practice, but even more so from your own artistic exploration. It is imperative to treat this text and your experience with its information as a formal introduction to a new language and way of working for yourself. The rest of it, the gorgeous still frames and eloquent animations, come with furthering your study of your own art, working diligently to achieve your vision, and truly having fun on the way. Enjoy and good luck.

Index

Note to the reader: Throughout this index **boldfaced** page numbers indicate primary discussions of a topic. *Italicized* page numbers indicate illustrations.